The Study of Stolen Love

AMERICAN ACADEMY OF RELIGION
TEXTS AND TRANSLATIONS SERIES

Edited by

Terry Godlove
Hofstra University

Number 18
THE STUDY OF STOLEN LOVE

translated by
David C. Buck
K. Paramasivam

The Study of Stolen Love
A Translation of Kaḷaviyal eṉṟa Iṟaiyaṉār Akapporuḷ with Commentary by Nakkīraṉār

by
David C. Buck
K. Paramasivam

Scholars Press
Atlanta, Georgia

The Study of Stolen Love
A Translation of Kaḷaviyal eṉṟa Iṟaiyaṉār Akapporuḷ with Commentary by Nakkīraṉār

by

David C. Buck
K. Paramasivam

Cover photo of sculpture on the exterior of the imperial Chola temple at Gangaikondacolapuram, Tamil Nadu, courtesy of Glenn Yocum.

Library of Congress Cataloging in Publication Data
Nakkīraṉār.
[Kaḷaviyal eṉṟa Iṟaiyaṉār Akapporuḷ. English]
The study of stolen love / translated by David C. Buck, K. Paramasivam.
p. cm. — (Texts and translations series ; no. 18)
Includes bibliographical references.
ISBN 0-7885-0331-6 (cloth : alk. paper). — ISBN 0-7885-0332-4 (pbk. : alk. paper)
1. Tamil poetry to 1500—Translations into English. 2. Tamil poetry—History and criticism. 3. Love in literature. I. Buck, David C. II. Paramasivam, K., 1933–1992. III. Title. IV. Series: Texts and translations series (American Academy of Religion) ; no. 18.
PL4758.65.E5N36 1997
894.8'1111—dc20 96-6539
CIP

Printed in the United States of America
on acid-free paper

TABLE OF CONTENTS

ACKNOWLEDGMENTS

The translators would like to thank the American Institute of Indian Studies and the National Endowment for the Humanities for funding work on this project during the summers of 1986 and 1987, respectively. Our special thanks also go to Professor Norman Cutler of the University of Chicago for checking portions of the translation for accuracy. We would also like to thank all who put up with our preoccupation during the course of the work.

Of course, errors and other weaknesses that come to light as the translation is read must be seen as the sole responsibility of the translators. Interested readers are urged to communicate their comments, suggestions, and criticisms to us.

David C. Buck
Upton, Kentucky, U.S.A.

K. Paramasivam
Madurai, Tamil Nadu, India

NOTE

It is with a tremendous sense of loss that I join with others in mourning the passing of Dr. K. Paramasivam in January, 1992.

David C. Buck

Introduction

The Study of Stolen Love was composed in Tamil in southern India something over a millennium ago. It is a composite work, consisting of sixty terse verses on the poetry of love, Nakkīraṉār's commentary on those verses, and the hundreds of poems he selected to illustrate principles that the sixty verses lay down. The commentator identifies himself as a man, and attributes to God the authorship of the sixty verses. The earliest extant book-length Tamil prose composition, this commentary explicated earlier poetic conventions and ushered in a new era of its own. It exemplified and outlined Tamil interpretive method. Even today its method structures all traditional interpretive Tamil commentary on all subjects. In subject matter it addresses issues ranging from religion to social structure and, of course, it focuses on the delicate relationships between the sexes.

Title of the Work

The English title is a direct translation from the Tamil, and it reflects both the purpose and the content of the work as commentator Nakkīraṉār details it in his treatment of the first verse; however, it is open to serious misunderstanding. The book builds an approach to spiritual fulfillment through a study of cross-gender relations; its purpose is spiritual, and its method, says Nakkīraṉār, is one of benevolent deception. To people caught in the tangles of everyday life, as most of us are, the book presents a vision of pure love between idealized lovers. He presents a picture that is not so far removed from ordinary experience as to be unrecognizable, yet is removed enough that readers do not identify, through these lovers, with sordid realities, but focus instead on purity of thought, intention, word, and deed.

Nakkīraṉār puts it this way:

> It is like pointing out a mirage to one who has been drinking murky water: a wise person points to it and says, "Look there, that's good water—drink it. What are you doing, drinking this dirty water?" but actually leads him to good water, and gives it to him to drink.[1]

Nakkīraṉār himself perceived a need to justify the use of the title *Stolen Love*. He wrote,

---

[1] Page 10.

"What?" you ask, "Is this not a volume on thievery? How can we attain the gift of Release by learning this? Aren't stealing, murder, passion, and fornication all condemned by both the religious and the worldly? And is this not one of those?"

It is not so.

When one hears the word "stolen," it does not necessarily indicate evil; it is not to be called evil every time you hear the words "stealing" or "passion." Rather, these can also be good.

Once there was a woman who had quarreled with her family. She concocted some poison, intending to drink it and die, but there were some who would impede her. As she was waiting for them to leave, a compassionate man noticed it. He thought to himself, "I will take this poison and pour it out, so that she does not commit suicide." He took it without her seeing him, and poured it out. Later, when nobody was around, she went to drink it and kill herself; but as she could not find it, she avoided death. Because he saved her life through that act of stealing, he would have good karma. Other things of this sort also are not thievery, but produce good.[2]

The book does focus entirely on the development of love between a woman and a man, as their love grows and changes from their first meeting through their entry into middle age; this flow dictates the use of the word "love" in the title. Yet it does so with an ulterior end in view, an end that dictates the use of the word "stolen." Again, in the words of the commentator,

It is because of the deception used in setting him upon the correct path that this takes the designation "stolen."[3]

Poetic Tradition

Tamil possesses a proud and vibrant tradition of love poetry, and some of that poetry is available in excellent English translations. The earliest literary works that we have from ancient Tamil are love poems, dating from the Caṅkam period, which seems to have extended from the first few centuries BCE to the first century or so CE.

Caṅkam poetry was broadly divided into two categories, identified by the Tamil words akam and puṟam. Puṟam poems deal with regal glory and are analyzed with an apparatus parallel to the one developed for the akam poems. But they are not directly related to the love poetry tradition with which the present volume deals.

Akam poems from the Caṅkam period, on the other hand, initiated the Tamil tradition of love poetry. The term "love poetry" is a loose term, used to designate poems that fall into the akam category: it is not a translation of the term akam. Akam means "interior," as opposed to the "exterior" world of kings

---

[2] Page 9.

[3] Page 11.

and war. In fact, though, the interior poems deal only with relations between women and men who are defined as being in love.

Tamil Poetic Convention: Five Modes of Love Poetry

To address this love relationship, akam poetry has been sorted into five modes (tiṇai) on the basis of the stage of development in the relations between the hero and the heroine. Each mode is extensively described in the traditional literature; the *Commentary* which forms the most substantial part of the present translation is the earliest extant discursive exposition of them. A mode is a set of intertwined poetic characteristics designed to heighten the poignancy of a certain emotion, and poems were to be analyzed in terms of their mode, before all else. Set out in detail for each mode are the time, place, and seasons of the year appropriate to the stage of love the mode epitomizes, as well as numerous images to be used, including flowers, animals, trees, social backdrop, and so forth. In naming the five major modes of love, scholars normally utilize the name of the principal flower appearing in each mode. Nakkīraṉār also utilized this convention in naming the modes, but we have opted to name them in English on the basis of the ecological regions portrayed,[4] following a lead Nakkīraṉār presents in his discourse on the essence of the modes, from his comments on the first verse:

> ... a region in which the conduct termed "mountain-country mode" occurs may also be called "mountain-country mode," [although] this usage follows simply in the way that we use the term "light" not only for a flame, which really is light, but also for the object in which the flame burns.[5]

Here then, against this background, is an overview of the modes:

1. The mountain-country mode provides an array of imagery and situations appropriate to the varied emotions involved in the lovers' first meeting, as the young heroine and her hero fall in love for the first and only time in their lives. The poet uses waterfalls, peacocks, mountain millet fields, hunter tribes, springtime nights, clear mountain pools, and other items to evoke these emotions, and for the connoisseur in appreciating them. The quintessential flower in this mode is the kuṟiñci, or conehead flower, which blooms in profusion, but only once in twelve years, on the mountain slopes of the Tamil country.
2. The forest mode sets out poetic materials with which to portray the patient waiting of a temporarily abandoned heroine. She knows the hero will return,

[4] Our reason for this choice is that the flowers named are not well known to many English-language readers.

[5] Pages 22–23.

and the emotions are played out against a thickly wooded backdrop with forest pools, rabbits, deer, and laburnum and wild lime trees; the people in the social background of the forest mode are busy harvesting and threshing millet, and tending cattle. These poems are set in the rainy evenings of the monsoon, when lovers lie idle, reminiscing.

3. The middle of the five modes is reserved for the wastelands, stark in both emotions and imagery. Hot deserts peopled with highway thieves frame poems on the separation from home and loved ones. Vultures, dry wells, and a merciless noontime summer sun are typical of the imagery in these poems on the wrenching of ties with family, home, and lover, as the hero pursues his fortune in distant lands. The same mode is used for a large corpus of poetry on the elopement of the two young lovers, in an attempt to flee the stings of neighborhood gossip.
4. Seaside imagery is prescribed for the evocation of the emotions of impatient lovers who must undergo enforced separation through fear of being found out. Drying fish, thieving seagulls, and rough and ready fisherfolk appear in these poems. The quintessential flower is the neytal, or water lily, although many other flowers and odors also permeate the mode. These poems are set in the evening.
5. The last of the five modes is that of the river-plain. It is placed in a fertile agricultural region, in a populous town on the banks of a river. Technology and complex social structures are the backdrop for these poems, set in the wealth of centers of culture. Hero and heroine are older in these poems, and they may have children. Although they are married, most of these poems deal with the triangular relationships created by the hero's interest in courtesans. The dominant flower is that of the marutam, or queen's-flower tree, although other flowers also assume great importance, particularly lotus flowers blooming in artificial ponds and reservoirs. The time for these poems is the period just before dawn.

There are two other modes, considered "outer" modes, as they are normally enumerated one before and one after the central five modes. However, as the types of love portrayed in them are considered decidedly inferior and of sullied emotional purity, they play no significant part in the present work.

The Present Work

The present work is the oldest extant discursive codification of Tamil poetic conventions. It contains, as its name implies, *The Study of Stolen Love* and Nakkīraṉār's *Commentary* upon it, but it also contains a third important work, *Pāṇṭi-k-Kōvai*, whose authorship is unknown. The *Study of Stolen Love* itself is a series of 60 terse epigrams, whose meaning is often enigmatic. The *Commentary* explains and expands the *Study*, and utilizes citation of poetic examples in the process: *Pāṇṭi-k-Kōvai* is a poetry collection which provides the vast majority of these illustrative citations. These three portions can be viewed as threads which have been woven together by the commentator into the received form of the book.

Because of its tripartite character the work is hard to date. *Pāṇṭi-k-Kōvai*, which is a series of some 325 poems, is a kōvai, a type of love poem that also functions as a panegyric upon a king—in this case Neṭumāṟaṉ of Madurai, who must have ruled during the last part of the 7th century.[6] Thus it must have been composed either during or after Neṭumāṟaṉ's reign.

The sixty verses of *The Study of Stolen Love*, however, are practically impossible to date. The commentary declares that *The Study of Stolen Love* was composed during the Caṅkam age itself, although there is a fragile consensus among scholars relegating it to a considerably later period, perhaps about the 8th century.

Nakkīraṉār's *Commentary* also claims to have been composed during the Caṅkam age, at the same time as the *Study of Stolen Love*. But then again, it includes an enumeration of ten people following Nakkīraṉār, through whom it was handed down to posterity. Thus while it may or may not have been authored with the *Study of Stolen Love*, the received text evidently dates from a century or more later.

Despite such difficulties, it has become standard to date the whole work in the 8th century. Given the qualifications noted above, we also accept this date as a working reference-point for a general understanding of the historical situation of the work.[7]

The Study of Stolen Love is the basic text for the whole work. It is a series of sixty terse epigrams, known in Tamil as nūṟpās and in Tamilized Sanskrit as cūttirams. These cūttirams or nūṟpās are meant to be discoursed upon by teachers and students, and Nakkīraṉār's *Commentary* is the classical written example of such a discourse. *Pāṇṭi-k-Kōvai*, for its part, is a book of poetry. It is a string of independent verses that function step-by-step as well, as a progressive whole. For the most part it is these verses that Nakkīraṉār uses to illustrate his arguments on poetics. His genius was to interweave terse epigrams of authority

---

[6] For further discussion of this date see, for example, Subrahmanian (1986), page 335.

[7] For example, the *Encyclopedia of Tamil Literature, Volume 1* (1990), dates the sixty verses in the 8th century (p. 91), the commentary "most probably of the 8th century" (p. 73), and the verses, the commentary, and the bulk of the illustrative poems in the 8th century (p. 149). Mu. Varadarajan (1988) dates the sixty verses in the 7th or 8th century but gives no date for the commentary. T. P. Meenakshisundaran (1965) believes the commentary was written "probably in the 7th century." Nilakanta Sastri (1955) dates the entire work in the 8th or 9th century. N. Subrahmanian (1986) claims the 7th century as the date for the composition of the commentary.

with poetic illustrations into an integrated prose piece in such a way as to highlight his argument.

Given the tripartite character of the work, we must postulate three primary authors. The author of the sixty nūṟpās is known as Iṟaiyaṉār, which means nothing more nor less than "Lord," undoubtedly intended in the sense of the Divine Lord; nothing further is known about the possible identity of a human who might have composed the work. The commentary, however, was composed by a man named Nakkīraṉār, whose identity with a Caṅkam poet of the same name must be doubted because of the probable gap of centuries between them, although it is impossible to reject categorically the possibility of their identity. In any case, the primary author of the commentary clearly had access to both Caṅkam-age works and *Cilappatikāram*, an epic poem from an age just after that of the Caṅkam poems. *Pāṇṭi-k-Kōvai* also was composed by an unknown person,[8] although its poetic style indicates that it must have appeared after the Caṅkam age. In addition, certain passages, particularly in the commentarial sections, suggest the possibility of later interpolation, indicating a series of secondary authors and editors from later centuries. Despite the likely plurality of authorship, the work is tightly knit into a cohesive whole: whoever the successive editors were, the form of our received text leaves no doubt as to their sensitivity to the work, and their skill in preserving its integrity.

The Tamil text is something over two hundred pages long. It is composed in what has since become a classical commentarial style, in which each verse (nūṟpā) is followed by its carefully constructed commentary. The comments on the first few nūṟpās, and on the last few, present material above and beyond straightforward explanation and illustration of the verses. Among other things, they include prescriptions for the content and structure of a commentary and the presentation of love-poetry conventions, the basis for a serialization of love-story scenes, and observations on history. The commentary to verse 59—the next-to-last verse—presents a fairly complete summary of the entire work.

Editions of the Work

We have been guided in our translation by two critical editions, each based on all palm-leaf manuscripts available at the time of their compilation: one by the Bavanandam Kaḻakam (1939) and one by the South India Saiva Siddhantha Works Publishing Society (1976). In addition, we have consulted palm-leaf manuscripts from the libraries of the Tamil University and Saraswathi Mahal, both in Thanjavur. Despite a number of minor differences, such as repositioned blocks of commentary, we noted little substantial variation in these sources;

---

8 We do not even know with certainty whether the author was a woman or a man.

presumably this comprehensive agreement reflects a relatively in-tact transfer of the work from copyist to copyist. Such an understanding is supported by the tightly knit character of the tripartite work itself: a tightly knit work is likely neither to reflect nor to encourage serious editorial emendation. Nonetheless, a few cases presented enough discrepancy to demand a choice between two possible readings, primarily where one edition contains short passages absent in the other. Where the two critical editions do not agree, our translation follows the South India Saiva Siddhantha Works Publishing Society edition.[9] Since the two critical editions were based on careful readings of many old manuscripts, we considered variant readings in the two old manuscripts noted above much less significant.

Place of the Work in History

One reason for the enduring influence of Nakkīraṉār's *Commentary* is the fact that, for the first time in Tamil, he utilized a prose style throughout a major work. Moreover, the work also lays out the nature of the commentarial endeavor. His own prose is engaging and forceful, while it retains an air of elegant sophistication. The commentary is cast conversationally, like a discourse that one might present to the Caṅkam, the literary academy in the court of ancient Pāṇṭiyaṉ kings.[10] It makes heavy use of a rhetorical device in which the commentator phrases hypothetical questions and objections—again, such as those one might hear in a literary academy—which he proceeds to dissect, accepting the good, rejecting the spurious, and occasionally simply developing alternative lines of thought.

Although Nakkīraṉār's is the earliest prose commentary on the Tamil love-poetry tradition, the *Study of Stolen Love* itself was preceded by other versified works on the subject. Most notable of these is Tamil's oldest extant grammar and poetics treatise, *Tolkāppiyam*, which has been dated variously but was probably composed during the first few centuries BCE. Like the *Study of Stolen Love*, it is a series of epigrammatic *nūṟpās*. Covering much the same ground as *Tolkāppiyam*'s sections on "Stolen Love," "Marital Love, and "Meaning in Poetry," the *Study of Stolen Love* recasts traditional ideas only slightly; it retains the authority of acknowledged grammatical and stylistic referents, and it does so through citation as well as argumentation. Nakkīraṉār's *Commentary* quotes copiously from *Tolkāppiyam* and other, no longer identifiable, works on grammar and poetics, and refers with obvious deference to

[9] We favored this edition because of its much greater availability, given that differences are not substantive.

[10] The Caṅkam period of Tamil literature, referred to on page viii, takes its name from this academy. The word *caṅkam* is akin to the Sanskrit word *sangha*.

Akattiyam, a similar work now lost, but which he assigns to a period prior to *Tolkāppiyam*. Although *Tolkāppiyam* is the oldest extant work treating the poetics of love, it is certain that all of its existing commentaries date from periods considerably later than that of Nakkīraṉār's *Commentary* on Iṟaiyaṉār's *Study of Stolen Love*. Thus, scholars typically accept the following chronological relationship: first, *Akattiyam* (now lost), then *Tolkāppiyam*, then *The Study of Stolen Love* and its *Commentary*, and finally, a number of commentaries on *Tolkāppiyam*.[11]

Significantly, we find the earliest clear description of the literary academies known as Caṅkams in Nakkīraṉār's *Commentary*. These academies were instituted by various Pāṇṭiyaṉ kings, and Nakkīraṉār's account details the who, what, when, and where of the three successive Tamil Caṅkams. *Akattiyam*, said to be composed by the sage Agastya, he assigns to the period of the First Caṅkam, which he locates in a city he calls "Madurai which the sea claimed." According to tradition, there once was an unbroken land mass to the south and east of present-day Tamil Nadu, which was inundated and wiped off the map 3,700 years before the Final Caṅkam was established at Upper Madurai, which is taken to be the current city of Madurai.

Iṟaiyaṉār and Nakkīraṉār's most striking contributions came not in the clarification of ancient tradition, however, but in codifying a next step that was developing within the tradition. They put the poetic course of love in order. Prior to Nakkīraṉār's *Commentary* on the *Study of Stolen Love*, love poems dealt with individual scenes, like little, condensed crystals of reality drawn from the lives of lovers. *Tolkāppiyam* laid down conventions for constructing "snapshots" of love life, and may well embody an earlier tradition of serialized continuity. But it was Nakkīraṉār who, in the present detailed commentary, first ordered those poetic moments unmistakably into a serialized plot. The sequel to this serialization of moments in love poetry was nothing short of spectacular. What had begun in the beautiful, succinct poetry of the Caṅkam age blossomed in a plethora of literary forms that developed in succeeding centuries.

The kōvai form, of which *Pāṇṭi-k-Kōvai* is likely the earliest example, is itself the earliest in a whole class of literary forms that came to be known as Shorter Works, ciṟṟilakkiyam, by reason of their contrast in length to the earlier Great Epics, peruṅkāppiyam. By far the greatest bulk of what was written in Tamil from the time of Nakkīraṉār's *Commentary* to the nineteenth century falls into the class of Shorter Works. The point of a kōvai is precisely to order love scenes serially; so *Pāṇṭi-k-Kōvai* was well suited to Nakkīraṉār's commentarial purpose.

[11] See, for example, T. P. Meenakshisundaran (1965).

But the present commentary did not single-handedly spawn this gigantic literary development. In the first place, it is likely that the kōvai form was around before this commentary became crystallized, since *Pāṇṭi-k-Kōvai* was available to cite. Also, seeds had been sown elsewhere for such a development. *Cilappatikāram*, one of Tamil's magnificent Twin Epics of the third century CE, for example, displays the full development of a serialized love story, albeit on an epic scale instead of a snapshot scale; it even has extensive, if disconnected, prose passages.

By drawing illustrations from *Cilappatikāram* and from the poetry of the Caṅkam age, Nakkīraṉār related the Shorter Works to their own heritage in the *akam* tradition as he codified an approach to literature that blossomed in later centuries.

This revivification of ancient literary tradition seems to have occurred contemporaneously with the bhakti revival in Tamil Nadu. Indeed Neṭumāṟaṉ of Madurai, eulogized in these pages, was converted to the Saiva religion by the bhakti saint Tiruñāṉa Campantar, in an event that gave the bhakti movement one of its greatest boosts.[12] Both movements developed a changed and revitalized way of life in opposition to what sometimes are referred to as "foreign" forms instituted by Buddhists and Jains.

Dramatis Personae and Their Scenes

A text of this sort must delimit identities within the world of poetry: it notes who speaks and acts in love poems, prescribes many of their governing characteristics, categorizes their activities, and plots the effects of their actions on one another.

The framework for all of this detail is taken wholesale from the poetics of the Caṅkam age. The snapshot quality of love scenes is taken for granted, and all plot and character development takes place within one of the specified situations portrayed in these glimpses into the lives of two people in love, and of people associated with them. With this in mind, we can look at some of the people who populate love poems, and at the situations in which they find themselves.

Like the formulators of the Caṅkam poetry conventions that he inherited, Nakkīraṉār assumed love poetry to take the form of actual utterances by dramatic characters in the story of a continuing love. Every poem is spoken by someone specified and addressed to someone or something, also specified.

But it is not real. That is, the scenes, the characters, and what they say, do, and feel, are not to be realistic portraiture of life in the world. The commentary is explicit on this point. It lists eight different types of marriage, the eight that

12 See, for example, T. P. Meenakshisundaran (1965), page 137.

are enumerated in Sanskrit treatises, it says, and in comparing the union described in the *Study of Stolen Love* with one of them, the Gandharva convention, it says:

> Further, if you say that those eight forms of marriage and this one then make nine nuptials, it is not so. Those eight exist in the real world, but this one does not; it is a conduct established by poets as "the nonexistent, the sweet, and the good," and he does not add it to the world's customs.[13]

Only certain people appear in the poems, and only some of them may actually speak. There are, of course, a woman and a man who are the central characters, the heroine and the hero, the talaivi and the talaivaṉ. But the hero also has a close friend with whom he shares his feelings, as does the heroine; and her friend's mother doubles as the heroine's foster mother. There is also an assortment of other characters: some Brahmins, eventually a courtesan, and bards who attempt to mediate between a wronged wife and her husband are among them. Each has identifiable places within specific thematic moments throughout the love story. But it is only the characters of the hero and the heroine that are scrupulously identified throughout the history of their love.

The hero, says Nakkīraṉār in his comments to the second nūṟpā,[14]

> has the four qualities of wisdom, constancy, investigation, and resolve

while

> the heroine's four qualities are modesty, innocence, fear, and loathing.

Nakkīraṉār then defines these qualities more fully; he asks rhetorically,

> What is wisdom, you ask?

and quotes couplet 355 from the *Tirukkuṟaḷ* of Tiruvaḷḷuvar:

> Whatever the nature of whatever thing, wisdom
> is seeing its true substance.

He then goes on to discuss the rest of the hero's qualities:

> What is constancy, you ask? It is the protection of what is to be protected, while discarding what is to be discarded.
> Investigation is researching a thing and understanding it.
> And resolve is not forgetting a thing undertaken.

But, the commentator goes on to say,

---

[13] Page 26.

[14] Pages 32–33.

> All four of these are overwhelmed in the hero by his desire and lie bent, as grass lies bent in the path of a flooding stream.

For her, then, Nakkīraṉār explains simply that

> Modesty is a natural characteristic of women.

He then says, for her other characteristics,

> Innocence is holding on to what she knows, without letting go.

Fear, he explains, is

> fearing something that she has never seen before, due to her femininity.
> And loathing is the state of loathing things that are unfamiliar.

For the heroine also, Nakkīraṉār adds, concerning the heroine's four characteristics, that

> All four of these lie bent like grass in the path of a flooding stream, overwhelmed by desire.
> It is this that is called the Union of Love.

Nakkīraṉār further considers the ages of these protagonists in some detail: he is just turning sixteen, "the age at which he becomes confirmed in manhood," and she is just turning twelve, and about to enter "the childbearing age." Both manhood and the childbearing age are "eschewed as inappropriate for Stolen Love," more appropriate to Married Love.[15] Marriage at such a young age seems to have been the ideal in ancient Indian Literature.[16] Given its actual existence in more modern India,[17] it may have been preferred in earlier practice as well. The protagonists in *The Study of Stolen Love* appear to begin their life together immediately upon marrying—or even earlier.[18]

The stage is now set for the tension between the essential characteristics of the two lovers and their behavior under the influence of love and desire for each other. Other characters in the poems—their friends, relations, and acquaintances—all serve as backdrop figures to highlight this relationship. And all of the thematic moments pictured in the individual poems develop reactions of the hero and the heroine to each other in specified social and emotional settings.

---

[15] *The Study of Stolen Love*, commentary to Verse 32, pages 240–241.

[16] Kaṇṇaki, the bride in *Cilappatikāram*, for example, also was twelve, and her husband Kōvalaṉ was sixteen. See R. Parthasarathy (1993), pages 25–26.

[17] Gandhi, for example, and his wife Kasturbai were 13 years old when they were married. See Gandhi (1927), Chapter III.

[18] In certain situations they eloped, and married upon their return. See pages xx–xxi.

Here, for example, is what the hero says to a friend who has just teased him about his brand-new love affair:

> Sure, make
> fun of me!
> If your warning could stop
> my body from melting,
> nothing would be better!
>
> But inside me
> it spreads
> like a slab of butter
> melting on a scorching rock
> set in the summer sun,
>   a dumb boy with no arms
>   trying to corral it
>   with his eyes.
>
> It is so hard
> to contain
> this disease.[19]

The example this time is not from *Pāṇṭi-k-Kōvai*, but from one of the anthologies of Caṅkam love poetry, *Kuṟuntokai.*

Then when his friend finally eases up on his teasing, realizing that the boy is really serious about her, he asks the hero where he met such a girl. Here is the hero's response, and one of the four illustrative poems brought in by the commentator:

> The hero was overjoyed when he heard this: it was though he had just attained her again, as a withering sandalwood tree, scorched by the summer sun, sprouts when it rains. He said, "The form I saw was in such-and-such a place, and of such-and-such a nature." Here are some poems for that:
>
> ...
> I did not know
> that there in the sea grove,
> fragrant with flowers,
> lives a bewitching goddess,
> holding in her hands
> a bouquet of screwpine blooms,
> pretending to chase birds
> from fatty fish set to dry—
>
> had I known,
> I never

[19] *Kuṟuntokai* 58, pages 61–62.

would have gone
there.[20]

Finally he does get to meet her again. But the immediate joy of that meeting can become complicated, as the commentator explains. He presents a number of possible scenarios, one of which is this:

> There he comes upon the heroine, standing alone. She sees him, and they meet. The moment she sees him, her fear of his death disperses, and she becomes herself again. Becoming herself, remember, means regaining her modesty, innocence, fear, and loathing; but as she stands reunited with her old nature, he becomes upset, since he cannot draw near without some sign from her! Being upset means there can be no other emotion. Now, his distraction grabs for anything it can find in consolation; but there is nothing. So he says something. What does he say, you ask? He says things like this: "You must be the goddess of this grove; if you are not, please open your mouth! If I lost my life, it would be very difficult to get it back, would it not?"

Nakkīraṉār then quotes two stanzas from *Pāṇṭi-k-Kōvai* illustrating this speech of the hero, and continues,

> Is it the hero who said these things, you ask? It is not: it is the anguish born within him. That, too, must be considered the hero. The moment she heard these words she looked up at him, afraid that he might actually die, and she saw the truth: when she saw him, she felt a tremendous thrill, like picking up a fine jewel that you had lost and searched for. Her joy made her teeth appear in a smile, but then she became distracted, thinking, "I have committed a great immodesty before my lord!" Then she thought, "My lord grieves even while I stand here before him! If he were now to see me in anguish, he would most surely die!" As she thinks in this vein, her anguish leaves and her modesty returns.
>
> Yet though it returns, she can find nowhere to hide. So, with a loving glance, she covers her long, flower-like eyes with her gentle fingers, like a good jewel, the glory lily.
>
> When she covers her eyes, he thinks it will console her if he comes to her side. "You covered your long black eyes because you figured they cause me anguish, didn't you?" he says, "But what about your shoulders, with their tracings of sugarcane! Are they any less important to me?"
>
> Here are some poems for that:[21]

The commentator then quotes three poems illustrating this speech of the hero, including this one from the Caṅkam anthology *Naṟṟiṇai*:

> You do not respond when I speak,
> you are modest, you bow
> your beautiful face.
> When love strangles me
> like this, how can I bear it?

---

[20] Pages 63–65. The poem is *Cilappatikāram: Kāṉalvari*, 9.

[21] Pages 71–73.

It's not just your eyes
that gouge me out with their corners red
like the tips of the tusks of an elephant
stinking of flesh after it bullied
a tiger, and gored its great, striped back,
leaving it shuddering—
It's your shoulders, too, they
bewitch me with their tracings
of sugar cane, your shoulders
like the celebrated city of Kūṭal,
city of Ceḻiyaṉ, victor in battles,
  who took up the drums of war
  and stormed garrisoned castles
  and towns, even as his enemies
  swarmed their battlements![22]

Inner allusions in this poem, as in all akam poems, tie it together into an integrated whole. Her eyes are powerful enough to cause him to tremble, as the tusks of the elephant, to which they are compared, reduce the mighty tiger to helpless trembling. And even if they are concealed, there is no concealing her beautiful shoulders. As her eyes are compared to the powerful tusks of an elephant, her shoulders are compared to Kūṭal (another name for Madurai), the beautiful capital city of an emperor: those shoulders belong to her who has conquered him, as Kūṭal belongs to the king who captured impregnable fortresses and carried off the royal drums signifying the strength of enemy kings. So the poem declares his love, his surrender to her, his own strength under normal circumstances (remember that modesty is her virtue, not his), and the futility of trying to deny their love; and it beseeches her to open up to him.

At a later point in their love story, her neighbors start gossiping and causing problems. When that happens, the commentator points out various options for the poet. Among the possibilities is that of elopement. While it is not the course that the commentator praises as the most virtuous, it is the one upon which he lavishes most of his comments, and for which he adduces the most example verses. After considerable soul-searching, the hero might decide that it is the best way out. If so, he is to inform the heroine's friend, according to convention. She returns to the heroine, the commentary informs us:

> "Our lady," she says, "Our lord is thinking of eloping with you! What do you think?"
>
> Now there are only two alternatives for the heroine when she hears this: approval or denial of his wish. If she honors him and elopes, she loses her modesty; yet if she declines, she loses fidelity! Of those two, which type of woman will she be, you ask?

[22] *Naṟṟiṇai* 39, page 74.

> She has both modesty and fidelity, does she not? Of the two, fidelity is the stronger. Why is it stronger, you ask? Since he has said,

and here Nakkīraṉār quotes *Tolkāppiyam*:

> Modesty is more important than life; fidelity with faultless perception is even more important than modesty,

> she would never think of letting her fidelity go to ruin, even if it meant her modesty were ruined. So she agrees to elope, as she inclines her head and stands scratching the earth with her big toe: standing like that amounts to agreeing.[23]

At this point the commentary includes three poems illustrating the general theme of the moment of her deciding to elope with him. The speaker is the heroine and she speaks to her friend, who has just announced the elopement proposal to her. Here is one of those poems, again from the Caṅkam anthology *Naṟṟiṇai*:

> In little groups
> and in crowds, leering
> at me out of the corners
> of their eyes, and touching
> their fingers to their noses
> in contempt, my neighbors
> are whispering!
> And mother! She
> struck me!
>
> But tonight
> he's coming
> in his fine chariot
> he's forcing fast horses
> to fly even faster,
> horses whose beautiful backs
> have the smells of the flowers
> they brushed in the backwaters,
>
> and I have decided
>
> to go with him.
>
> This stupid village
> can just sit here
> and gossip![24]

The hero and heroine do get married, and there are several ways for this to happen. But once they are married and she bears children, she faces new

---

[23] Page 181. The quotation is *Tolkāppiyam: Kaḷaviyal*, 23.

[24] *Naṟṟiṇai* 149, page 182.

problems in the form of his prolonged absences. These absences may have any of six causes, according to the verses and their commentary. Verse 35 declares,

> Learning, defense, peace-mission,
> service to the emperor, amassing wealth, and courtesans:
> these six are the separations in that case.[25]

The commentator goes to great pains to prove that none of these activities in any way compromises the incomparable character of the hero. He first postulates objections to the hero's incomparable nature that might arise in considering these reasons for his absence; then he counters them. Take the departure for amassing wealth, for example. Nakkīraṉār poses a possible objection this way:

> Next, if you say that he leaves to amass wealth, then he becomes someone who had no wealth before. Since people who have no wealth cannot command scorners, nor give to beggars and so on, he must also have all of those shortcomings, and where is the incomparability of a man like that?[26]

He counters the argument thus:

> Next, departing for wealth does not mean he has none. All the various types of wealth that his parents had amassed may lie there for him to use, but he does not think it manly to enjoy his life in using that up; so he departs to amass wealth by his own enterprise, that he might live on that. Moreover, affairs of the gods and the ancestors will not bear fruit unless they are carried out with wealth that one has amassed by his own enterprise. Why? Gods and ancestors are not pleased with rites performed with inherited wealth. Thus, he departs in order to make them happy as well.[27]

In other places, Iṟaiyaṉār identifies who among men is to leave his wife for which reasons. For example, Verse 39 goes,

> Departure for service to the emperor and amassing wealth:
> those two also belong to the lower people.

By lower people, he means merchants and farmers, the lower pair of the four castes, *varṇas*, Nakkīraṉār explains. But then he has another problem to face, which he tackles in this way:

> You think it contradicts their incomparability to say they are low? It does not. Since this treatise both accords with and does not accord with the world, these people are called "low" by virtue of the distinction of worldly castes. In all other respects, incomparability is theirs as well.[28]

---

[25] Page 245.

[26] Page 246.

[27] Pages 247–248.

[28] Page 251.

When he has finished his work away from home, whatever it may have been, the hero sets his sights once again toward home and his wife. To urge his charioteer to drive faster, he soliloquizes in such a way that the charioteer will overhear him. Here is an illustrative poem for that moment:

In the southern lands
  of the Lion to His Enemies,
  who fought the scorching
  Battle of Pāḻi,
  the descendant of the king
  who gave a thousand elephants
  in alms,
winter *piṭavu* is blooming now,
like a fragrant, woven
wreath in the cool woodlands.
I watch the dark clouds:

is that doll, that girl,
whose wide mound of love
is covered with silk
watching them too?
I wonder.[29]

When he arrives drums beat, conches sound, and he re-unites happily with his wife.

But the case of his departure to visit courtesans is rather different. His reception at home after this sort of absence may be much less enthusiastic. Here is a poem, says the commentator, spoken by the heroine's friend to the hero. He has just returned from a stay with a courtesan. In this verse, the heroine's friend announces at the door that she has told the heroine of his coming and relates the result. He is *not* permitted to come home.

I said,
"You with impeccable jewels,
who are like the lands in the south
  of Neṭumāṟaṉ with a well-oiled lance,
  who granted heaven to his enemies at Vallam,
  with its great groves
  where clouds settle!
  Our lover
  is coming this way."

---

[29] *Pāṇṭi-k-Kōvai* 252, pages 257–258.

> And right in front of me,
> her red lips quivered,
> and her black eyes reddened.[30]

There are also stanzas to be spoken by the courtesan. One illustrates Verse 47, which says,

> The heroine's self-praise before the hero,
> even in times of quarrel, is not great.

The commentator explains:

> The heroine will never get to praise herself; and thus we see her greatness.
>
> Next, by saying that the heroine never gets to praise herself, he implies that the courtesan does get to praise herself. Here is a poem on the courtesan praising herself:

> If I do not
> make him turn to me,
> like a thistle
> turns to face the sun,
> right in front of her
> with her white teeth,
> and her sunshine face,
> then may my white
> conch bracelets break
> like the army
> of gleaming swords
> that broke
> for those who fled
> the fertile lands
> taken by the Lion to His Enemies,
> who clutches
> that glistening lance![31]

Some poems are spoken by people other than the hero and heroine or their close friends. Through the eyes of these people poets present other facets of the hero and heroine to their audiences. One such group of poems is spoken by the heroine's foster mother. She has visited the couple in their marital home, and reports to the heroine's real mother on the happy state of affairs there. In addition to three verses from *Pāṇṭi-k-Kōvai*, Nakkīraṉār cites one from the Caṅkam anthology *Naṟṟiṇai*; here is one from *Pāṇṭi-k-Kōvai*:

> In the cool Kolli Mountains
> of the Goad to His Enemies,
> the king of this world

---

[30] *Pāṇṭi-k-Kōvai* 273, page 271.

[31] Page 285. The poem is *Pāṇṭi-k-Kōvai* 292.

with his righteous scepter,
she, her hair dark
as a raincloud,
is as constant
as the pole star,
and those magnificent horses
harnessed to the grand,
golden chariot of the lord
whose lance never rests in war—
they don't know what it means
to stay long in the battlefield,

even when he goes to carry out
his king's commands![32]

Literary Patron

Throughout these examples, Nakkīraṉār makes unmistakable reference to a king with a name, the only person referred to by name in *any* poem. No one else in these interior, or love, poems, is named, according to a convention first laid down in *Tolkāppiyam*. Naming a lover would particularize the poem and detract from the universality of emotion that the poems are to invoke, say the pundits. So who is this king, this Goad to His Enemies, this Lion to His Enemies, in *Pāṇṭi-k-Kōvai*? He is the Pāṇṭiyaṉ king Neṭumāṟaṉ, who ruled during the latter part of the 7th century in Madurai, and was converted to Saivism by Tiruñāṉa Campantar.[33]

Neṭumāṟaṉ is known as the Literary Patron of the piece, the pāṭṭuṭai-t-talaivaṉ. *Pāṇṭi-k-Kōvai* probably was composed in, or at least presented to, his court. Every verse in the kōvai refers to him somewhere in glowing terms. Sometimes it is just a fleeting mention, and other times imagery associated directly with the panegyric claims most of the words in the verse. But he is always there.

The poet's mastery shows in the use of the imagery in the panegyric as a foil for depicting the theme of the love-story moment. Sometimes there is a transparent relation between the panegyric and the love theme, as in *Pāṇṭi-k-Kōvai* 317, spoken to the heroine by her friend, who wants to reassure her that the hero will return from his trip:

I know
that he who left
is coming back.

---

[32] *Pāṇṭi-k-Kōvai* 311, pages 302–303.

[33] For further information about the history of this period and about Neṭumāṟaṉ, see for example T. P. Meenakshisundaran (1965) or Nilakanta Sastri (1955).

Girl, don't
grow thin
    like the enemies of him
    who conquered Cennilam
    in war
    ...[34]

Sometimes it is further removed, as in *Pāṇṭi-k-Kōvai* 67, from nearer the beginning of the love story. Here the heroine has just told her friend that the reason she looks so blooming and beautiful is that she took a bath in a certain mountain pool. Actually, she has just returned from her first-ever union with the man with whom she is to spend the rest of her life. Her friend does not know what happened, but she evidently suspects that something of the sort is afoot. Here is what she says to the heroine:

If it will make me
as beautiful as you,
like a peacock
in the Potiyil Mountains
of him who witnessed
    the confederacy
    of garlanded kings
    wage war at Pūlantai
    in the South,
    suffer wounds
    in their precious chests,
    and reach heaven
    right there,
woman!

I too will bathe
in that bright
mountain pool,
like you.[35]

No explicit relation is drawn between the war imagery and the love imagery. But take out the regal terms and what do you have? Wounds in the chest, where your heart is, and immediate entry into heaven, familiar feelings to attribute to lovers. And the regal imagery also is appropriate in terms of her accepting him as her lord, in light of the probably patriarchal society through which these poems circulated.

---

[34] Page 309.

[35] Pages 91–92.

Conclusion

Finally, a word on the art of literary translation: We have all heard that poetry and prose both "lose in translation," and we unhappily agree. A masterpiece in Tamil *is* in Tamil, and there is no literary or social decree that there must exist an equivalently good piece in English, simply waiting to be found. On the contrary, the excellence of any turn of phrase is always tied to its words and syntax, and their nuances, which in their turn are part and parcel of the original language. One way out of this quandary is to posit an inner feeling out of which the original expression grew. As an "expression," then, the original work expresses something deeper, and presumably more universally reachable, than any expression in any language; and it is its appeal to such a universally understood base that makes any writing good or excellent. One's task as a translator, then, is not to change a literary masterpiece into a new language, but, first, to understand its deeper emotional significance as thoroughly as possible, and then to write it out anew in the target language.

Readers who feel at home in both Tamil and English will have to judge our attempts in this light. Readers who do not have access to the Tamil original, however, clearly form the bulk of our intended audience; they will have to judge our efforts solely on the basis of the emotional appeal, or lack of it, that they find in the translation. Of necessity, they will judge the translation, as well as the original, on the basis of its literary success in English.

The Study of Stolen Love, with its *Commentary* and illustrative poems, raises issues in a great many areas in the context of ancient southern India. These areas include women's studies; gender relations; religion; political, economic, and social history; anthropology and sociology; literary criticism; and intellectual history, among others. We hope this translation will render its viewpoints on such issues accessible to English-language scholars and general readers around the world.

ஓம்:

களவியல்

என்னும்

இறையனார் அகப்பொருள்

1. களவு

க. அன்பின் ஐந்திணைக் களவெனப் படுவ
தந்தணர் அருமறை மன்றல் எட்டனுள்
கந்தருவ வழக்கம் என்மனார் புலவர்

என்பது சூத்திரம். 'எந்நூல் உரைப்பினும், அந்நூற்குப் பாயிரம் உரைத்து உரைக்க,' என்பது மரபு; என்னை?

"ஆயிர முகத்தான் அகன்ற தாயினும்
பாயிரம் இல்லது பனுவல் அன்றே"

என்றாராகலானும், 'பருப்பொருட்டாகிய பாயிரம் கேட்டார்க்கு நுண்பொருட்டாகிய நூல் இனிது விளங்கும்,' என்பவாகலானும், 'பாயிரம் உரைத்துரைக்கவேண்டும்,' என்பது மரபு. 'என் போல?' எனின், 'கொழுச் சென்ற வழித் துன்னூசி இனிது செல்லும்; அது போல,' என்பது.

அப்பாயிரம் இரு வகைப்படும், பொதுவும் சிறப்புமென. அவற்றுள் பொதுப்பாயிரம் என்பது, எல்லா நூன்முகத்தும் உரைக்கப்படுவது; சிறப்புப்பாயிரம் என்பது, தன்னால் உரைக்கப்படும் நூற்கு இன்றியமையாதது.

'பாயிரம் என்ற சொற்குப் பொருள் யாதோ?' எனின், புறவுரை என்றவாறு. 'ஆயின், நூல் கேட்பான் புகுந்தோன்* நூல் கேளானே? புறவுரை[1] கேட்டென்னை?'

---

* 'நூல் கேளாமுன் புறவுரை கேட்பதென்னையோவெனின்' என்பதும் பாடம்.

1. 'கேட்டலால் யாது பயன்?' எனின்

PART I
The Study of Stolen Love

Verse 1.[1]

> **What is called Stolen Love, in five modes of affection,[2]**
> **is, among the pleasant ones' rare secret's eight nuptials,**
> **the Kantaruva Convention, say the poets.**

Such is the verse.

Now, whatever the book you undertake to interpret, it is always best to present a preface before beginning your commentary. We know it is traditional to expound a preface first because he has said,

> Though it expand in a thousand dimensions,
> without a preface, it is no book,[3]

and

> For those who attend to its synoptic preface,
> a book's subtle nuances shine sweetly.[4]

Now what is this preface to be like, you ask? It shall be like this:

> Where a plowpoint has gone, a needle
> will easily follow.[5]

Prefaces themselves are of two sorts: the general and the specific. All books need general prefaces, but you must compose a specific preface only for a book you write yourself.

---

[1] The verses themselves, throughout the *Study of Stolen Love*, are quite opaque even in the Tamil; thus the commentary is absolutely essential. Such a relationship between verses and their commentary is standard in ancient Tamil scholarly writing; it is discussed at greater length in the Introduction, pages x–xv.

[2] "Affection" is used here to translate **aṉpu**, which is to be distinguished from "Stolen Love," **kaḷavu**. Often, **aṉpu** will require translation by the single word "love," but the phrase "Stolen Love" will be reserved as the exclusive translation of **kaḷavu** in all contexts where **kaḷavu** refers to love.

[3] Unidentified verse which also occurs as Verse 54 of the 12th century grammar treatise *Naṉṉūl*. Footnotes will be provided for Nakkīraṉār's commentary whenever he cites other works even if they are not identifiable (as in the case of this footnote), and when they can aid in interpretation by explaining the Tamil literary background relevant to otherwise opaque passages.

[4] Unidentified verse.

[5] Unidentified verse.

What, then, is the meaning of this word "preface," you ask? It means an external exposition. In that case, what is the point in learning an external exposition when one is learning the entire book itself, you ask? It is indispensable to the book, even if it is placed outside it. What is it like, you ask? It is like a gatehouse to a great, fortified city; it is like the sun and the moon, lights in endless space; it is like a fine fresco on a massive wall. Thus, the book is to be studied only after the preface has been mastered.

Now a general preface is divided into four parts: the nature of the donor, the nature of his giving, the nature of the recipient, and his method of receiving. This we know because he has said,

> Donor's nature, giving's nature,
> recipient's nature, and receiving's method:
> this double pair is the nature of the general.[6]

The nature of the donor is the character of the author, or teacher; the nature of his giving is his plan in composing the book; the nature of the recipient is the character of the reader, or pupil; and his method of receiving is his learning style. It would be superfluous to expound upon all of these here: see the rest of the present volume.

Next, a specific preface has eight parts. What are they, you ask? They are: author's name, school, boundary, book's title, prosodic structure, content, audience, and purpose. This we know because he has said,

> Author's name, school, bounds,
> book's title, structure, content,
> audience, and purpose: to place these eight
> subjects on display is the nature of a preface.[7]

There are also those who would add time, location, and cause of composition, to make eleven. Why? Because he has said,

> There are also those who admit
> time, location, and cause.[8]

Author's name is the name of the scholar who created the work. Who created the present work, you ask? The answer is the Vedic God with the Light of the Sun, Who Holds as a Wreath in His Hair the Crescent Moon with Tender Milky Rays, in Kūṭal City where the palace of the Grand One stands.

---

[6] Unidentified verse.

[7] Unidentified verse.

[8] Unidentified verse.

School is the scholastic tradition into which a book falls. This book, however, is not to be placed in any tradition, because it was created by Him Who is Foremost in That Wisdom Which Removes Karma; it is an original treatise.[9]

By **boundary** we mean that each book pertains to a certain geographical area. What are this book's boundaries, you ask? They are the Vēṅkaṭam Mountains in the north, Cape Kumari in the south, and the ocean on the east and west. This we know because Kākkaippāṭiṉiyār and Tolkāppiyaṉār have said,

> In the north and the south, the west and the east,
> Vēṅkaṭam, Kumari, and the sweet-water seas:
> the range of a book lies within these four bounds
> when one expounds with clarity,[10]

and

> Northern Vēṅkaṭam and southern Kumari:
> in between
> is the good world where people speak Tamil.[11]

Book's title means the title of the book. Books may take titles of various types. Which types? A book may take its title from the name of its author, or from the name of someone who commissioned the work; it may take a specially designed name as its title; it may take a title from its length; or its title may derive from its particular significance. *Akattiyam* and *Tolkāppiyam* took their titles from the names of their authors;[12] *Catavākaṉam* and *Iḷantiraiyam* took theirs from the names of the people who commissioned them;[13] *Nikaṇṭu Nūl* and *Kalai-k-Kōṭṭu-t-Taṇṭu* took specially designed names;[14] *Twelve Paṭalams* took its name from

---

[9] See also Nakkīraṉār's discussion of the "original treatise" on pages 12–13.

[10] Unidentified verse, presumably drawn from the ancient treatise *Kākkaippāṭiṉiyam*, now lost.

[11] These are the opening words of Paṉampāraṉār's Specific Preface to *Tolkāppiyam*. See the Introduction, pages xiii–xiv for more about *Tolkāppiyam*.

[12] Akattiyaṉār and Tolkāppiyaṉār wrote these two formative grammars of Tamil some centuries before *The Study of Stolen Love*; *Akattiyam* has been lost, but *Tolkāppiyam* still functions as the last word in Tamil grammar and poetics. See the Introduction, pages xiii–xiv.

[13] They were commissioned by Catavākaṉaṉ and Iḷantiraiyaṉ, respectively. Catavākaṉaṉ was probably a king from the Catavākaṉa dynasty; Iḷantiraiyaṉ was a king who ruled in northern Tamil Nadu during the Caṅkam Age.

[14] Although some scholars, such as Singaravelu Mudaliar in his encyclopedic *Abithana Chintamani* (page 974), treat these two as a single book, they most likely are two; still, their exact nature is not known, and the books themselves are lost.

its length;[15] and *The Study of Stolen Love* takes its title from its particular significance: the author regards Stolen Love as more significant than Married Love;[16] we know this because he insists that,

> As there is no speech before uniting,
> what is known as Marital Love follows Stolen Love.[17]

Marital Love does not involve as firm an affection as Stolen Love.

Next, **prosodic structure**: A book may be structured in any of four ways: collection, exposition, collection and exposition, or translation. As it is said,

> Collecting, expounding, collecting and expounding, and translating:
> structuring in these ways is within the tradition.[18]

This book is structured as a collection, because in it he has collected, within these sixty verses, all characteristics of love poetry that are abroad in the world.

Next, we turn to the **content** of a book. What does this book describe, you ask? It describes Tamil.[19]

Audience, then, means those who heard the book's debut. And who heard this book's debut, you ask? When it is possible that a book might have flaws, it is necessary to have a board of reviewers to hear it and establish its perfection. But as this book was created by The Source, it can have no flaws. There was no audience then, for this book, because of its positive lack of flaws. Yet when one looks at the commentary, one sees that it did have an audience. And who heard it, you ask? It was Uppūri Kuṭi Kiḻār's son Uruttiracaṉmaṉ. We shall relate the reason he came to hear it:

History Of The Three Caṅkams

The Pāṇṭiyaṉ kings instituted three Caṅkams:[20] the Premier Caṅkam, the Middle Caṅkam, and the Final Caṅkam. They say that five hundred and forty-

[15] This book is said to have been composed by twelve disciples of Akattiyaṉār; it is a treatise on exterior poetry, perhaps analogous to *The Study of Stolen Love*, although its exact nature is not known since it also is lost.

[16] Married Love is also covered in this treatise.

[17] *The Study of Stolen Love*, 15. This verse is explained in detail on pages 147–148.

[18] *Tolkāppiyam: Marapiyal*, 99

[19] As opposed to Sanskrit, presumably. In Sanskrit there is no emphasis on the Stolen/Married Love distinction.

[20] **Caṅkam** means "gathering;" it refers to gatherings of literary men and women in an academic setting at the king's court; the word is related to the Sanskrit word **sangha**. Although the word appears occasionally in earlier poems, this is the earliest discussion of the tradition of Tamil Caṅkams, which since the time of *The Study of Stolen Love* have constituted a serious subject in the study of Tamil.

nine people participated in the Premier Caṅkam, including Akattiyaṉār,[21] the Lord with Spreading Locks Who Burnt Three Cities,[22] Lord Murukaṉ Who Destroyed the Hill, Muriñciyūr Muṭinākarāyar, the Owner of Wealth,[23] and others. Including them, four thousand, four hundred and forty-nine people presented poems,[24] they say. Ever so many *paripāṭals* were sung, as well as *Mutunārai*, *Mutukuruku*, *Kaḷariyāvirai*, and so on. They remained convened in that Caṅkam for four thousand, four hundred forty years. They say eighty-nine kings kept the Caṅkam convened, from Kāyciṉavaḻuti at first to Kaṭuṅkōṉ at the end, and that seven of those Pāṇṭiyaṉ kings even presented poems. The Madurai that the sea claimed[25] is where they held their sessions and researched into Tamil, they say. They also say that the reference work for that Caṅkam was *Akattiyam*.

Next, fifty-nine people participated in the Middle Caṅkam, they say, including Akattiyaṉār, Tolkāppiyaṉār, Iruntaiyūr-k-Karuṅkōḻi Mōci, Veḷḷūr-k-Kāppiyaṉ, Pāṇṭaraṅkaṉ the Younger, Tiraiyaṉ Māṟaṉ, Tuvarai-k-Kōmāṉ, Kīrantai, and others. Including them, three thousand, seven hundred people presented poems, they say. They presented *Kali*, *Kuruku*, *Veṇṭāḷi*, *Viyāḻamālai Akaval*, and other works, they say. Their reference works were *Akattiyam*, *Tolkāppiyam*, *Māpurāṇam*, *Icainuṇukkam*, and *Pūta Purāṇam*. They remained convened in that Caṅkam for three thousand, seven hundred years, they say. Fifty-nine kings kept the Caṅkam in session, from Ceḻiyaṉ of the White Chariot to Tirumāṟaṉ the Lame; and five of them presented poems, they say. Kapāṭapuram is the city in which they held their sessions and researched into Tamil. Perhaps the sea took Tamil Nadu then as well.

And further, forty-nine people researched into Tamil during the institution of the Final Caṅkam. Among them were Mētāviyār the Younger, Cēntampūtaṉār, Aṟivuṭaiyaṉār, Kuṉṟūr-k-Kiḻār the Elder, Tirumāṟaṉ the Younger, the Madurai Professor Nallantuvaṉār, Madurai Marutaṉiḷa Nākaṉār, Nakkīrar the son of Kaṇakkāyaṉār, and others, they say. Including them, four hundred forty-nine people presented poems, they say. They sang the *Anthology of Four Hundred*

---

[21] Presumably the author of the treatise *Akattiyam*, referred to above and throughout Nakkīraṉār's commentary. See also the Introduction, pages xiii–xiv.

[22] Lord Siva.

[23] Lord Kubera.

[24] Literally, "they sang," **pāṭiṉār**.

[25] It is said that the seas destroyed two early Pāṇṭiyaṉ capitals, the Madurai mentioned here and Kapāṭapuram mentioned below. The third Pāṇṭiyaṉ capital, Upper Madurai, is said to be the same as the present city of Madurai in Tamil Nadu.

Long Poems,[26] the *Anthology of Four Hundred Short Poems*,[27] the *Four Hundred Good Poems On The Modes*,[28] the *Four Hundred Outward Poems*,[29] the *Five Hundred Short Poems*,[30] the *Ten Decades*,[31] the *Hundred and Fifty Kalis*,[32] the *Seventy Paripāṭals*,[33] the *Dance*,[34] *Vari*, the *Lesser Musical Treatise*,[35] the *Greater Musical Treatise*,[36] and others. *Akattiyam* and *Tolkāppiyam* were their reference works, they say. They remained in session and researched into Tamil for one thousand, eight hundred fifty years, they say. Forty-nine kings maintained that Caṅkam, from Tirumāraṉ the Lame, whom the sea took, to Ukkira-p-Peruvaḻuti: three of them presented poems, they say. They held their sessions and researched into Tamil in the city of Upper Madurai, they say.

History of *The Study of Stolen Love*

In those days famine visited the Pāṇṭiyaṉ land for twelve years, and as hunger grew the king summoned all his court scholars.

"Come," he said, "My country is suffering horribly, and I can no longer support you: go wherever you can find a place. When this land becomes a real country again, think of me and return."

Thus they left the king, and twelve years passed with no reckoning of the time.

But in time the rains fell, and the land prospered: the king sent men in all directions saying, "As this land has now become a real country once again, bring back all those people well versed in literature."

So they found and brought back all the scholars in the fields of letters, words, and structures; but they had to report, "Nowhere could we find a scholar in the field of meaning."[37]

---

[26] *Neṭuntokai*, currently also known as *Akanāṉūṟu*.

[27] Currently also known as *Kuṟuntokai*.

[28] Currently also known as *Naṟṟiṇai*.

[29] Currently also known as *Puṟanāṉūṟu*.

[30] Currently also known as *Aiṅkuṟunūṟu*.

[31] Currently also known as *Patiṟṟu-p-pattu*.

[32] *Nūṟṟaimpatu-k-Kali*.

[33] *Eḻupatu Paripāṭal*.

[34] *Kūttu*.

[35] *Ciṟṟicai*.

[36] *Pēricai*.

[37] The *Field of Meaning* referred to here is the *Study of Stolen Love*, the sixty Verses of the present work.

The king was stricken, and he worried.

"What is the point in researching into letters, words, and structures, if not for the field of meaning? Without the field of meaning, gaining the other fields is no gain at all!" he exclaimed, and gave himself to meditation upon the fire-colored God at the Madurai temple.

"Shame!" thought God, "The king is really far too upset! But as it is in the cause of Wisdom, we shall end it." He then created these sixty verses, inscribed them upon three copper plates, and placed them beneath the altar.

There was one of the worshippers of the Divine Family who would polish the entire temple; he sprinkled water and arranged the flowers, but he always missed that spot beneath the altar. That one day, however, he received a sign from God and thought, "I think I shall sweep there today." With elation in his heart, he swept under the altar, and his broom struck the copper plates. He picked them up and looked at them: it proved to be the Field of Meaning, full of possibilities.

That Brahmin thought to himself, "Our Lord must have graciously made these, when he heard that the king was so upset at losing the Field of Meaning."

Instead of going home, he went straight to the front gate of the palace and informed the gatekeepers. They informed the king, who called out to the Brahmin and said, "Enter!"

The Brahmin entered and showed them to the king, who received and inspected them.

"The Field of Meaning!" he cried, "Our Lord must have created these when he saw our suffering!" And he turned toward God and stood in worship. Then he caused the members of the Caṅkam to be summoned.

"Here is the Field of Meaning," he said, "Our Lord created this when he saw how we suffered. Take it, and interpret it."

They took it with them and mounted the dais of deliberation to investigate its meaning. Several days passed as each one declared his own interpretation to be correct.

Determining the Commentary to the *Study of Stolen Love*

"No matter how we work over the commentary, we cannot agree; we must return to the king and ask him to grant us an arbitrator. We will accept whatever he declares the true meaning to be, and reject whatever he says it is not," they concluded, and proceeded to the king.

The king rose to receive them, saying, "So, you have determined the meaning of the book?"

"In order to determine that, you must grant us an arbitrator," they reported.

"Where am I to find such an arbitrator?" the king demanded. "There are forty-nine of you, and none can equal you. Go away, leave me!"

So they left, and mounted again upon the dais of deliberation.

"Now how are we to get an arbitrator, since the king has answered us thus?" they wondered.

But He who created this book is the Lord of the Temple, He with the spreading locks, is He not? So they prayed to Him to grant them an arbitrator as a divine boon.

Then, in the middle watch, they heard the Voice that sounds through all three times,[38] saying, "In this city there lives a five-year-old boy with innocent eyes and thin hair; he is Uruttiracaṉmaṉ, the son of Uppūri Kuṭi Kiḻār, and he is a mute. Do not deprecate him for that, but bring him here and cause him to sit upon this seat. Then, when beneath him you utter the true meaning of a verse, tears will come to his eyes, and his body hair will bristle; when he hears a commentary that is not the true meaning, he will simply sit quietly. He is really the God Kumāraṉ,[39] who has been made to appear here through a curse."

As this was agreeable to them all, the entire Caṅkam arose, circumambulated the temple, and went to Uppūri Kuṭi Kiḻār. They related the story, and spoke these words: "The Brahmin must give us Uruttiracaṉmaṉ."

They brought him, dressed him in white, garlanded him with white flowers, anointed him with sandal paste, and installed him upon the dais of deliberation. Then they sat beneath him, and interpreted the verses.

He sat quietly as they all expounded their commentaries in turn; when Madurai Marutaṉiḷa Nākaṉār explained his interpretation, there were a few points at which tears welled in the boy's eyes and his body hair stood on end.

But later, when Kaṇakkāyaṉār's son Nakkīraṉār explained his interpretations, his eyes watered at every word, and his body hair bristled. Then they all made a tumultuous noise, crying, "We have come to the true interpretation for this book!"

There are some, therefore, who claim that it was Uppūri Kuṭi Kiḻār's son Uruttiracaṉmaṉ who wrote the commentary to this book, but he did not; he heard the commentary, you may say. Actually, one really should say that the commentary determined by Nakkīraṉār to the book written by the Great Lord of the Madurai Temple was heard by Lord Kumāraṉ.

Next, we shall relate the manner in which this commentary has come down to us.

---

[38] Past, present, and future.

[39] Son of Siva; Kumāraṉ, which translates as "son," is another name for Murukaṉ, also known as Subramanian or Kārttikkēyaṉ.

The Transmission of the Commentary

Madurai Kaṇakkāyaṉār's son Nakkīraṉār taught it to his son Kīraṅkoṟṟaṉār. He taught it to Tēṉūr-k-kiḻār, who taught it to Paṭiyaṅkoṟṟaṉār. He taught it to Celvattāciriyar Peruñcuvaṉār, who taught it to the Maṇalūr Professor Puḷiyaṅkāy-p-Peruñcēntaṉār. He taught it to the Cellūr Professor Āṇṭai-p-Peruṅkumāraṉār, who taught it to the Tirukkuṉṟam Professor. He taught it to Mātaḷavaṉār Iḷanākaṉār, and he taught it to the Muciṟi Professor Nīlakaṇṭaṉār. This is how the commentary has come down to us.

Next, the **benefit**: That is, by learning such-and-such a work, such-and-such a benefit will result. If one says, "I know the meaning of the book, but I do not understand the benefit in having learned it," he will be met with the rejoinder, "If you do not understand a terse statement of benefit, composed in but a few words, how can you possibly understand the meaning of a work that is composed of a tremendous number of words? Get out!" Therefore, one must learn what benefit is to accrue from learning a book.

So, what will it benefit us to learn this book, you ask? It will result in the attainment of Release.[40]

Rationale for the Term "Stolen Love"

"What?" you ask, "Is this a not volume on thievery? How can we attain the gift of Release by learning this? Aren't stealing, murder, passion, and fornication all condemned by both the religious and the worldly? And is this not one of those?"

It is not so.

When one hears the word "stolen," it does not necessarily indicate evil; it is not to be called evil every time you hear the words "stealing" or "passion." Rather, these can also be good.

Once there was a woman who had quarreled with her family. She concocted some poison, intending to drink it and die, but there were some who would impede her. As she was waiting for them to leave, a compassionate man noticed it. He thought to himself, "I will take this poison and pour it out, so that she does not commit suicide." He took it without her seeing him, and poured it out. Later, when nobody was around, she went to drink it and kill herself; but as she could not find it, she avoided death. Because he saved her life through that act of stealing, he would have good karma. Other things of this sort also are not thievery, but produce good.

---

[40] "Release," **vīṭu**, has very similar connotations in Tamil to those of the word **mokṣa** in Sanskrit.

Next, passion also can be good. You must have seen passion that arises through thinking, "I shall enjoy the delights of heaven," or, "I shall go to the highest Guru and absorb his teachings," or, "I shall learn true wisdom and attain Release," or, "I shall worship God," haven't you? These passions are exceptionally beneficial: they are praised by superior people, and they yield benefits in the next world as well.

Here is how passion can be beneficial:

How Sexual Passion Can Be Beneficial

All six schools of philosophy regard sexual intercourse as evil; whenever it occurs, they point out, family ties develop. Then vices like murder, thievery, anger, haughtiness, and shame will follow, they say. The greatest people understand this and eschew intercourse.

Next, the middle rank of people hold that woman is a scaffold of bone, a nest of flesh, a multitude of worms, which, when viewed from the inside, is a sight to cause vultures to cry out in joy. Phlegm, bile, gas, bowels, fat, blood, nerves, urine, and feces—the combination of these is not ultimately real; if it were, we would have no need to adorn it with flowers, sandal paste, unguents, oils, and jewels because it would be inherently good, would it not? These people understand this point; they hear its unwholesome nature expounded, and eschew intercourse.

The last rank of people do not eschew intercourse at all: they have performed it in many births as men and as women, and they enjoy its delights. In accord with the saying, "Show love to an ignoramus and let him go," then, here is how to teach these people: one shows that there is a great kernel of truth in this debased fornication. In it there is no old age, no disease, no death, and no enduring poverty or distress. He is a youth of sixteen, and she a girl of twelve. They possess comparable qualities: similar virtues, affection, wealth, and education. They can indeed enjoy their delights without jeopardizing anything else, and thus the point is made, they claim.

To what can it be compared, you ask? As one coats bitter medicine with sugar, one can display great conduct "coated" in the very intercourse in which a man indulges. It is like pointing out a mirage to one who has been drinking murky water: a wise person points to it and says, "Look there, that's good water—drink it. What are you doing, drinking this dirty water?" but actually leads him to good water, and gives it to him to drink. Once he is shown, he will ask, "How does one get this kind of water?"

Now our object is attained through austerities, not through human effort, strength, beauty, or wealth. It is said,

> As one gets what one wants in the ways one wants,
> the performance of austerities is to be tried here.[41]

When one learns that, he will think, "I also shall perform austerities to obtain that." And thus his craving for fornication will lead him to the performance of austerities.

At that point one says, "You poor fellow, do you really think the bliss of attaining Release depends on this?" and expands upon the bliss of attaining Release. Once he learns that Release is a great flood of bliss that comes from within, like the iridescence of a gem, or the fragrance of a flower, or the coolness of sandal paste, he will shed his helpless worries about birth, disease, old age, and death, and fix in himself the desire to attain Release; then he will pursue austerity and wisdom, and he will indeed attain Release.

It is because of the deception used in setting him upon the correct path that this takes the designation "stolen."

The Four Goals Will Derive From Learning This

Further, becoming well versed in this book will lead to these four: fame, wealth, friendship, and merit. There is no fame greater than that of being well educated, since then you are praised by both the religious and the worldly. And it will also produce wealth. Why? Because wealthy people will give you part of their wealth in order to learn. Next, it will also bring friendship. Why? Because many people will cling to you, thinking, "My wisdom will grow as I move with this educated person." Next, it will also grant you merit. Why? Because there is no better gift than that of wisdom.

That is the benefit.

Next, the **time**: It was composed during the period of the Final Caṅkam.

Next, the **place**: It was in the court of Ukkira-p-Peruvaḻuti.

The **cause**: It was produced by the Lord of the Temple, who had noted that the Pāṇṭiyaṉs and the members of the Caṅkam were suffering because they could not obtain a grammar of meaning in poetics.

And now the Preface is complete.

The Treatise

After composing a preface, it is time to comment upon the work itself. A commentary is to be written in four parts. What are they, you ask? They are: comments upon what the work says, comments upon what the chapters say,

---

[41] *Tirukkuṟaḷ* 265.

comments upon what the subdivisions within the chapters say, and comments upon what the verses within the subdivisions say.

Of those, when one comments upon what a treatise says, it is appropriate to begin with a discussion of what constitutes a treatise, and what is meant by the word "treatise."

Three Types of Treatises, and Oppositional Treatises

In discussing what constitutes a treatise, note that treatises are of three types: original, derivative, and offshoot. This we know because he has written,

> Original, derivative, and offshoot are the three
> types of treatise.[42]

Of those, original treatises are those produced by one whose knowledge has no bounds.[43] This we know because they have written,

> What one who is foremost in knowledge, who glows
> in the avoidance of karma, has constructed:
> those are original treatises.[44]

and,

> In an original author's treatise
> there is no quotation of another's opinion.[45]

and,

> An original treatise is one with no precedent
> in these three areas: technique, verses, or exposition.[46]

Next, a work that discourses in a vein similar to one of those, providing variations on an original author's views, is a derivative treatise. This we know because he has said,

> Ones that come later and relate necessary variations
> in line with the conclusions of earlier treatises
> are derivative treatises of an undying tradition.[47]

---

[42] This quotation appears as verse 5 in the 12th-century grammar *Naṉṉūl*.

[43] This may refer either to an author unfettered by fidelity to a previously established school, or, as an extension of that idea, to God Himself as an author.

[44] *Tolkāppiyam: Marapiyal*, 96.

[45] Unidentified verse.

[46] Unidentified verse.

[47] Unidentified verse.

And a new arrangement of ideas covered previously in specific ways in those two types of treatises, but with a particular benefit in mind, is an offshoot treatise. This we know because he has said,

Beginning with one side of treatises that these two have written,
and changing and varying (them) is an offshoot treatise.[48]

Next, there is also something known as an oppositional treatise. What is that, you ask? If a writer for some reason alters a point made in an original treatise, and a brilliant author then shows up his contradictions and demonstrates the lack of accord, that is called an oppositional treatise. Why? Because he has said,

That which establishes his own and refutes others' ideas
some call an oppositional treatise.[49]

Moreover, it is only such works as can be described in these ways that are to be called treatises, they say, because he has declared,

What is called a treatise
points out in the very beginning the subject under treatment,
sets its subdivisions in order and presents its verses,
falls into one of the three categories known as original, derivative, and offshoot,
faultlessly selects global statements, classifications, and expansions,
naturally contains verses that flow in two ways, whether linear or back and forth,
is structured,
contains something of substance,
sets its own limits, and
draws its own conclusions.[50]

Not only that, but he has also declared,

In speaking of that which we call a treatise,
first, it declares what the subject under discussion is;
it has no contradictions between the beginning and the end;
it presents its substance globally and in classifications;
it has a commentary that is composed from within itself;
and it has the nature of explaining minutely.[51]

---

[48] Unidentified verse.

[49] Unidentified verse.

[50] Unidentified verse.

[51] Unidentified verse.

The Meaning of the Word "Treatise"[52]

Next, the meaning of the word "treatise" will be discussed. It is called a "treatise" because it is like a thread, as we call a woman who is like a doll a "doll." Being like a thread means this: as a skillful woman spins a thread out of many small cotton filaments, that which is spun through her craftsmanship becomes apparent, and this is what is known in the world as spinning thread. In like manner, a great scholar cards extensive verbiage and strings together the aggregate, the chapters, the subsections, and the verses through his sensibility to structuring; because it is "spun" in this way, it is called a treatise.

Next, some say it is called a treatise because it is refined, like a thread.

Next, take it as Tamil usage to appropriate the meaning of the Sanskrit word "tantiram,"[53] which means "thread."

This is the meaning of the word "treatise."

What This Treatise Discusses

Now it is time to state what this treatise discusses; but we have already noted that in the Preface: it discusses Tamil. Tamil is divided in four—letters, words, themes, and structure.

What This Chapter Discusses

Which of those is it that this chapter discusses, you ask? It places thematics under investigation.

What This Subsection Discusses

Now no subsection may treat all of the substance of a chapter, as there must be several subsections in one chapter if there are any at all. What does this subsection of this chapter take up for discussion, you ask? Because of the absence of a plurality of subsections here, there is no subsection at all.

What This Verse Discusses

Now it is proper to note what this verse discusses. What does it discuss, you ask? When one composes comments upon a single verse, one is to do so in a four-fold manner, by telling the substance of the verse, by dissecting it phrase by phrase, by paraphrasing it, and by commenting extensively.

---

[52] The Tamil word is **nūl**, whose root meaning is "thread," from the verb **nūl-tal**, "spin."

[53] **Tantra**.

What is the substance of this verse, you ask? It announces the subject matter of the chapter, and notes what it resembles. How this verse does that will become clear through the phrase-by-phrase dissection.

A phrase-by-phrase dissection is the glossing of words—its meaning:

What is called Stolen Love, in five modes of affection—that conduct known as 'Stolen Love' in five modes, which arises through affection.[54]

among the pleasant ones' rare secret's eight nuptials—the pleasant ones are the Brahmins; the rare secrets are the Vedas; nuptials means types of marriage arrangements; and eight is their number.

is the Kantaruva Convention, say the poets—people who are well educated declare that Stolen Love is a course of conduct that resembles the Kantaruva[55] Convention.

Next, the paraphrase: The conduct known as 'Stolen Love,' which arises through love in five modes, resembles the Kantaruva Convention, which is one of the eight ways of taking a woman that are described in the Vedas of the Brahmins; it is called 'Stolen Love' by learned scholars.

Next, all other comments made in order to clarify the meaning of the verse, including questions and their answers, constitute the extended commentary:

Love

In saying, 'the five modes of affection,' one must understand love itself in order to understand its five modes, you say? But love cannot be openly displayed: we cannot say, "Look, this is love," like a lamp inside a pot, or a sword in a scabbard. It is only when one observes the qualities of a person in love that it is correct to infer that, since they exist, love also exists.

So, what are the qualities of a person in love, you ask? They are these: dying if there is death, becoming ill if there is illness, giving abundantly of wealth, speaking the good and the sweet, craving union, and pining in separation. Yet these also may have distortions. But how can they have distortions, you ask?

"Dying if there is death" does not necessarily occur only through love. A woman who is diseased and hates life may opt to die, simply using this as a pretext.[56] Or, you must have seen a woman who thinks to herself, "People will say of me, 'She pours on her perfumed hair oils, eats her meals, and just goes on living as though nothing happened after her husband died. Look, she is really

---

[54] See footnote 2 on page 1 for the uses of the words "affection," "love," and "Stolen Love" in this translation.

[55] Cognate to the Sanskrit word **gandharva**.

[56] The reference in this paragraph is to a new widow's throwing herself upon her dead husband's funeral pyre in total dedication to him, a practice often called **sati**.

wicked!'" haven't you? Such a woman might even die, thinking, "People are going to talk about me like that every day I live, and some day I will die anyway; let me just die today." Then again, she may die in hopes of becoming famous. And some women have heard that if they die with their husbands they will go to heaven, and may die through desire for that. Still, beyond these reasons, one may also die truly for love; it doesn't happen for one reason only.

"Becoming ill if there is illness": we don't know what the disease might be, so this also can have distortions; it can appear both when there is love, and when there isn't. Thus it is refuted.

"Giving abundantly of wealth": union with courtesans also occurs through wealth; thus, that also is without love.

"Speaking the good and the sweet": your enemy also may accomplish his ends by speaking the good and the sweet; thus, that also is not love.

"Craving union": some unite as though they craved union, but really do so only out of fear; thus, that also is a distortion.

"Pining in separation": there are also some people who do not bathe, nor wear flowers or sandal paste, and wither away as if they were separated from a lover; thus, that also has a distortion.

Now, take it that there can also be love, with no distortion, when these qualities occur. How will this be, you ask? If she dies just exactly as he dies, take it that it happened through love. Take the others also as happening through love when they occur in this way, with no distortions.

Moreover, what we call love is a phenomenon of the emotions: it arises inside oneself, directed toward the thing one desires. Since he himself comprehends it, a man does not put it on display and say, "See this!" does he? Why not? A thirsty student would not ask his teacher, "Demonstrate thirst to me," since it is something that he already understands; if he were to ask, he would be cheating. And if his professor began to inform him, he would be an ignoramus.

Things Are of Two Types

Moreover, things in the world are to be understood in two categories: those whose existence alone is evident without form, and those which exhibit both existence and form.

Of those, the existence of lust, anger, confusion, pleasure, pain, and so on, is evident, but not their form. Why? Because he has said,

> Similarity, form, hatred,
> fidelity, luster, and beauty,
> softness, modesty, and credulity,
> disease, desire, and enjoyment:

according to established traditions,
the meanings of all these words
cannot be demonstrated, other than
by getting them in the heart.[57]

Next, take "Kūṭal of many mansions," "district," and so on as things that are known in terms both of their existence and of their form.

The thing called love is known by its existence alone, not by form.

Love is a desire that wells up toward something about which one thinks, is it not? Here what we specify as love has no distortion. So what is it, you ask? Take it that love between a man and a woman acquires its special characteristics when modesty shrinks, and the desire for union swells.

The Five Modes

Now that I understand love, what are its five modes, you ask? They are: mountain-country, seaside, wasteland, woodland, and river-plain.[58] But, you point out, beyond mentioning the five modes he did not indicate these names, nor their order, nor their definitions. He did not indicate them here because his is a terse book; they are to be commented upon in the completed volume. In the commentary, they are to be treated in terms of three aspects: First Aspect, Matrix Aspect, and Propriety Aspect. We know this because he has said,

First, Matrix, and Propriety: when one speaks
of these three, they are superior in order.[59]

The First Aspects of the Five Modes

Here is what they are like: of those three, the First is divided into two categories, place and time. Why? Because he has said,

What is known as the First has the nature of both
place and time, say those who know its nature.[60]

---

[57] *Tolkāppiyam: Poruḷatikāram, Poruḷiyal*, 51.

[58] Much of the following discusses these five modes in detail so we shall not add to Nakkīraṉār's explanation here; but a note on the translations of their names is in order. Conventionally these modes are referred to by the names of the principal flowers prescribed for imagery within each mode; we have chosen rather to identify them by the landscapes indicated, following the precedent set by A. K. Ramanujan when he selected the title *The Interior Landscape* for his ground-breaking translation and study of Caṅkam poems in English (Bloomington, Indiana, USA: Indiana University Press, 1967).

[59] *Tolkāppiyam: Akattiṇaiyiyal*, 3.

[60] *Tolkāppiyam: Akattiṇaiyiyal*, 4.

The place for the mountain-country mode is the mountains, and the areas surrounding them. The time is autumn,[61] the middle watch of the night, and early winter.[62]

The place for the seaside mode is the sea, and the areas around it; the time is sunset.

The wasteland mode has no place of its own. We know this because Tolkāppiyaṉār has said,

> Except the middle one of the five modes,
> they are natural divisions of the sea-girt earth.[63]

Its time is midday, in the summer[64] and the late-dew season.[65] But can it be a mode, you ask, with only a time, and no place? Notice the fact that locations near mountains or woodlands become wastelands during those seasons.

The place for the woodland mode is in the forests, and in areas around forests. The time is the rainy season,[66] in the evening.

The place for the river-plain mode is in cultivated fields, and in areas around fields. The time is the period just before dawn.

How do we know these things, you ask?

> The world of the woodlands, ruled by the Dark One,
> the world of black mountains, ruled by the Red One,
> the world of sweet waters, ruled by the Emperor,
> the world of great sands, ruled by Varuṇaṉ,[67]
> are called, in their order declared,
> woodland mode, mountain-country mode, river-plain mode, and seaside mode.[68]

> Rainy season and evening is the woodland mode.[69]

---

[61] The Tamil calendar, like calendars in much of the rest of India, is divided into six two-month seasons. What is meant by "autumn " is the months of Aippaci and Kārttikai, from roughly half-way through October to half-way through December.

[62] The months of Mārkaḻi and Tai, from halfway through December to halfway through February.

[63] *Tolkāppiyam: Akattiṇaiyiyal*, 2.

[64] The months of Cittirai and Vaikāci, from halfway through April to halfway through June.

[65] The months of Māci and Paṅkuṉi, from halfway through February to halfway through April, when the dew falls late at night.

[66] The months of Āvaṇi and Puraṭṭāci, from halfway through August to halfway through October. The Tamil areas receive most of their yearly rainfall during these two months.

[67] Sanskrit **Varuṇa**.

[68] *Tolkāppiyam: Akattiṇaiyiyal*, 5.

[69] *Tolkāppiyam: Akattiṇaiyiyal*, 6.

Mountain-country mode:
autumn and midnight, say the learned.[70]

It also has the early winter, they say.[71]

Pre-dawn and dawn: river-plain mode.[72]

Sunset
appears truly in the seaside mode.[73]

The mode in the middle position: it is of the nature
of midday and summer, when it is determined.[74]

It also has the late-dew season, they say.[75]

As no seasons are specified for the river-plain and seaside modes, take it that they may appropriate all six seasons.

These are the elements of the First Aspect of the modes.

Matrix Aspect of the Five Modes

Next, the Matrix Aspect concerns gods, foods, animals, trees, birds, drums, activities, music, and so on, as they relate to each mode. Why? Because he has said,

God, food, beast, tree, bird, drum,
activity, music categories, and so on collected,
and other things of that sort: they are called the Matrix Aspect.[76]

We shall list them in that order:

For the mountain-country mode,

God—Murukaṉ

Food—wild rice and millet

Animals—tiger, wild boar, and elephant

Trees—eagle-wood, sandalwood, neem, teak, and kino

Birds—parrot and peacock

Drums—the drum of the possession-dance, the hill people's toṇṭaka drums, and the hill-people's kuṟavai drums

---

70 *Tolkāppiyam: Akattiṇaiyiyal*, 7.

71 *Tolkāppiyam: Akattiṇaiyiyal*, 8.

72 *Tolkāppiyam: Akattiṇaiyiyal*, 9.

73 *Tolkāppiyam: Akattiṇaiyiyal*, 10.

74 *Tolkāppiyam: Akattiṇaiyiyal*, 11.

75 *Tolkāppiyam: Akattiṇaiyiyal*, 12.

76 *Tolkāppiyam: Akattiṇaiyiyal*, 20.

Activities—robbing honey, digging roots, roaming the hills, and driving parrots from millet crops

Music—kuriñci melodies

By 'other things of that sort' is meant:

Names for the hero—Cilampaṉ, Vēṟpaṉ, and Poruppaṉ

Names for the heroine—Koṭicci and Kuṟatti

Water—waterfalls and mountain pools

Towns—small villages and hill settlements

Flowers—conehead, glory-lily, kino, and waterlilies in mountain pools

Names for the people—Kuṟavar, Iṟavuḷar, and Kuṉṟavar

For the seaside mode,

God—Varuṇaṉ[77]

Foods—things bought with fish and with salt

Animals—shark and crocodile

Trees—mastwood, screwpine, and mangrove

Birds—swan, aṉṟil, and makaṉṟil

Drums—fishing drums and boat drums

Activities—producing and selling fish and salt

Music—laments

By 'other things of that sort' is meant:

Names for the hero—Tuṟaivaṉ, Koṇkaṉ, Cērppaṉ

Names for the heroine—Nuḷaicci, Paratti

Water—sand wells and brackish backwaters

Flowers—silver-petaled screwpine and dark waterlily

Towns—seaports, small villages, and fishing settlements

Names for the people—Paratar and Parattiyar, Nuḷaiyar and Nuḷaicciyar

Tolkāppiyaṉār does not want a place for the wasteland mode, and, therefore, he does not want a god for it either. Others, however, claim Pakavati[78] and Ātittaṉ[79] as gods.

Foods—whatever is waylaid and plundered

Animals—weakened elephants, tigers, and red dogs

Trees—iruppai and the toothbrush-tree

Birds—vulture, kite, and dove

Drums—lamentation drum, burnt-village drum, and cattle-raid drum

Activities—cattle raiding, preying upon caravans, and plundering villages

Music—pañcuram melodies

---

77 Sanskrit **Varuṇa**.

78 Sanskrit **Bhagavati**.

79 Sanskrit **Āditya**.

By 'other things of that sort' is meant:

Names for the hero—Mīḷi, Viṭalai, Kāḷai

Names for the heroine—Eyiṟṟi, Pētai

Flowers—small-oakflower, bottle-flower, and trumpet-flower

Water—dried up wells and pools

Towns—villages of murderers

Names for the people—Eyiṉar and Eyiṟṟiyar, Maṟavar and Maṟattiyar

For the woodland mode,

God—Vācutēvaṉ[80]

Foods—common millet and poor-man's millet

Animals—rabbit and little deer

Trees—laburnum and wild lime

Birds—jungle-fowl, peacock, and partridge

Drums—bullfight drum and tabor

Activities—weeding millet, harvesting it, threshing it; and herding cattle

Music—mullai melodies

By 'other things of that sort' is meant:

Name for the hero—Lord of Kuṟumpoṟai

Names for the heroine—Kiḻatti and Wife (these names also belong to heroines in the river-plain mode)

Flowers—jasmine and white glory-lily

Water—woodland stream

Towns—hamlet and woodland settlement

Names for the people—Iṭaiyar and Iṭaicciyar, Āyar and Āycciyar

For the river-plain mode,

God—Intiraṉ[81]

Foods—red rice and white rice

Animals—water buffalo and otter

Trees—willow, ṛiver-portia, and queen's flower

Birds—waterfowl and heron

Drums—wedding drum and harvest drum

Activities—harvesting rice, threshing it, and weeding the crop

Music—marutam melodies

By 'other things of that sort' is meant:

Names for the hero—Townsman, Makiḻnaṉ

Names for the heroine—Kiḻatti, Wife

Flowers—lotus and the red waterlily

---

[80] Sanskrit **Vāsudeva**.

[81] Sanskrit **Indra**.

Water—household wells and reservoirs
Names for the people—Kaṭaiyar and Kaṭaicciyar, Uḻavar and Uḻattiyar
Town—large town

These Matrix Aspects may also come mixed together:

> Flowers and birds of whatever mode,
> even when they do not occur in a certain mode and its time,
> come as results of the mode in which they do occur.[82]

The Propriety Aspect of the Five Modes

Next, it is declared that the Propriety Aspects are the themes that belong to the modes. What are they, you ask? They are union, separation, waiting, pining, quarreling, and the causes of these. We know this because he has said,

> When examining union, separation, waiting,
> pining, quarreling, and their causes, these are
> the properties of the themes of the modes.[83]

Among those,

> Union and the causes of union are the mountain-country mode;
> Separation and the causes of separation are the wasteland mode;
> Waiting and the causes of waiting are the woodland mode;
> Pining and the causes of pining are the seaside mode;
> Quarreling and the causes of quarreling are the river-plain mode.[84]

But isn't the mountain-country mode just for union alone, you ask? It is not only for union: the fear of separation, reassurance, the hero's avoidance, his speaking to his friend, his friend's taunting, the hero's retort, meeting through his friend, seeing the heroine, the hero's grieving, the hero's going, the hero's reuniting the heroine with her friends, and such occurrences as well as permutations of themes involving the heroine and her friends, and many others, all are included in 'union and the causes of union.' Take the rest in the same way.

What a Mode Is

Next, critics are of two types: some say that a mode is a type of conduct, and some, inappropriately, say it is a geographical region. Conduct alone is the mode. While a region in which the conduct termed "mountain-country mode"

---

[82] *Tolkāppiyam: Akattiṇaiyiyal*, 21.

[83] *Tolkāppiyam: Akattiṇaiyiyal*, 16.

[84] Unidentified verse. The *Bavanandam* edition has it printed not as a verse at all, but in prose paragraph form.

occurs may also be called "mountain-country mode," this usage follows simply in the way that we use the term "light" not only for a flame, which really is light, but also for the object in which the flame burns.

Next, some maintain that a mode is both a conduct and a region; otherwise, they claim, saying "five modes of love" would be like saying "five pieces of clothing" or "five compartments of a box." But their idea also is incorrect. If that were what he meant, he would not have said, later,

> The mode and conduct.[85]

He would have said, "Both are lovers' conduct."[86]

Well, still he should have said, "The modes, five in number," like "the spans, five in number," or, "the groups, five in number," you say?[87] You ask in ignorance: one calls a five-headed snake both "a snake with heads, five in number," and "a five-headed snake;" it can have either form. This we know because he has said, in *The Study of the Shortened 'U,'*

> If, after a number-word, a hard letter follows,
> or if ña, na, or ma follows, or if ya or va follows,
> the first word remains unchanged, say the scholars.[88]

Stolen Love of the Five Modes

Further, to one who thinks, "I shall take the conduct that arises through love to be something apart from that love, just as a mansion that arises through a carpenter is different from the carpenter," we say that it is not so; take it to be like a vessel that arises through gold, which is not different from the gold. The third grammatical case[89] can indicate either a difference between a cause and its

---

[85] *The Study of Stolen Love*, 56. This Verse is explained in greater detail on pages 307–312.

[86] With the word "both" referring to both conduct and region.

[87] At issue is a point of grammar. In a nutshell, Nakkīraṉār's grammatical analysis forces the five modes to be considered as a unit, and never separately. The hypothetical questioner claims that the form **aintiṇai**, as used in the verse, would have to have been **aintu tiṇai** for the meaning to be as Nakkīraṉār argues; Nakkīraṉār counters that the compound form **aintiṇai**, used adjectivally in the verse, lends precedence to the noun **aṉpu**, "affection," as an integral unit: thus he stresses the integrity of the poetic idea of love. Without the compound form, the emphasis would shift to the individual modes, like focusing on the individual compartments in a box, or the individual heads on a five-headed snake.

[88] *Tolkāppiyam: Kuṟṟiyalukarappuṇariyal*, 72

[89] Termed the "instrumental case," it indicates who or what did or caused an action. One example in English would be the phrase "by the carpenter" in saying, "a house built *by the carpenter*." There are also other, subtly different usages; all usages, though, retain the element

effect or a lack of difference between them. Here, take it that of those two possibilities, it indicates a lack of difference.

Then in what capacity does the term 'Stolen Love' follow 'five modes?'[90] When one phrase follows another, it does so in one of three capacities: as a predicate, as a compound, or as a listing. In which of those ways does this one occur, you ask? It is a compound. Now there are many types of compounds: which of them is it, you ask? It is a case compound.[91] And there are many case compounds, too: so which of those is it, you ask? It is a seventh-case compound. And the seventh case[92] itself has many suffixes: which one is elided here, you ask? 'Within'[93] is elided.

Now, you say, a love that is within[94] the five modes must be different from them, since he said "Stolen Love, in five modes." And when you claim it to be different, like a light within a pot, or a sword within a scabbard, the seventh-case suffix is cited as an indicator of the difference between the location and the thing in that location; but "within" can just as well indicate their non-difference. In posing your question, you gave an example of its standing for their difference. But take, rather, an active example that indicates their non-difference, as in saying, "He dug within the mound," or "He dug within the mansion." Stolen Love simply is not different from the five modes.

But if that is so, would it not be phrased simply, "Stolen Love, in five modes of affection, among the gracious ones' rare secrets...?" What is the "What is called..." phrase for, you ask? One school argues that it is simply for euphony in the verse, but that is not so. Another says, "We shall interpret a meaning through it," and strength lies on that side. But what is that meaning, you ask? It is to give particular emphasis to the phrase 'Stolen Love.' When people say, "Uṟaiyūr is *what is called* a city," they note the existence of all cities, but give particular importance to Uṟaiyūr. Here, noting the existence of all other 'stealings,' he gives this 'stealing' particular importance, because it can result in heaven and the attainment of Release. This importance was given to it by his having said,

---

of instrumentality. The third case ending is present in the word **aṉpiṉāṉāya**, which means "arising because of love," and modifies "five modes." The argument centers on a case ending, **āṉ**, which itself is elided in the Verse, leaving its nature, and hence its implications, completely in the hands of the commentator.

[90] It does, in the Tamil original of the verse: **aṉpiṉ aintiṇai-k-kaḷavu**. Their order had to be reversed in translation, due to the exigencies of English grammar and word order.

[91] Case compounds are compound words in which a case-ending is implied after the first word. It is understood that the ending itself has been elided between the two words.

[92] The seventh case is called the locative, as it indicates the location of something.

[93] **uḷ**

[94] **uḷ**

"What is called..." We noted that in the Preface as well. All other stealings bring one disgrace and sin; they end in shortening of the hands, piercing of the eyes, and impaling, and lead one to such bad places as Hell. It is because this one partakes of the nature of wise conduct, because it has been praised by great people, and because it entails no sin or disgrace, that he distinguished it by saying, "What is called..."

Eight Types of Nuptials

Next, the line, "among the pleasant ones' rare secret's eight nuptials:"

The pleasant ones are the Brahmins; rare secrets are the Vedas; nuptials are marriage rites; eight simply gives their number. And what are they, you ask? They are: Piramam, Piracāpattiyam, Āriṭam, Teyvam, Kāntarvam, Acuram, Irākkaṭam, and Paicācam.[95] Note the meaning of these lines:

> State of Virtue, Consent, Obtaining Wealth, and Divine,
> Harpists' Union, Rare Feat, Demonic, and Devilish:
> among these eight nuptials of the Vedic people,
> the nature of the mating of good harpists with divisions
> is the meaning of this, say the scholars.[96]

Piramam: the giving of a twelve-year-old girl bedecked with jewels to a man who has maintained celibacy for forty-eight years. If one does not give her away, and she menstruates before she unites with a man, it is comparable to the murder of a Brahmin.[97] This is what is understood by the phrase, "State of Virtue."

Piracāpattiyam: the giving of the girl, with no denials, when someone of her brother-in-law's lineage comes and asks for her. This is what is understood by the phrase, "Consent."

Āriṭam: Placing her between a cow and bull whose horns and hooves have been gilded, and then pouring water over them. This is what is understood by the phrase, "Obtaining Wealth."

Teyvam: giving her to a sacrificial priest before the sacrificial fire. This is what has come to be honored as "Divine."

---

[95] Known in Sanskrit as **Brahma, Prajāpatya, Arṣa, Daiva, Gandharva, Aśura, Rākṣaśa, and Paisāśa**, these names can be translated, respectively, as Brahminic, Prajāpati's (Prajāpati is the lord of creation), the Sages', Divine, Harpists', Demonic, Fiendish, and Devilish.

[96] Unidentified verse in non-Sanskritized Tamil. Nakkīraṉār proceeds immediately to explain the relationships between the Sanskrit terms for the eight nuptials, and their Tamil meanings, as given in this verse.

[97] The most heinous of all offenses.

Kāntarvam: the joining together on their own of two people who are similar. This is what is understood by the phrase, "Harpists' Union."[98]
Acuram: giving her away with a declaration like, "Whoever can control this murderous bull will get her," or "Whoever bends this bow will get her," or "Whoever hits this moving-boar target will get her," or "Whoever receives her garlanding will get her," or other such things. This is the performance of a "Rare feat."
Irākkaṭam: taking her by force, without either her or her family's consent.
Paicācam: Joining with an older woman, a sleeping woman, or an intoxicated woman. This is called "Devilish."
Understand these eight marriages to be the eight nuptials mentioned.

Next, **the Kantaruva Convention**: Those whom we call here Kantaruvas are two lovers. Without anyone giving or receiving either of them, they come across each other in a grove of trees and unite, as though their union is the fruit of some good deeds they had done in the past. This is the Kantaruva Wedding, and this author wants situations like it to be called 'Stolen Love.'

If that be the case, then since he said, "the Kantaruva Convention..." and not, "like the Kantaruva Convention...," should we not take it actually to be the very same thing as Stolen Love, you ask? We do not take it that way. The intent of the treatise as a whole is not like that; therefore it is correct to take it as a mere comparison. Comparison implies that the things compared are somewhat similar, and somewhat dissimilar. Thus when one says, "Eyes like a water lily...," we take it that only the dark blue color is comparable, and that the rest, which is not comparable, is the greater part. When one says, "A mouth like coral...," only the redness is compared; the other, non-comparable portion is larger. And here, the comparison is made between their joining without a giver or receiver, their coming from comparable families, and their having comparable feelings of love; all other areas are not comparable.

Still, should the verse not read, "like the Kantaruva Convention...," you ask? It need not. We may elide the comparative post-position[99] when we say, for example, "cow" for "she who is like a cow," or when we say, "doll" for "she who is like a doll."

Further, if you say that those eight forms of marriage and this one then make nine nuptials, it is not so. Those eight exist in the real world, but this one does not; it is a conduct established by poets as "the nonexistent, the sweet, and the good," and he does not add it to the world's customs.

---

[98] Kāntarvam (Sanskrit **gandharva**), refers to a marriage like that supposed to be performed by the Gandharvas, the heavenly harpists.

[99] The post-position in Tamil functions something like a preposition in English. The post-position under discussion here is **pōl**, with the meaning "like."

Now, as we have determined that this is an Original Treatise, he should have ended the verse with the words, "Kantaruva Convention," without adding, "they say;" as it is it follows the formulation of a Derivative Treatise: so goes the question. Its answer is this: If you ask whether this work has only a single author's views, as other works do, it does not. He fashioned it this way because Stolen Love is reminiscent of the Kantaruva Convention to all the scholars of all three times.[100] Now, if you say that there is no scholar comparable to him because he is the Principal, because he knows all, well that is just your opinion; you do not know. Though he composed it by himself, he took in everything else as well, with or without modification; he stated it in such a way as to declare that all people accept his work with no modifications. He calls people who understand his tenets "scholars" because it is possible for others to be scholars with respect to such materials as they understand.

Next, "(they) say," eṉmaṉār,[101] is a finite form of the verb eṉpa. The pa drops because of the verse,

> It shortens when there is shortening,[102]

and it expands by the two particles maṉ and ār because of the verse,

> It expands when there is expanding.[103]

"(They) say" is completed by taking the grammatical subject "scholars" because a finite verb is always completed by the addition of an implied subject.

* * *

Verse 2.

> **That,**
> **when he and she see alone, is the accord**
> **on both sides of the union of love.**

What does this declare, you ask? Above, he did not indicate the characteristics of Stolen Love; he merely said that it must resemble the Kantaruva Convention. Here he presents an understanding of it; the subject matter of this verse is consistent with that of the previous one.

Its meaning:

---

[100] Past, present, and future; it means people who have supernatural insight.

[101] What follows, completing Nakkīraṉār's comments on Verse 1, is a grammatical explanation of the verbal endings and subject-predicate relationship in the verse.

[102] *Tolkāppiyam: Eccaviyal*, 7.

[103] *Tolkāppiyam: Eccaviyal*, 7.

That—a demonstrative particle implicating previous knowledge; in this case its antecedent is the above-mentioned Stolen Love, which resembles the Kantaruva Convention.

he and she—he is she, and she is he. What does that mean, you ask? It means there is no differentiation between him and her.

Even though they are indicated by different words, assume that it means they do not differ one from the other in love, character, education, beauty, or wealth. What is that like, you wonder? It would be inappropriate if one were to say that it is like a coriander seed and coriander. For what reason, you ask? Their lack of differentiation had already been clinched back when he compared this to the Kantaruva Convention. Since they are already known to be without differentiation, it would be a tautology for him to say the same thing again in another statement. Why? Because tautology means saying a thing many times in different idioms.

Now, one school maintains that the hero can never be alone unless he strays from his normal company of many hundreds of thousands of other young men with sharpened spears, because he is such a great man; and similarly, the heroine cannot be alone unless she strays from the company of many hundreds of thousands of women, since she is such a great woman. He leaves his company and stands alone, as she leaves hers and stands just by herself, and they unite in this way, these people say. "He and she" was said in order to establish that he has been separated from the young men, and she from the women, they maintain. This commentary also is not proper. For what reason, you ask? Because it was clinched that they unite alone as soon as he compared this to the Kantaruva Convention; to have said the same thing again would have been a tautology.

Then what is the commentary, you ask? "He and she" indicates that there is none like him among men, none greater than he; rather, they are all less than he: in all times and places, in wisdom, in beauty, and in wealth, he is without equal, and she is the same. Thus they are both beyond comparison.

Which of the five possible ones are the final particles appended to "he" and "she," you ask?[104] Since they distinguish him from the group of men, and her from the group of women, they are final particles of distinction. That particle which distinguishes one from many is called the final particle of distinction.

Granted all that, does it not then also indicate that they have no shortcomings at all, as this situation is said to resemble the Kantaruva Convention, you ask? It

---

[104] "He," **tāṉē**, and "she," **avaḷē**, both exhibit the grammatical suffix **ē**, which can indicate any of five meanings, according to Tamil grammar. Here the commentator assigns to them both the meaning of distinction, whereby the particle serves to distinguish the noun to which it is appended from others like it.

does not. The Kantaruvas too have their shortcomings—in wisdom, virtue, and effort. He assesses their shortcomings and finds them to be minuscule; hence, he wishes to say in this verse that they are beyond comparison.

when he and she see alone—to encounter each other without being aware of themselves.[105]

Now then, you ask: if one says that, will they lose self-awareness before they see each other, after they see each other, or at the very moment of seeing each other?[106]

If one says that they were unaware of themselves before they see each other, then their seeing each other would not be the cause for their becoming unaware of themselves. Moreover, it would have occurred without a cause, and therefore they must always have lacked self-awareness.

Next, if one says that they become unaware of themselves after they see each other, then they would have to remain unaware of themselves even after the sight of each other is removed; it would be like this: if you say, "Cāttaṉ arrived after he ate," then he must have come after the act of eating had passed away. Moreover, if one says that they become unaware of themselves after they see each other, then it must happen back in their respective groups; but why would they become disoriented when they see their familiar groups?

Yet even if one says that the sight of each other and their becoming unaware of themselves occur simultaneously, note that it is still inappropriate to claim automatically that the sight of each other causes them to become unaware of themselves. We know that, like the two horns of a cow, it is not necessarily true that one thing must have caused another, even if they do occur together at the same time and place. Yet as there is no third or fourth time, we must conclude that they did indeed become unaware of themselves because of seeing one another. Why do we draw this conclusion, you ask? Because they already had a proclivity toward becoming unaware of themselves, even before they saw each other. Why? When one receives a title and its emblematic ring, it is not that he attains that good fortune just at the moment of the award; it lay in wait for him. And the fortune of being crowned king does not occur only at the moment of coronation; it, too, lay in wait for him. Such fortunes cause people to attain things at later points, in certain places, and for certain reasons. Likewise, his becoming unaware of himself due to her on such and such a day, upon such and such a development, and in such and such a place, as well as her becoming

[105] That is, losing their self-consciousness.

[106] This point is critical to the development of the poetic theme for the moment, **tuṟai,** at which they meet; the poet must know when to portray the protagonists as being aware of their own actions, and when to portray them as oblivious to everything but their love.

unaware of herself due to him, were ordained earlier. Their fortunes cause it to occur at a later time. Why? Because it is said,

> Even if you hide, fate will not pass by
> without getting at you.[107]

The sight of each other is the instrumental cause[108] of their fate's fruition, just as earth, water, and the season are instrumental causes of a seed's sprouting, or just as such causes as a cook are instrumental in the transformation of rice-grains, which hold the potential for turning into cooked rice, into food. Having said that, then if one still maintains that the sight of each other and the instrumental cause of their becoming unaware of themselves are different things, then the earlier question remains: does that occurrence in the mind arise before, after, or during the sight of each other? It arises right with the sight itself. How? When you enter a dark place with a light, the darkness does not leave before the light arrives, nor does it leave after the light arrives; the light's arrival and the departure of the darkness occur together. Just like that, the sighting of each other and the dissolution of their wisdom, good conduct, and good character occur at once; consider the light as the sighting of each other, and wisdom and good conduct as the darkness.

Next, what is called **the union of love** is the encounter between the hero and the heroine alone in a grove, their being unaware of themselves, and their uniting in an excess of desire.

Now as he has said earlier that the hero and heroine are beyond comparison, we conclude that he travels with a retinue of many hundreds of thousands of youths with sharp lances and the strength of lions and yāḻis,[109] who bring to mind such things as stone pillars, male porcupines, cruel-eyed elephants, fearless wild boars, black mountains, the wide earth, and the sky.

And she, too, is surrounded by many hundreds of thousands of women, among whom she was born and raised, with whom she has bathed, gained distinctions, listened to lullabies, drunk milk, teethed, learned to speak, and established long-term friendships and intimacy, who have excellent character, fellowship, general excellence, good conduct, and splendor. They all have bright foreheads, which appeal to the eye and to the mind. It is to be concluded that she moves as the cool moon in the midst of these stars.

---

[107] Unidentified verse.

[108] Causes are of three kinds: material, instrumental, and agentive. The common example is the making of a pot: clay is the material cause, the potter's wheel is the instrumental cause, and the potter is the agentive cause.

[109] Mythical beasts with the faces of lions and the tusks and trunks of elephants; the word may also mean simply "elephants."

Do such conclusions contradict the statement that they are alone when they unite, you ask? They do not. How? As soon as they enter the grove, her friends disperse from her in their desire to play. How do they disperse, you ask? They say, "Let's race each other in stringing pretty leaf skirts!" or, "Let's make cool, fragrant garlands!" or, "Let's pick these wonderful flowers!" or, "Let's have a dance contest with the peacocks!" They say, "Let's compete with the cuckoos in singing!" or, "Let's bathe in the waterfalls and splash in the pretty mountain pools!" or, "Let's swing on these fragrant flowering vines!" and they disperse. As they separate from each other they wonder, "Is so-and-so really over here, or over there?"

But would they really separate from her and leave her alone for these reasons, you ask? They would, because she does not come from a family that people point out and talk about from a distance; and she has such good character that they would never give it a second thought. But would she herself really stand there alone, when she has never before been separated from her girlfriends, you ask? She would, because she is as familiar with the place as she is with her girlfriends.

How does she stand there, you ask? All about her are sandalwood trees, champak trees, sweet mango trees, sweet jackfruit trees, breadfruit trees, asoka trees, caung trees, kino trees, and ipecacuanha trees. Gamboge, barbadoes pride, crocus-vines, copperleaf, delight-of-the-woods, jasmine, and Arabian jasmine combine their fragrances. Trumpetflowers, screwpine, and fresh laburnum burst open; waterthorn, purslane, and lemon flowers blossom. Bees buzz and suck nectar, and the musical cuckoo sings as the cool south breeze meanders through the grove. In the midst of this grove, which causes lonely people to feel resentment, upon a mound of rubies, she sees a kino tree brushing the sky and blooming pure gold with intoxicatingly aromatic blossoms yielding their honey as bees buzz by. At the very sight of it, she feels a swelling love. The anklets on her pretty little feet jingle as she walks, as though a marvelous flowering vine had learned how to walk, and she plucks some of those honey-filled fresh kino flowers. As she plucks them, in a jasmine bower by an emerald-bordered pool of rubies, under the rich shade of flowery fragrance, she grabs hold of a kaṭikkurukkatti vine. Pursuing diadems of pure gold, washing gold nuggets and pushing diamonds and rubies along, a waterfall of rising beauty falls upon a golden rock, sounding with the voice of a drum. Beetles and bees sound the lute, and the musical cuckoos sing. On a crystal seat covered with pleasant pollens, a peacock fans its beautiful feathers, as though a royal blue fan were opened, and the tender young sun tosses in its warmth. And so she stands watching that young peacock dance.

Meanwhile, the hero also came to the cool mountainsides to hunt, with his many hundreds of thousands of young men with sharp spears. He chased after a lion that sprang up there, and left the youths who were protecting him. He ordered his charioteer to stand by with the chariot and its great horses, on the moon-like sands of a wild river bed. His warrior's anklets jangled, and he tied up his dark curly hair with a golden cord, as honeybees wedded themselves to the fragrant wreath on his head, and the aroma of his sandal paste spread through the wide grove. Holding an arrow with his killing bow, he moved like the god of love reincarnate,[110] and entered the great grove where she was. How could that be, you ask? As a yoke-pin tossed into the southern seas might drift north and fit into the pinhole of a yoke floating in the northern seas; or just as the sun with its hot rays, and the moon with its cool ones, might slip from their orbits and meet, these two will meet. And they will be all alone when they first see each other. Being alone implies that they are unaware of themselves. What does being unaware of themselves mean, you ask?

The Four Qualities of the Hero

The hero has the four qualities of wisdom, constancy, investigation, and resolve.

What is wisdom, you ask? Because he has said,

> Whatever the nature of whatever thing, wisdom
> is seeing its true substance,[111]

no matter what the thing may be, wisdom means standing within that thing and truly understanding it.

What is constancy, you ask? It is the protection of what is to be protected, while discarding what is to be discarded.

Investigation is researching a thing and understanding it.

And resolve is not forgetting a thing undertaken.

All four of these are overwhelmed in the hero by his desire and lie bent, as grass lies bent in the path of a flooding stream.

The Four Qualities of the Heroine

Next, the heroine's four qualities are modesty, innocence, fear, and loathing.

Modesty is a natural characteristic of women.

Innocence is holding on to what she has learned, without letting go.

Fear is fearing something that she has never seen before, due to her femininity.

And loathing is the state of loathing things that are unfamiliar.

---

[110] Siva once reduced the god of love to a pile of ash for disturbing him in his meditations.

[111] *Tirukkuṟaḷ*, 355.

All four of these lie bent like grass in the path of a flooding stream, overwhelmed by desire.

And what is desire, you ask? It is being indispensable to each other. Desire, which becomes so indispensable, pushes out all other emotions; it stands on its own. Like gold coins strung on a string, or like a raft drifting on the tides, it operates through fate and unites two people. Therefore uniting when they are all alone does not contradict their superiority.

It is this that is called the union of love.

The Union of Stolen Love is Emotional Union[112]

This, says one author, means that they unite only in their hearts. Why? Because bodily union would contradict their incomparability. How would it contradict that, you ask? One who seizes upon another's property opportunistically is not highly spoken of. Yet just like that, he gets this girl without having her given to him, and without properly receiving her; he just chanced to meet her when he embraced her. Since the property of others is not easily acquired, he can thus pass as a great man. But if that is so, most of the men in the world must be great: they do not take what belongs to others when there is no opportunity, yet steal it whenever they can.

Next, she also would lose her greatness, because she would have met him accidentally, swooned, and worshipped him when she ought to have worshipped him only at her parents' command. Why? Because her heart just flowed wherever it flowed, without her searching for and finding him. There is nothing that the heart would not want, is there? Yet she lets her heart flow wherever it flows, among all the things it wants, without investigating into their propriety for her, or whether they might cause a fall from virtue or rectitude; that is not proper, and therefore it also would contradict her superiority.

Then how can one interpret it, you ask?[113] They did not unite with each other in body; only their passion united them. Their union is thus in their hearts. Their separation comes as they leave each other with the thought that it would not be possible to stay united like that for a long period of time, because somebody would come to know about them. Poems spoken in their separation are appropriate for all that is to be said about their physical union. All material in

---

112 This section and the next one, "The Union of Stolen Love is Physical Union," consist of arguments first against, then for, the occurrence of sexual intimacy as a given in *akam* poetry. In the end, Nakkīraṉār decides that sexual intimacy must be assumed: he concludes this discussion on page 34 by saying that "...emotional union is not the correct exposition; physical union is required."

113 This paragraph is the capstone of the argument against sexual intimacy in this poetry. Nakkīraṉār refutes this entire argument below.

the themes of union through the hero's friend and union through the heroine's friend is the same.[114]

Physical union, they say, occurs when they are married.

The Union of Stolen Love is Physical Union

Critics who want there to be physical union claim that argument is inappropriate; they say this: those people think that physical union is inappropriate, yet they want there to be emotional union, don't they? If we think as they do, then since letting the heart run to others' property is not right, we couldn't redeem the heart later, either, could we? Moreover, even if their desire goes only to the heart, it still amounts to having had physical union. In emotional union it is impossible to think of them as two people; if it were possible, she would lose her chastity through worshipping someone else. Next, even if the above author claims there is no thought at all of two people when their hearts unite, it still amounts to physical union. And what is wrong with that anyway? Further, deed and speech follow thought, don't they? Once such a thought has emerged, what won't follow? Moreover, if a Brahmin so much as thinks a sin, he must expiate himself; that is, thought and deed are the same. Moreover, if there exists such a clear feeling that there should be no physical union, then that contradicts their being all alone.

Moreover, these two people unite merely in their hearts only if Kantaruvas do the same. Why? Because it says this is comparable to the Kantaruva Convention.[115]

Further, if there is such a clear emotion, then one can not say they are full of love. Why? Because it is like a vessel that is full—there is no room for anything else.

And if it is claimed that their union is consummated when their hearts unite, since they are such exemplary people, then they ought never to have physical union. If one answers that they unite physically, and without passion, for the gift of children, then there is no union of love, just union for a specified purpose.

Therefore, emotional union is not the correct exposition; physical union is required.

---

[114] In this paragraph Nakkīraṉār alludes to several of the poetic moments, **tuṟai**, discussed more fully in the Introduction (pages xiv–xxv): separation, union through the hero's (or heroine's) friend, etc.

[115] Kantaruva lovers are *not* "platonic" lovers.

The Occurrence of Speech

Next, one school claims that physical union is appropriate, yet adds that it would be inappropriate to have them unite without sweet words and speech, like cattle; and when such speech does occur, then their union is to develop in the proper order. What is the proper order of events, you ask? The Sight, the Doubt, the Clarity, and the Determination.[116]

The Sight occurs when the eyes of those two people meet; a poem for that:

I took her two eyes,
like blossoms,
to be honeybees,

her two young breasts
to be flower buds,

her scarlet mouth,
like honey,
to be the bud
of a leaf,

when I first saw
this beautiful,
alluring,
flowering vine
in that grove
by the Vaiyai River
of His Majesty
who conquered Cennilam
with his army of elephants—

both my eyes
rejoiced.[117]

The Doubt is doubting what you've seen. In what manner does it occur, you ask? He wonders whether she might be a hill fairy, or a celestial damsel, or a water nymph—or maybe just a human girl. A poem for that:

Here in the South,
in the lands of the Pāṇṭiyaṉ,
the Supreme, the renowned
Emperor of Sweet Tamil,

is she a heavenly goddess
who lives in this grove

[116] These are the first four of the multifarious moments of love, **tuṟai**, presented in the Introduction (pages xiv–xxv).

[117] *Pāṇṭi-k-Kōvai*, 1.

sparkling with fragrant
flowers—

or is she a goddess
from the mountains
that brush against
the sky—

is she a goddess
of the very sky itself—

or a spirit
living on the waves
of the waters?

She makes me wonder,
this girl
with her beautiful
eyebrows.[118]

And she wonders about him, too: is he that god who is partial to cadamba,[119] or is he a wood sprite—or, maybe, is he a human being? That is how she wonders.

Here then is how Clarity comes to him after they have expressed such wonder: he realizes the truth because her clothing has specks of dust, because her feet touch the ground, because her eyes blink, because her garlands have withered, and because her sandal paste looks dried out. And after the Clarity comes Determination; a poem for that:

The Goad
to His Enemies,
the king whose lances
are perfect and sharp, whose
elephants' feet are enormous,
who brought down his foes
at Pāḻi,

he owns
these fresh waters,
where bees suck
water lilies.

Her long eyes, bright
like those lilies,
blinked, and I saw
her red feet touching
the ground.

---

118 *Pāṇṭi-k-Kōvai*, 2.

119 Murukaṉ.

> She is no goddess,
> this girl with perfect
> jewels.[120]

She also determines that he is human in the same way. And when they have realized it, their desire swells to the point that they join each other; when they unite in this way, it is with great beauty.

But that interpretation is inappropriate. For what reason, you ask? Because it smacks of mismatched love: his wondering whether she might be a goddess instead of a woman, and his determination that she is not on the grounds that she lacks the pertinent indicators, are signs of mismatching. Since we are commenting here only within the inner modes, this interpretation would be a confusion of modes, and the interpretation given above must be correct.[121]

If one thinks their love must be different from their union because he said "the union of love," like "a vine taken by a sword," it is not. Take it that they are non-differentiable, like "a chest made of gold," or "a pot made of clay."

This is also called "natural union," because they united through nature, as described by poets, similar to the Kantaruva Convention.

Next, it is also called "divine union" because the two of them unite through the nature of divinity. Whenever karma is fulfilled for someone through no effort or intent on his part, it occurs through the deity; likewise here, since union occurs for these two people through no effort or intent on their part, it is called "divine union."

It is also called "the union of meeting," since he attains her beauty in meeting her, and she attains his beauty in meeting him.

Next, what is the reason he said "the union of love" instead of "divine union," or "the union of meeting," or "natural union," you ask? It would have been appropriate for him to have said any of them, but he chose to say "the union of love" because all three of the others occur through love. When you mention only one of several causes for something, you note its specific importance. What do we mean? When they call a combination of earth, water, time, and seed a "rice-sprout," the rice is noted as the specific cause of the

---

[120] *Pāṇṭi-k-Kōvai*, 3.

[121] There are actually seven modes of love poetry in Caṅkam Tamil, the tradition to which this entire work appeals for authority. Yet two of those seven—the ones listed first and last—are regarded as decidedly inferior, and are rejected from consideration here because of the note in Verse 1 concerning the "five modes," a common reference to the five "inner modes," i.e., the ones other than the first and the last. It is the last of the seven modes that Nakkīraṉār cites when he speaks of "mismatched love." Called **peruntiṇai**, it includes poems about love between men and women who are ill matched in age, class, etc., a situation he explicitly avoided through his earlier statement of their equality. It would be mismatching, he implies, for a human to fall in love with a deity.

sprout. Earth, water and so forth are general causes because they serve as causes for lentils and so on as well. Likewise here, deity, nature, and meeting are general causes, but love is the specific cause; therefore, it is called "the union of love."

Next, what does he mean by **the accord on both sides of the union of love**, you ask? It is like saying their affection will remain the same in degree before and after their union. One might object that this does not accord with the ways of the world; a passion that is firm before union may grow weak afterwards, as a strong thirst goes away after drinking. But to him we reply, "You speak with no comprehension. You asked earlier about the nature of the world, didn't you? Must we repeat that at times this does not agree with the ways of the world, even though the author stated when he undertook this work that a treatise is something established by scholars, and deals with "the non-existent, the sweet, and the good?"

Yet even if one stipulates that this is not love as it is found in the world, there may still be an objection: if love as it stands before union remains just the same after the union, then there must have been no benefit in uniting, just as there is no use in drinking if the thirst that precedes drinking remains the same after you drink. To him, we reply, "Not so." Desire, as it stood before the union, will in fact diminish during their union; yet that reduction will be replenished by an affection born through the active qualities in which they engage themselves. Replenished, their love as it stood before their union will not diminish, but will remain always in the same degree.

Now this hero, whose love remains unchanged both before and after their union: will he leave her or not? If we say he is to depart, then it will seem as though he does not love her. Why? Leaving her is the opposite of loving her. Yet even if we stipulate that he shall not depart, he will still be thought not to love her. Why? Because if he does not leave, others will realize what they are up to, and then she would die; he could even be thought unsympathetic to her death. Is there no third alternative, you ask? He is to depart. When he does, will he leave behind an absence of love, you ask? He will not. We shall now explain how even his departure occurs through love.

Driven by both natural and developed love, the hero has united with her in divine union; now he makes his love known. Natural love is that which arises without any cause at all, while developed love arises in response to her qualities. What the hero actually says as he is driven by those two types of love is designated his Expression of Love.

What we call the Expression of Love occurs when the hero speaks as though to a bee, but in such a way that the heroine hears him express his love. How does it work, you ask? He lets her know by saying,

"You think her arm is a red glory-lily, her eye a dark water lily, and her mouth a red lotus! You stagger and buzz about her hair and her garlands! But you do know the fragrance of her red mouth, do you not? And you visit all the water flowers and all the land flowers, all the flowers that grow on twigs and on vines—all these kinds of flowers! You know the fragrance of the red lotus, don't you? You do! Is there a fragrant lotus blossom that smells like the red mouth of such a girl? Tell me: I trust you, o bee."

Here is a poem for that:

Certain of victory
his enemies joined him
in battle at Viḻiñam,
but our king witnessed
their exploits in climbing to heaven:
in his grand grove
here on Mount Potiyil,
deep in the south
you live in your search—

Tell me now,
little bee!
Do there exist
any gorgeous,
fragrant lotus blooms
with aroma to match
this delicate girl's
coral-red mouth?[122]

It is the bee's nature to search among the flowers in its home in the grand grove on southern Mount Potiyil, which belongs to the king who witnessed the exploits of his foes at Viḻiñam in their ascent into heaven, thinking they might yet win the battle.

This is what the poem means: "When he caused so many kings to fall as they fought him on the Viḻiñam seacoast, our king did not think of them as enemies, but granted them heaven, which otherwise cannot be entered except through austerities or through gifting. Because you are a bee from the land of such a noble man, you also are noble, and hence you are to be trusted. Moreover, Potiyil is home to all the gods, and that grand grove is their woods; you also live in that grove and partake of their nature, don't you? Therefore again, you are to be trusted. As that is your nature, you would never lie. Now, is there a lotus blossom which smells as fragrant as her mouth?" In saying this, the hero made his love known.

---

[122] *Pāṇṭi-k-Kōvai*, 4.

Next, the word, "delicate:" It means that delicacy is her nature. Delicacy is something that is extremely natural to women; he means that it is not something she has developed, but something natural in her. In this way also, he expresses his love.

Next, "coral-red mouth" means a mouth that is very elegant. Elegant people do not conceal their good qualities, and this girl's mouth glows with the qualities of shape, speech, and fragrance. In saying this, too, he expresses his love.

Next, in the phrase "Do there exist..." take the final particle as the interrogative indicator, among the five possibilities.[123] He has said,

> Certainty, interrogation, distinction,
> enumeration, and metrical completion are the five kinds
> of final particles.[124]

Next, the phrase, "gorgeous, fragrant lotus blooms" means beautiful aromatic lotus flowers. It follows from this phrase that other qualities of handsome people are also mostly beautiful; he described the fragrance in the lotus in order to make just this point. "Could that sort of very fragrant lotus smell like her mouth?" it implies.

The final particle at the very end of the poem is the final particle of metrical completion.

Our next point to examine is this: You note that he said merely, "with aroma to match her coral-red mouth," and did not utilize the comparative particle "like," do you? Take it that the comparative particle is elided. Why? Because he has said,

> Case compound, comparative compound,
> verbal compound, compound of quality,
> conjunctive compound, other-word compound:
> these are the six types of compound construction,[125]

consider the comparative particle elided.

But now you assert, "You have drawn the simile incorrectly. In the world the lotus is used as a simile for the mouths of women. Why? They have written,

> The coral-red mouth,
> filled with honey,

---

[123] See footnote 104, page 28. This final particle is the same ē, but here it is to be interpreted as an interrogative marker.

[124] *Tolkappiyam: Iṭaiyiyal*, 9.

[125] *Tolkappiyam: Eccaviyal*, 16.

and smelling like a lotus
...[126]

Instead, you said, 'is there a fragrant lotus like her mouth,' which makes the mouth the simile for the lotus, and that is wrong."

You don't know what you're talking about: things in the world are not established as similes and what they are compared to. Through a poet's volition, the simile may become the object to which something is compared, and the object may become the simile. Why? Because he has said,

Comparisons of things come through the intent
of him who brings them together,
in this tradition with no confusions.[127]

Also, it says,

Like an eye,
it blossoms
in a heap of grain
...[128]

and,

A lily that blooms
as an eye
...[129]

and,

This girl with mascara eyes,
like the lotus,
and I ...[130]

and,

the lotus eye, rimmed in
collyrium, grew
in misery
...[131]

They express it both ways, so it is appropriate to construct the simile in either way.

---

[126] From *Kuṟuntokai*, 300.

[127] Unidentified verse.

[128] From *Naṟṟiṇai*, 8.

[129] From an unidentified poem.

[130] From *Akanāṉūṟu*, 156.

[131] From *Naṟṟiṇai*, 113.

Next, if you contend that a water lily of the river-plain mode can become a water lily from the mountain-country mode, it cannot. That bee from the mountain country does not wander only among the mountains—it travels through all the landscapes and feeds at all flowers. Moreover, the poem is constructed in line with the saying,

> Flowers and birds of whatever mode,
> even when they do not occur in a certain mode and its time,
> come as results of the mode in which they do occur.[132]

Also, it is appropriate since seaside lotuses and mountain-country lotuses both actually exist; note that in the *Peruṅkuṟiñci*.[133]

Next, if you say that it would conflict with the title "hero" to say that he unites with her in the land of another hero,[134] it does not. Why? Because the poem gave Mount Potiyil as the place of their union; that mountain belongs to a real Pāṇṭiyaṉ king, and all who appear in his lineage are gods. Now the hero we want is not the greatest among the gods, just the greatest of humans; thus there is no conflict in saying that he unites with her in the Pāṇṭiyaṉ's land.

Moreover, it says,

> There in Uṟaiyūr,
> with its mountains of rice,
> Uṟaiyūr of great, munificent Tittaṉ,
> who gives wealth as the rains,
> in the floods of the river Kāviri,
> where boat poles don't touch bottom,
> you played in the water yesterday
> with the girl of your desire,
> dazzling in her earrings
> and her jewelry:
> you made a raft
> of white reeds,
> and your faces bloomed
> like those of elephants
> looking for ponds in Pūḻiyūr,
> while the flower garlands
> hanging from your great,

---

[132] *Tolkāppiyam: Akattiṇaiyiyal*, 21.

[133] An alternate title for the Caṅkam Tamil work known more commonly as *Kuṟiñci-p-pattu*, one of the Ten Long Songs.

[134] That is, the hero of the love poem is said, in the poem itself, to unite with his heroine in the country of the Pāṇṭiyaṉ king.

handsome chest
withered.[135]

and,

the large male murrelfish,
with many stripes, its mouth
gaping ...[136]

Also, it is appropriate because it says that the hero of the poem played in the water in the lands of the Literary Patron,[137] and he has united there with her in the poems of other ancient authors.

The substance that comes through in this poem is that the hero makes explicit the love that rests within him—that he makes his love known. Some more poems:

All you bees, cavorting
and pure, come
to me, speak!

In those seaside glades of yours,
there in Koṅku province
of the king who crushed hosts
of enemy kings at Kōṭṭāṟu,
are there flower clusters
with fragrance as enticing
as that of her hair,
she whose glance wilts
clusters of young mangoes,
gleaming red?[138]

Tell me,
all you bees,
swarming the flowering slopes
of the southland's Mount Potiyil,
that mountain of Pūḻiyaṉ Māṟaṉ
with his warrior's anklet,
who sapped the strength
at Āṟrukkuṭi
of the great Cēra king
with his warrior's
anklet:

---

135 *Akanāṉūṟu*, 6.

136 From *Akanāṉūṟu*, 36.

137 See Introduction, pages xxv–xxvi.

138 *Pāṇṭi-k-Kōvai*, 5.

is there
a delicate blossom
as fragrant
as her black hair,
anywhere in
your grand
grove?[139]

Stubborn enemy kings
fell at Viḻiñam
to our monarch
with his glittering chariot,
and you swarm the slopes
of his Mount Kolli
sucking nectar
from all the riotous
blossoms—
you would know,
would you not?

Is there, o bees,
a flower as intoxicating
and fragrant
as her hair?
Tell me![140]

They joined battle at Pūlantai
hoping to help that Cēra king,
but they just climbed
the funeral pyre
together
as he demolished
them:
his
are those slopes
on Mount Kolli
where you swarm,
o bees, among
brilliant flowers—
you know: so tell me!

Are there anywhere
any splendidly aromatic blooms

---

139 *Pāṇṭi-k-Kōvai*, 6.

140 *Pāṇṭi-k-Kōvai*, 7.

as fragrant as this girl's
dark hair?[141]

He was their death,
destroying in battle
those enemy kings
who never understood
there at Cēvūr—
and it's on the slopes
of his Mount Kolli
that you swarm, devouring
flower nectar, you bees:
Answer me!

Do you know of any
sweet blossoms
with the fragrance
of her flowing
hair?[142]

Now, little bee
with such pretty wings,
you make it your life
to look for honey:
don't just tell me
what I'd love to hear,
tell me what
you've really seen:

Do you know of any flowers
that smell as nice
as the hair
of this girl
with close-set teeth,
the beauty of a peacock,
and a close and cultivated
love?[143]

Take these also in that manner.

When he praised her thus she became embarrassed. Why? Even children become uncomfortable through modesty if you praise them to their faces: need we note that she, with her excellence and her great modesty, was embarrassed when the hero stood right there and praised her?

---

141 *Pāṇṭi-k-Kōvai*, 8.

142 *Pāṇṭi-k-Kōvai*, 9.

143 *Kuṟuntokai*, 2.

When he observed her discomfiture he considered, "Such a change ought not to come over her while I am by her side, just as a tall tree growing on well watered land is not hurt by heat; how did it happen?" Then he understood. "Now I know," he thought, "Maybe it was caused by the way I praised her in the excess of my love." When he realized that, he felt a great anguish, thinking, "If she weakens so in her great modesty just when I praise her here, she might even die if it occurs to her that some outsider could come to know of our behavior." Being anguished implies that he becomes that anguish, with no other emotion.

Then she began to worry about his anguish; her embarrassment left, while she felt a new anguish herself, like the vanishing of a scorpion sting when you suffer a javelin wound. The hero observed that and thought, "She has no character of her own; she takes mine. When I feel consoled, she feels consoled; and when I am afflicted, so is she. And so she will not die when I leave, unless I were to intend her to. Moreover, outsiders surely will realize what we're doing if I do not leave soon, and then she will be really distraught. But no outsiders will know about us if I leave now. Thus she will be consoled."

With these thoughts in his mind he adjusted the edges of her thick black hair, smoothed her hair and forehead so they looked proper, caressed her breasts and shoulders so they glowed with beauty, and spoke to console her. He decided, "I shall embrace her so she springs back to life; then I will leave."

Having made that decision, he then speaks a poem on the Fear of Separation.

Fear of Separation

The Fear of Separation is his own fear of their separating, and his causing her to fear it; that is why it is called Fear of Separation. How does he express it, you ask? He declares, "I will not leave you; if I did, I would languish!" Here are some poems for that:

He is victorious!
his reddened lance gleams
like a lightning streak,
this king with the righteous
scepter:
he granted heaven
to the king
who challenged him
at Viḻiñam,
    and you are like
    his Vañci City.

I will not leave you,
  if I did I would languish:
so why do you weep?
It makes your long,

bamboo shoulders
lose their luster
like sallowed gold.[144]

Kings with grand,
colorful, bejewelled crowns
came to ruin at Āṟṟukkuṭi
when the Pāṇṭiyaṉ displayed
the cutting force
of his bright lance!

Girl, you are like
his Toṇṭi City!
The hue of your long hair
brings me the sickness
of love!
And such armlets you wear
on your arms!

I will not leave you—why
do you grieve?
It turns your ruby complexion
yellow, like gold.[145]

Pūlantai crumbled
when the Scholar, the
Pāṇṭiyaṉ, the emperor
whose warrior's anklet
is of gold, merely grabbed
his javelin, glistening
like lightning.
He is the Lord
who stood upon
white waves, yet
none knew he was the First
in those old days.

Girl,
you are like
his Muciṟi City—
I will not leave you;
if I did, I would languish!

---

[144] *Pāṇṭi-k-Kōvai*, 10.

[145] *Pāṇṭi-k-Kōvai*, 11.

Don't
grieve.[146]

When the heroine hears him say these things, she thinks, "My lord says, 'I will not leave you; if I did, I would languish!' There must be such a thing as separating."

Then she gets upset: she thinks about not seeing her lord, nor hearing him, nor touching him, and being separated from his body. This girl, who was like lightning among the clouds, a vine over the water, or a beautiful liana rising thick with buds and leaves and trembling with beauty in brisk air, tarnished a little; her mind melted like a wax doll before fire, and her luster dimmed like that of a round mirror upon which one breathes. Yet even then her pain subsided as she thought, "If I were to languish and die, my lord also would die."

He watched her console herself in that way, and felt overwhelmed with a great and tender joy, thinking to himself, "It seems she has no character of her own; she just takes on mine." So he then speaks a poem called The Reassurance.

The Reassurance

The Reassurance is the speech of reassuring. How does it work, you ask? It works because he says, "Our home is nearby." Here are some poems for that:

The king of poetic, sweet Tamil,
that Goad to His Enemies,
holds arrows and a cruel bow:
it is he
who conquered Pāḻi—
  girl, you are like
  his Vañci City!

Ranks of tall banners
steeped in brilliance
on the pure, colorful
roof terraces
of our town
shade all the bazaars
in your town:
it's really
that close.[147]

The king simply
took up his bright,

---

[146] *Pāṇṭi-k-Kōvai*, 12. This poem identifies King Neṭumāṟaṉ with Vishnu, who stood on white waves, and is called First among the gods.

[147] *Pāṇṭi-k-Kōvai*, 13.

slicing, lightning lance,
and the rest of the kings,
with their strong shoulders,
broad and fine of complexion,
perished at Naṟaiyāṟu
in the South—
    and you are like
    his Toṇṭi City!

Don't grieve:
gems strung and hung out
on brilliantly colored
terraces in our town
illuminate pretty
colored terraces
in yours, like
the sun:
it's that
close.[148]

The king took to arms,
and warriors who disagreed
died in camaraderie
at Naṟaiyāṟu—
    you're like
    his Cōḻa lands!

When your people light
bright lamps to guard
their mountain millet fields,
they rout the darkness
from our assembly grounds.[149]

The king,
the Gift of the Gods,
bewildered the Cēra king
who opposed him at Cēvūr,
where carp meander through
wet rice fields—
    innocent girl,
    you are like
    his Vañci City!
Your hair is fragrant
with perfume.

---

[148] *Pāṇṭi-k-Kōvai*, 14.

[149] *Pāṇṭi-k-Kōvai*, 15.

Cotton banners
on bejewelled terraces
in your town
brush tridents set out
on pretty terraces
in ours.[150]

When the heroine hears this, she says to herself, “My lord tells me his home is nearby, and it won’t be hard for him to come by here. I guess that means I will be able to see him and hear him often, and people who see and hear each other often are content, aren’t they? I guess that will satisfy my lord,” and she is consoled.

Then, after he has ascertained that she has calmed down, he will leave.

Next, note that he utters both the Fear of Separation and the Reassurance because he thinks, “She has tremendous modesty; if I don’t leave, our behavior will become known to outsiders and then she would surely die.” In these ways, then, even their separation occurs through love.

The Hero Realizing the Preciousness of the Heroine

Will he leave her all alone, after he has consoled her by saying these things, you ask? He will not. He hides in a nearby thicket, where she cannot see him, but where he can see her; he is like lightning hiding in a rain cloud. And she walks past as he hides there, her thick braids and her garlands swaying, her liana waist growing tired,[151] her broad buttocks-cloth shimmering, her fine gold earrings flashing lightning, her pure gold anklets jingling on her pretty little red feet, those feet like the inner petals of a lotus, where noisy bees buzz. She steps softly, softly, like a swan. She walks as though a golden vine with tender leaves from the celestial tree of desire took her steps. She sits upon a squared ruby rock by an emerald slab and a fresh, blue mountain pool with crystal banks, near a beautiful cascade thundering on that cool mountainside. She sits by a seat covered with fine pollens, deep in shade, fragrant with blossoms, in a jasmine bower.

As she sat there, a bunch of her friends returned from making little wreaths, great garlands, and skirts of mixed leaves, flower garlands, grand bracelets, and so forth, from pollens, young leaves, flower buds, and other fine things. Beetles and bees frightened them by their sides as they held out these offerings to her, praised her, and called for her long life. As they stood there she seemed as radiant as the cool moon among the stars.

---

[150] *Pāṇṭi-k-Kōvai*, 16.

[151] From the heavy burden of bearing the weight of her breasts.

He saw her there and thought, "I thought I had attained this girl, but it just seems like a dream. Even if it were true, it will be hard for me to reach her again." Here are some poems for that:

He took up his furious,
victorious lance,
and he conquered:
enemy kings who opposed him
at Cennilam
climbed the hill
where bamboo thickets
rattle,[152]
and it was all just
a dream
in a terraced field
on his tall cool mountains:

I dreamed I caressed
the breasts of this girl
with shoulders soft
as bamboo shoots!
Even if it were true,
never again
will I ever attain
her awake.[153]

The Protector
of grand lands
used his sharp-tipped
lance to force enemy kings
from earth to rule in heaven,
kings who battled in Naṟaiyāṟu
over his grand, well watered
lands in the South, over lands
her feminine allure resembles—

and all my enjoyment
of her rich beauty
was nothing
but a dream,
I fear.[154]

---

[152] A figure for the cremation ground.

[153] *Pāṇṭi-k-Kōvai*, 17.

[154] *Pāṇṭi-k-Kōvai*, 18.

The king of the Nēri Mountains,
with fire in his eyes,
took up his exquisite
oiled lance
at Kaṭaiyal,
and other kings
who had held their bows
so elegantly in their hands
just ran away—

It cannot be
that I caressed
the breasts
of this girl
with her wide eyes lined
in kohl, in that grand grove
on his Kolli Mountains!
Even if it were true,
there is no way
ever to join
with her
again.[155]

When he thinks of her preciousness like this, he will marry her if he feels that such an opportunity really will never come again. But if he thinks to himself, "How can I manage to join with such a girl?" he will just try for another meeting with her. He leaves at this point, thinking thoughts such as these, and still gawking at the heroine, who by now is running about with her girlfriends. He speaks about her as he leaves, and here are some poems for that:

When the Pāṇṭiyaṉ strung his bow,
swift arrows pierced
his enemies' vital parts,
then, flaming, sped on
to desiccate the reddened
battlefield—
and here she wanders
with her friends
inside this grove
with its delicate flowers
in his Vañci City:
    isn't she my own
    precious soul?

And people say
you cannot perceive

---

[155] *Pāṇṭi-k-Kōvai*, 19.

the soul with your
senses![156]

Our king won
the Battle of Kaṭaiyal,
and the eternal souls
of those who began the war
reached heaven—
he supports this world
as though it were
his own soul.

But isn't this my
own soul, wandering
among her friends
here on Mount Kolli,
in this grove,
where branches hang
so low?

And they would say
no one has seen
his own sweet
soul![157]

As he speaks, he languishes, worrying that he will never get to join with her again. But his pain grabs onto something for consolation. What will console it, you ask? He will think of that bewitching beauty he has just attained, and hope that his own best friend will help him reach her again. Using that thought as a crutch, he leaves, content for the moment.

* * *

Verse 3.

The hero who has thus united,
in two fashions shall he meet her again,
according to tradition:
a rendezvous arranged by his friends, and
coming upon her alone, without his friend.

What does this declare, you ask? The best thing for a hero who has united with her in natural union is to decide to marry her. What do we mean? As a wayfarer who slips and steps in mud or cow dung cleans his feet to restore their purity before he enters his home, it would be great if the hero too, who walks the path

[156] *Pāṇṭi-k-Kōvai*, 20.

[157] *Pāṇṭi-k-Kōvai*, 21.

of wisdom and good conduct, were to redeem himself when he slips, acknowledging that his slip was a failing. But this is how he acts if he does not redeem himself: this verse relates the manner in which he behaves.

Its meaning:

The hero who has thus united—the hero who united and departed in that way.

a rendezvous arranged by his friends—meeting at a tryst set up by his best friend.

coming upon her alone, without his friend—encountering the girl alone, without his friend.

There is an empty word at the beginning of the last line.[158]

two—the total.

in ... fashions shall he meet her again, according to tradition—the definition of the manners in which he meets her again.

It means that, by stipulation, his meeting her can occur along only one of these two lines: meeting her at a rendezvous arranged by his friend, and encountering her alone, without his friend; either of these may occur after the hero has united with her, and departed from her, in the way noted above.

"The hero who has thus united" signifies a hero who met his heroine in a place where there was no one else, driven by providence, with God in the background. And thus it was that the heroine came to unite with him. He is called a "man of rights"[159] because he has his rights, and a "head man"[160] because he holds headship. Take the terms for her also in like manner.[161]

Rendezvous Arranged By His Friend

Next we shall relate how a rendezvous arranged by his friend comes about. After the hero leaves her content, following their natural union, he muses over all that has been said. What does he think about, you ask? He frets, "Will she be distraught, worrying about me when I cannot see her, since I said, 'I will not leave you; if I did I would languish!' Or will she suffer because she does not know how to hide the changes that have come over her from outsiders?" and so on.

---

[158] The word is **āṅka**, one of several words called **acai-c-col**, which serve to fill metrical spaces in the verse, but convey no particular meaning.

[159] The word **kiḻavōṉ**, or **kiḻavaṉ**, "man of rights," often substitutes for the term **talaivaṉ**, "hero." See the Introduction, page xvi.

[160] The word **talaimakaṉ**, "head man," often substitutes for the word **talaivaṉ**, "hero." See the Introduction, page xvi.

[161] She often is called **kiḻavi**, "woman of rights," and **talaimakaḷ**, "head woman," in place of the term **talaivi**, "heroine."

Questioning What Happened

After a while, his languor will strike his best friend. When this happens, his friend will look him over from head to foot, and he will find faded that splendid radiance that exiles the beauty of the young sun with its swelling light, as it appears at the peak of the gorgeous dawn mountain, with its high summits, resplendent with gems and cascades that toss down gold to rout the night's darkness and dislodge the world's sleep. He will say, "And why does our lord suffer this wilting change today?" Here are some poems for that:

What could make this
generous man's heart wilt
and suffer like the foes
of the Lion to His Enemies
    who owns victorious elephants,
    who sheathed his honed
    and glistening lance
    when he saw his foes flee
    at Nelvēli,
    with its vast
    cool fields and
    flowers?[162]

Lord of the cool
lake fronts!
Why do you languish,
why do you let
your mind wilt?
Did your heart chase
bright themes in
rich Tamil poetry
in Kūṭal City
    of the Southern King
    who unsheathed
    and took up
    his sharp lance
    to make other kings flee
    Naṟaiyāṟu, surrounded
    by vast groves
    where bees
    live?

---

[162] *Pāṇṭi-k-Kōvai*, 22.

or has something
happened to you?[163]

This generous man's speech,
and his very body
are not as they have been:

Like foes of
Neṭumāṟaṉ,
    who crushed the pride
    of a Cēraṉ king who opposed him,
like foes of
Neṭumāṟaṉ,
    who seized all
    the tremendous wealth
    of his lands
    at one stroke,
    in Kaṭaiyal,
what is he thinking?

What is he
pondering?[164]

Telling What Happened

If his friend does not question him in this manner he has to give up, without ever finding out what happened to the hero. But the hero will reply to a friend who does ask; he will say, "Yesterday, I saw such-and-such a kind of person. My heart ran like a flood through an aqueduct, and it turned out like this." Here are some poems for that:

Just as an elephant
with its great trunk
loses its senses,
trembles, and grieves
when a baby snake
in its hole
bewitches it,
my own body
shrivels up
when this young girl
bewitches me
with her delicate teeth—
they are like pearls,

---

[163] *Pāṇṭi-k-Kōvai*, 23.

[164] *Pāṇṭi-k-Kōvai*, 24.

and she is like
Kūṭal City
of King Māṟaṉ.[165]

My heart blossomed
in her breast,
rounded out
in her soft shoulders,
bent
in the bow
of the god of Love
on her face,[166]
and curled up
in the hair
of this girl
who is like
Kūṭal City
    of the king
    with the murderous lance
    who fought at Āṟṟukkuṭi
    and made waves
    of enemy kings
    wearing warrior's anklets
    climb the funeral
    pyre.[167]

My love left me
for large, black eyes
in the lotus-red face
of a girl like that great
beautiful sculpture
in the cool Kolli Mountains[168]
    of the Goad to His Enemies,
    thick, strong-shouldered,
    who devastated foes fighting
    with huge armies
    in the land of
    Pūlantai.

---

165 *Pāṇṭi-k-Kōvai*, 25.

166 The reference is to her eyebrows.

167 *Pāṇṭi-k-Kōvai*, 26.

168 The figurine in the Kolli Mountains, **Kolli-p-pāvai**, is said to be so beautiful that any man who gazes upon it is entranced forever.

My love has not
returned.[169]

Like a little, pretty,
white-striped baby snake
bewitching a jungle
elephant,
a young girl
sprouting white
teeth, and wearing
bracelets on her arms,
has bewitched
me.[170]

My friend,
you make children
happy, and you
befriend poets—
now listen to me:
On the eighth day,
in the middle of
the great seas, fresh,
the white moon rises,
and it's just like that!

Her little brow,
shining by her
black hair,
snared me
like a newly trapped
elephant![171]

Admonishing

The hero's friend will admonish him when he hears him say these things. Admonishing him means exhorting him with words that do not forsake the love he holds for his friend, though he perceives evil in him. In his admonition he says, "Just as no seed could check a mountain if it started to roll, just as there is no way to cover a feed bin once an elephant breaks in, just as there would be no cooling waters to mix in if the seas were to boil, my lord: who is there to straighten you out if your heart runs amok and will not remain within the bounds

---

[169] *Pāṇṭi-k-Kōvai*, 27.

[170] *Kuṟuntokai*, 119.

[171] *Kuṟuntokai*, 129.

of wisdom, constancy, investigation, and resolve? It is for you to straighten others out! It is not seemly for someone like you to say, 'I saw such-and-such a form in such-and-such a place, and my understanding is undone.'" Here are some poems for that:

Is it nice
for our lord
of the mountains
to say,
"My heart
has worn thin
since I saw
that young liana
with her friends
gathered in the groves
by the Kolli Mountains
    of the king
    whose pearl parasol
    brushes the sky,
    the Lion to His Enemies,
    the Emperor
    who appreciates
    sweet Tamil poems?"[172]

You, wearing your
fragrant wreath
where bees buzz!

Who then is left
to be good
in this land
between the seas,
if you weaken
when you see
the moon-like face
of a girl
there in the lush grove
at Cape Kaṉṉi
    of the king
    who drove his
    powerful chariot
    and fought
    those kings at Āṟṟukkuṭi
    and caused them
to weaken,
wearing their cool,

---

[172] *Pāṇṭi-k-Kōvai*, 28.

fragrant garlands,
where bees buzz?[173]

Refutation of the Admonition

What a disconsolate hero says after his friend admonishes him is called Refutation of the Admonition; here are some poems for that:

If there be people
who have seen as I have
the soft, confused glance
of this innocent girl,
so like a vine in the mountains
west of Kūṭal City
    of the canopied king
    who took in his hand
    the victorious lance
    at the battlefield
    on the Viḻiñam coast
    and made his foes perish,

they never
would utter such
and other
tales.[174]

They came in anger,
they thought they'd grab
his land and live there,
but they lost their strength
and drowned in the blood
from their wounds
when our king conquered them
at Pūlantai, and she
is like our king's
Pukār City:

Once you see her eyes,
fresh and soft as glory lilies,
you'll never again utter
such tales as you've
just spoken.[175]

---

[173] *Pāṇṭi-k-Kōvai*, 29.

[174] *Pāṇṭi-k-Kōvai*, 30.

[175] *Pāṇṭi-k-Kōvai*, 31.

Long, my friends,
long may you live!

But you would never
admonish me so
if you had ever
stood before her
and seen in her beautiful,
lustrous face
the proud look
in those eyes, lined
with black, to which
the very lotus surrendered,
the lotus that opens its petals
to bees in the backwaters
on the Pāṇṭiyaṉ seacoast at Koṟkai
where great waves wash in pearls with cool rays
that hurt the hooves of fine-gaited horses
and block their way
through that expanse
where so many long, spiny outer petals
join to stand guard
so a bud inside
can bloom pure on the screwpine
with its scaly bark
and ghoulish head,
where the aroma of flowers
overpowers the stench of dead fish,
where the seashore is covered with sand dunes
littered with waterthorn
sporting luxuriant buds
and red stamens coated with fine
pollen.[176]

Sure, make
fun of me!
If your warning could stop
my body from melting,
nothing would be better!

But inside me
it spreads
like a slab of butter
melting on a scorching rock
set in the summer sun,
    a dumb boy with no arms

[176] *Akanāṉūṟu*, 130.

trying to corral it
with his eyes.

It is so hard
to contain
this disease.[177]

Speaking in Worry

When his friend hears the anguished hero refute the admonition in this way, he worries, thinking, "My lord is able to realize what is improper all by himself, yet he is still confused. And that is so even after I asked him if he thinks it proper to weaken like this! This must be due to the nature of the form he saw; otherwise, he would be convinced, wouldn't he?" Here is a poem for such worrying:

Who in the world
can convince him now?

He used to stand
like the solid gold mountain
with the carving of the carp[178]
cut by him who drove
his sure footed elephant
to cause kings to die
that day at Vallam—

but his constancy
and his wisdom
have been perverted
and weakened![179]

Asking Where It Happened

As he thought in this vein, his friend became chagrined. "What I said was out of line. It was my just fate that he rebuked my admonition," he thought. "If he had not spoken up, but simply died of grief, there was nothing I could have done. I have been a terrible boor." But the anguish of an anguished man will grab onto something for consolation; he thinks to himself, "If I die now of mortification, I will not be able to help him—remaining alive to console him is

---

[177] *Kuṟuntokai*, 58.

[178] The reference is to a tradition that the Pāṇṭiyaṉ king marched in triumph to the Himalaya Mountains and carved his royal insignium, the carp, on one of the peaks.

[179] *Pāṇṭi-k-Kōvai*, 32.

the thing to do!" and he does not die. Instead, he inquires, "In what place, and of what sort, is the form you saw?" Here are some poems for that:

Where
did my lord
see that vine?

Was it on the inner petals
of a broad lotus blossom
in the land of waters
of our king, on whose garland
are fastened, never to separate,
the tender, mango-like eyes
of women with little waists,
like vines, and broad shoulders?
Or was it on his Mount Kolli
in the West, filled
with his cool
grace?[180]

Was it on a lotus,
spreading its aroma,
and pleasant to those
who look upon it?

Or was it on Mount Kolli
in the West,
where clouds crawl,
Mount Kolli of him
  who conquered and plundered
  heaps of fine enemy wealth
  and herds of enemy elephants
  at Kaṭaiyal?

Tell me
where this girl,
who made your bright
garlanded chest slump,
resides.[181]

Relating Where It Happened

The hero was overjoyed when he heard this: it was as though he had just attained her again, as a withering sandalwood tree, scorched by the summer sun,

[180] *Pāṇṭi-k-Kōvai*, 33. The lotus blossom is an allusion to the seat of Goddess Lakshmi.

[181] *Pāṇṭi-k-Kōvai*, 34.

sprouts when it rains. He said, "The form I saw was in such-and-such a place, and of such-and-such a nature." Here are some poems for that:

On cool Mount Kolli
of the Goad to His Enemies,
who holds the righteous scepter,
that girl
whose brilliant brow
made me wither
has lotus blossoms
for feet,
a dancing snake
for her mound of love,
red water lilies
for the palms of her hands,
a liana
for a waist,
a red vine flower
for a mouth,
silk-cotton buds
for breasts,
and eyes sharp
as a fine javelin.[182]

On the pretty slopes
of Mount Kolli,
which belongs to the Lord of Cape Kaṉṉi,
the Gift of the Gods,
the southern king
who took the fortress at Kōṭṭāṟu
with its grand, colorful,
and long palisades, and made
the Cēraṉ king seek
the forest,[183]
that girl is like a vine,
but her fine face
is the moon,
her black-lined eyes
are red carp, and
her rising, grand
breasts, spotted with
pure gold, are
a pair of chalices,

---

[182] *Pāṇṭi-k-Kōvai*, 35.

[183] The reference is to the convention that a defeated king may wish to rescue his honor by starving to death while facing north in the woods.

topped with
sapphires.[184]

In a cool grove
on Mount Kolli
of the king who raised
    the banner of thunder
    that crashes forever,
    whose enemies perished
    in the land of Pūlantai,
a girl
with a brilliant forehead
made me wither
with her sharp, wide
flowery eyes—
her face is a grand
lotus bloom,
and her unbridled breasts
are lotus buds.[185]

I did not know
that there in the seagrove
fragrant with flowers
lives a bewitching goddess,
holding in her hands
a bouquet of screwpine blooms
crawling with honeybees,
pretending to chase birds
from fatty fish set to dry—

If I had known,
I never
would have gone
there.[186]

As soon as he gets this information, his friend begins to console the hero; he says, "Don't worry so much; let me see if there is anything I can do." Then he proceeds to the place the hero indicated. This, then, is the hero's situation.

Now for the heroine's situation: Some time after their union she is about to re-enter that playground grove with her friends when she is overpowered by a wave of great modesty. She imagines that the boy who had told her yesterday, "I will not leave you; if I did, I would languish!" might show up there, among the

---

[184] *Pāṇṭi-k-Kōvai*, 36.

[185] *Pāṇṭi-k-Kōvai*, 37.

[186] *Cilappatikāram: Kāṉalvari*, 9.

girls. She is also overpowered with fear, thinking that he might have died of grief. She is not herself; she just wanders around as the flood of her girlfriends meanders through the grove. When she comes upon the spot where yesterday she had honored the hero, she feels as though she has just seen him again. Why? Because it is in the nature of the world that simply seeing the spot where one met a sweet person will cause us to feel as though we had just met that person all over again. Her friends disperse as she stands there, just as they had the day before, saying, "Let's go and string some pretty leaf skirts!" or, "Let's go and make cool, sweet smelling garlands!" or, "Let's go and pick the best of the flowers!" Thus they disperse through their desire to play, and she stands still. How does she stand, you ask? She no longer feels the sense of modesty engendered by the thought that he might come. Why not? Because her friends have gone away. But she remains overwhelmed by the fear that he might have died. It is while she is standing like this that the hero's friend arrives.

He watches her from a place nearby where he can see her, but she cannot see him. "This is exactly the place he saw, and she is precisely the form he saw," he determines. Here are some poems for that:

Seeing Her At The Trysting Place

This is the girl
with hair where
bees buzz
who weakened
the heart of the lord
whose cool wreath
drips with nectar!

And this
is the terraced grainfield
he spoke of
in the Potiyil Mountains
of him who saw to it
  that vultures crawled
  all over mountains
  of enemy dead, and slept
  on their staring eyes
  at Maṇaṟṟimaṅkai
  with its great
  waters.[187]

[187] *Pāṇṭi-k-Kōvai*, 38.

This indeed
is the terraced grainfield
at Cape Kaṉṉi
    of the king
    on whose garland are fixed
    the minds and sharp eyes
    of black-haired women,
    the king who took Kaṭaiyal
    to make enemy kings, crushed
    in battle, lose their anger,
    leave, and
    day-dream.

And this
is the flowering
vine he
saw.[188]

Speaking in Amazement of the Hero

As he steeps in these reflections he thinks, "How could my lord have been consoled at all after he had seen this form? Such a thing is impossible even for the greatest of men: it must just be because he is so well learned that he could find any consolation. Anyone else would have died, but he did not; he came to me instead. It was quite improper of me to admonish him: he is my great friend, and a very worthy person." Here are some poems for that:

The lord's shoulders
are so very broad,
and he truly is
a great man!

Even after he gazed
into the wide, black eyes
in the red lotus face
of her who is like
the fine, tall figurine[189]
on dark Mount Kolli
    of the king
    who desiccated
    oncoming hordes
    of enemy armies
    that took him on
    at Vallam,

---

[188] *Pāṇṭi-k-Kōvai*, 39.

[189] This is the same statue referred to in *Pāṇṭi-k-Kōvai* 27 on page 57.

he actually
composed himself,
and faced
me.[190]

It is men
of great qualities
who really are
the best of men—

Even after he had gazed
into the rare,
flower-like eyes
of her who is like Vañci City
of the Gift of the Gods,
    the king with choice horses
    and well-built bows,
    who conquered Kaṭaiyal
    and made those who came at him,
    driving dark elephants
    with crescent tusks
    die,
my lord
composed himself.[191]

He will also muse in this vein:

In this grove by the sea
where a beautiful mastwood tree
spills its heavy load of flowers,
whose fine pollen fills
furrows left in the sand
by a right-whorled conch
feeding on the beach,
her eyes, like carp,
in her bright face,
full like the moon,
infected me
with a harsh disease
no medicine
can cure—

maybe its only cure
is the golden spottings

---

[190] *Pāṇṭi-k-Kōvai*, 40.

[191] *Pāṇṭi-k-Kōvai*, 41.

on her soft
breasts.[192]

and,

The hot,
delirious disease
caused by the sharp eyes
of this girl
with perfumed hair
cannot be cured
except by her
beautiful breasts,
with spottings
of gold.[193]

Musing thus he becomes consoled, although he is upset, as he thinks, "Since he did not actually die, I wonder what the best way would be to help him attain her again."

He returns to the hero and says, "That was a wonderful place!" Here are some poems for that:

Relating The Sight

Shade rich as the night
spreads all around,
and sands, white
as moonlight,
stretch on
and on,
beetles, bees,
and wasps sing
together, like
instrument strings
in tune!

That place
would make desire rise,
even in those
exceptional people
who have renounced
it.[194]

---

[192] *Cilappatikāram: Kāṉalvari*, 8.

[193] Unidentified verse.

[194] Unidentified poem.

On white sands littered
with pearls glinting
like lightning,
aromatic mastwood trees
spread their flowers,
fresh as gold,
as bees sing!

Today I saw a grove
of unequaled nature
at that oceanfront
on Cape Kaṉṉi
    of him who conquered Maṇaṟṟi,
    where enemy kings
    perished.[195]

The king whose pearl canopy
shines forever,
who triumphed
at Āṟṟukkuṭi,
the Wonderful One
with the scepter
of everlasting grace,
the descendant
of the cool moon,
to him belongs
that great grove
on Cape Kaṉṉi
    where screwpine blossoms mingle
    with waterthorn blooms,
    stirred by drunken bees,
    as cool droplets of honey
    trickle down vast
    white sands.[196]

There is a vast grove
which even gods
in the sky desire,
where fragrance spreads
and golden flowers
from woodland mastwoods
spill upon the vast sands
of the Vaiyai River
of the Supreme One

---

[195] *Pāṇṭi-k-Kōvai*, 42.

[196] *Pāṇṭi-k-Kōvai*, 43.

with his sharpened lance
covered with raw flesh,
whose rage destroyed
the Cēraṉ king
and his war-wreath,
dripping with nectar,
at Cēvūr.[197]

Suffering For A Word

His friend continues, "Aren't you fit to attain such exceptional things as these?" whereupon the hero returns to that place.

There he comes upon the heroine, standing alone. She sees him, and they meet. The moment she sees him, her fear of his death disperses, and she becomes herself again. Becoming herself, remember, means regaining her modesty, innocence, fear, and loathing; but as she stands reunited with her old nature, he becomes upset, since he cannot draw near without some sign from her! Being upset means there can be no other emotion. Now, his distraction grabs for anything it can find in consolation; but there is nothing. So he says something. What does he say, you ask? He says things like this: "You must be the goddess of this grove; if you are not, please open your mouth! If I lost my life, it would be very difficult to get it back, would it not?"[198] Here are some poems for that:

Your eyes hold
a network of fine
red lines,[199] they
vanquish the lotus
blossom—
I think of you
as the spirit
of this desirable
seashore
on Cape Kaṉṉi
    of him who vanquished
    his enemies, face
    to face at Veṇmāttu—
but if you
are not, please
open your mouth:

---

[197] *Pāṇṭi-k-Kōvai*, 44.

[198] The implication is that he will die if he cannot have a word from her.

[199] Tiny visible redness in the capillaries of the whites of a woman's eyes are signs of beauty; note that they are *not* to be mistaken for the English image of bloodshot eyes.

Who in this wide world
can retrieve his life
once it departs?[200]

You with your garland
where fragrance makes
its home—
I have called you
the spirit of brilliant,
beautiful Mount Potiyil,
owned by the Supreme One,
    the king of sweet Tamil
    in all its varieties,
    who destroyed the greatness
    of enemy kings
    at Cēvūr on the sea,
    swept with waves—
if you are not, please
open your mouth
for me:
if this life of mine
were to leave me,
who would be left
to bring it
back?[201]

Coming To Her Side

Is it the hero who said these things, you ask? It is not: it is the anguish born within him. That, too, must be considered the hero. The moment she heard these words she looked up at him, afraid that he might actually die, and she saw the truth: when she saw him, she felt a tremendous thrill, like picking up a fine jewel that you had lost and searched for. Her joy made her teeth appear in a smile, but then she became distracted, thinking, "I have committed a great immodesty before my lord." Then she thought, "My lord grieves even while I stand here before him; if he were now to see me in anguish, he would most surely die!" As she thinks in this vein, her anguish leaves and her modesty returns.

Yet though it returns, she can find nowhere to hide. So, with a loving glance, she covers her long, flower-like eyes with her fingers, gentle like good jewels, or glory lilies.

---

200 *Pāṇṭi-k-Kōvai*, 45.

201 *Pāṇṭi-k-Kōvai*, 46.

When she covers her eyes, he thinks it will console her if he comes to her side. "You covered your long black eyes because you figured they cause me anguish, didn't you?" he says, "But what about your honeyed garland, or your shoulders, with their tracings of sugarcane? Are they any less important to me?" Here are some poems for that:

> Good girl
> with your garland
> swarming with bees,
> you are like Kūṭal City
>   of the Lion to His Enemies
>   with his garland of flower buds
>   and his righteous
>   scepter!
> You covered up
> your large eyes, you
> thought they would
> grieve me!
>
> But don't your grand,
> lustrous shoulders,
> with their tracings
> of sugarcane, perturb
> my heart as well?[202]

> You covered up
> your wide, flower-like
> eyes—
> you thought
> they would make me
> waste away
> like the enemies
> of the Scholar,
>   the king who destroyed
>   the strength of his foes
>   at beautiful Cēvūr
>   filled with sweet,
>   cool groves!
>
> But don't
> your matchless
> red-lotus fingers
> hurt my heart as well?[203]

---

[202] *Pāṇṭi-k-Kōvai*, 47.

[203] *Pāṇṭi-k-Kōvai*, 48.

You do not respond when I speak,
you are modest, you bow
your beautiful face.
When love strangles me
like this, how can I bear it?
It's not just your eyes
that gouge me out with their corners red
like the tips of the tusks of an elephant
stinking of flesh after it bullied
a tiger, and gored its great, striped back,
leaving it shuddering—
It's your shoulders, too, they
bewitch me with their tracings
of sugarcane, your shoulders
like the celebrated city of Kūṭal,
city of Ce̱liyaṉ, victor in battles,
who took up the drums of war
and stormed garrisoned castles
and towns, even as enemies swarmed
the battlements.[204]

As he says this, he comes to her, as though to adjust her hair and garlands, and that is how the rendezvous arranged by his friend occurs.

Coming Upon The Place

Next, here is how the hero comes upon her alone, without his friend, at the trysting place.

He does not tell his friend anything, but just thinks to himself, "It was through fate that I attained her. Now if that fate will still give me a hand, I will be able to see her again," and he proceeds to the place where he had met her before. Here are some poems for that:

Who knows
what fate
will bring?

I will go again
to that wonderful,
pure grove
where I came upon
this innocent girl
with a brow
like a bow
equipped with
superb arrows,

---

[204] *Na̱ṟiṇai*, 39.

there on Mount Kolli
of Neṭumāṟaṉ
 the king of kings,
  of good family,
  the king of the sweet
  Tamil people.[205]

Fate, usually,
is hard to understand—
so I'll go
and try again
where bees buzz, and where
I saw and hugged that
innocent girl, whose
words are like sugarcane,
in the same vast grove
on Mount Potiyil
  of the king
  who desiccated
  those worldly kings
  who disagreed with him
  and fought at Pūlantai.[206]

Being Pleased With The Sight Of The Grove

As he is saying these things, he enters the grove where he had met her the day before. All his anguish leaves, and the grove comes to feel like a grand refuge to him. Why? Because simply seeing the place where one had met someone sweet is like seeing that sweet person all over again. Here are some poems for that:

This cool grove
cools off
my whole heart.
It feels as sweet
now as it did then,
when I united with her
who is like Kūṭal City
of the king
  with the curved bow,
  who conquered Pāḻi,
  the Pāṇṭiyaṉ who carved
  the sign of the carp

---

[205] *Pāṇṭi-k-Kōvai*, 49.

[206] *Pāṇṭi-k-Kōvai*, 50.

on a snow covered mountain
in the north, who protects
the world, and puts misery
to flight.[207]

This cool grove
is as sweet
as that eternally
pretty garland,
who is like
Pukār City,
beautiful and cool,
of the Lion to His Enemies
with his eversharp lance
and beautiful warrior's anklets,
who felt shame
when he saw the backs
of kings fleeing
the Battle of Cēvūr
in the South,
though they had fanned out
their armies, and battalions
of chariots.[208]

The hero unites with the heroine after he says these things; she is standing there as described before under the Rendezvous Arranged By His Friend, and he speaks as noted there. That is how he comes upon her alone at the trysting place, without his friend.

If there is a rendezvous arranged by his friend, he does not come upon her alone at the trysting place; and if he comes upon her alone at the trysting place, no rendezvous is arranged by his friend. Why? Because she is not that easy.

Now if all that is correct, should the verse not read, "Meeting her alone in the place without his friend, and meeting her through his friend at the trysting place," since coming upon her at the trysting place is the same as divine union? That is, even though he wrote it the way he did, may we not take it that the order of the ideas is to be exchanged? That would be inappropriate. Changing the order of ideas is to be done only when it is impossible to interpret a verse as it runs. For someone who might have thought it necessary to alter this verse to make it sound nice, this arrangement affirms that their reunion is to occur principally through the hero's friend, and only occasionally through fate: therefore, we see that the verse is constructed in the order he intended, and that it

---

[207] *Pāṇṭi-k-Kōvai*, 51.

[208] *Pāṇṭi-k-Kōvai*, 52.

is not a phrase-change verse. Moreover, when people in this world have troubles, they do not stay put and hope that their troubles will be settled by fate; they turn first to their friends and relatives to help solve them: that is another reason he constructed the verse in that order.

Granting that much, then, would this hero really go and tell his friend, when he has the feeling that the heroine might die if she realized outsiders knew about them, you ask? One commentator might argue that he could tell his friend without knowing for sure whether it is good or bad to do so, but that is inappropriate. If he were not sure of its propriety, why would he choose his friend; would it not do to tell any passer-by? Then what is the correct interpretation, you ask? He knew what he was doing, didn't he? And his friend's understanding equals his own, doesn't it? That point follows from his not thinking of his friend as different from himself.

Next, why should he use the plural form "his friends," instead of the singular in "a rendezvous arranged by his friends;" isn't his friend only one person, you ask? He used the honorific plural because the hero's friend is a Brahmin.[209] Moreover, his friend was given to the hero by his parents, who told him, "Act as though he were 'we;'" and the hero was given to his friend by his parents, who told him, "Act is though he were 'we.'" He utilized the plural form to bring out these things.

Then if all this is so, what will he do after natural union if her mother notices the changes in the girl and shuts her up in the house, you ask? Do you think his friend would go to her home with precious jewels, in the presence of Brahmins and exalted men, and cause the hero to attain her through marriage, assuming that is how their fate lies? Not so. If you leave it to fate to regularize this sort of union, then you might as well have it keep all knowledge of her changes from her mother to begin with. Then, you say, fate might cause these developments: the hero might miss a tryst when the heroine's friends take her to some seaside grove other than the one on the backwaters, or his friend might fail in his arrangements. Not so, because even if such things were to occur, he would still marry her.

Then again, could a fate that would cause their meeting later also generate in them the thought of entering yet another seaside grove? That is, you wonder, given that when he sees the hero after he had united in natural union, his friend asks, "Why has this change come over you?" why doesn't the heroine's friend ask her likewise, saying, "Why has this change come over you?" Fate will keep her friend from sensing the changes in the heroine. But then fate should also have kept his friend from sensing any change in the hero; or if it didn't, we must

[209] The reference is to the use of plural forms in Tamil to indicate social deference.

know the reason, you claim? One answer is that we cannot give reasons for fate. Yet if we were to give a reason, there would still be a purpose in his friend's sensing it: the rendezvous is possible only because his friend senses his changes and inquires about them. A rendezvous arranged by *his friend* is not furthered by having her friend sense a change in the heroine, nor is it possible through her friend alone; that is the reason.

Yet it should have been enough to say, "In two fashions shall he meet her again;" why did he add, "according to tradition," you ask? This is the definition of their reunion; and tradition, definition, and all such terms are just synonyms.

* * *

Verse 4.

> **Other than of that nature, union that is caused**
> **at no point exists in Stolen Love.**

What does this declare, you ask? It declares that this treatise sums up the definitions of both Stolen Love and Marital Love.

Verses can be ordered in any of four ways: river's flow, lion's glance, frog's jump, and falcon's dive.

Among those, verses lying as a river flows are sequential, like the continuous flowing of river water.

In the lion's glance, a verse relates to some other verse before, and one after it, just as a lion looks at those in front and those behind it.

In the frog's jump, verses are related with intervening spaces, as frogs jump over intervening space.

The falcon's dive evokes a falcon, in mid-glide, when it dives down and grabs an object about which it had been thinking; such a verse completes its intended sense with no relation to other verses.

Among those, this verse lies as the lion's glance. For what reason, you ask? Because it is concerned both with the previous rendezvous arranged by his friend, and with a rendezvous to be arranged later by her friend, as well as Marital Love and so forth, which are to follow.

Its meaning:

Other than of that nature—other than uniting in natural union, as described above.

union that is caused—union caused by someone who acts as a go-between.

at no point exists in Stolen Love—on no occasion occurs during the conduct known as Stolen Love.

Now this is not the sort of thing that occurs between a boy and a girl in the world, because there their unions may be either caused by others or not. Here we have a stipulated conduct, established by poets.

By saying, "Union that is caused at no point exists in Stolen Love," he implies that un-caused union is all there is.

Later, if she thinks that her married hero has gone away and stayed away with courtesans, the heroine gets angry; then they will reunite only when go-betweens[210] remove her anger. But, you say, there is a poem in *Neṭuntokai*,[211] beginning, "Sharp-thorned waterthorn...," in which their reunion is not caused by others? That union also is caused. Through what go-between did he re-unite with her, you ask? He joined her because of the go-between of anguish: you can find in that poem the way in which he united with her.

But if that is so, why is it said that no unions are caused during Stolen Love—here also might we not say that anguish causes union, you ask? Anguish does unite them, but here it does not fit the definition of a go-between; there it does. Why? Because go-betweens remove her jealousy, don't they? Does this not also remove her jealousy, you wonder? It does not. There it works because it fits the definition of a go-between.

Why does he add "at no point" when he says, "Other than of that nature, union that is caused does not exist in Stolen Love," you ask? He added that because there are occasions when a certain conviction develops, after somebody has informed someone of something. Who is informed, and who is convinced, you ask? The hero lets the heroine know of something her friend already knows.

It works this way: During a period of daytime trysts, one day near the end of their meeting, the hero was decorating the heroine's body. As he worked, she became extremely embarrassed, and the hero realized, "She suffered this change because what I am doing does not seem natural." In an attempt to console her he said, "I am just decorating you the way your friend does." At that point she thinks to herself, "Oh, so it seems he has met my friend!" Now, would she not die of embarrassment at this point, you ask? She would not, because she does not think of her friend as different from herself.

Then if she does not think of her friend as different from herself, would it not be proper for her to tell her friend all about the affair, you ask? She does not tell her friend because that would make her friend worry, thinking, "I have failed as a chaperon!"

Then what happens when the hero informs her friend about the affair, you ask? His intent is to prolong this affair for a long time, and as he tells her about it he thinks to himself, "She will console her when I am away," and "Some day

---

210 **Vāyil**, translated throughout this volume as "go-between," perhaps could be better translated here and in a few other contexts as "ambassador." It usually entails an effort to re-unite a couple suffering from jealousy.

211 This is poem 26 in the Caṅkam anthology known more commonly in modern times as *Akanāṉūṟu*.

she will come to know all about it anyway, and when she does, won't she be immediately upset? It would be some consolation to her for me to tell her in this manner."

There is a group of scholars who say this is inappropriate. Why? Such things, they say, do not occur during the period of daytime trysts: there are no poems of this sort by eminent poets. Because of that fact, "at no point" is said in proper refutation; it is not an extraneous phrase.[212]

If you say "union that is caused does not exist in Stolen Love," then what is the rationale behind stipulating rendezvous arranged by his friend and by her friend? That is because these rendezvous occur with their help. Can we not consider people who help them get together as people who cause their union, you ask? We cannot, because that is not their intent.

* * *

Verse 5.

> **After uniting, not behaving in that manner,**
> **through deferential speech to her friend,**
> **even accomplishing through entreaty exists for the hero.**

What does this declare, you ask? It is best if the hero decides to marry her after uniting with her either through a rendezvous arranged by his friend, or by coming upon her alone at the trysting place. But if he does not, he will act in this way; this verse declares how he will behave.

Its meaning:

After uniting—after uniting with her either through his friend, or by coming upon her at the trysting place.

not behaving in that manner—not behaving thus, even after that.

through deferential speech—by means of lowly speech; we say "lowly speech" in consideration of the unsavoriness of the terminology: it is deferential for him to say, "This leaf skirt is nice; this wreath is nice," in praise of his presents, but it does not fit his station; that would be for lowly people, would it not?

to her friend—to her friend.

even accomplishing through entreaty exists for the hero—it is permissible for the hero to entreat her friend in order to accomplish his ends.

---

[212] The reference is to the practice of defining certain phrases in verses as extraneous, and then constructing commentaries upon them which have no particular relevance to the phrases themselves, but which are nonetheless of substance. The bulk of the preceding argument is an example of this established commentarial technique.

Entreating means doing what one does when he needs to accomplish something. Accomplishing entails behaving affectionately, so that the accomplishment appears essential.

As he entreats her, will he think she is capable of accomplishing it for him or not, you ask? If we say that he thinks she can accomplish it, then he must have a low opinion of the heroine, since he considers her friend an errand-girl through whom he can attain her. But to esteem her so lightly would contradict the statement that he considers her difficult to attain by any means, since she has such precious excellence, and is so well protected.

Next, if we say that he does not think she can accomplish it for him, even as he entreats her, then there is no point in his entreating her at all: if you know that a man cannot do something and yet you go to him to get that thing done, you do not know how to go about things, do you?

Then what is the interpretation, you ask? When he entreats her, he does not evaluate whether or not she can accomplish it for him; he entreats her simply because his anguish is overwhelming. But if he does not consider whether or not it will be possible for her, he must consider other people also in the same way and entreat them as well, you think? Not so, because if this is to be accomplished at all, it is ordained that it must be done through her, and fate will generate the thought of approaching her. Do we not always say that encouragement comes to people of the world through their good qualities?[213]

And what does she think of all this, you ask? She has her doubts. She thinks, "He seems to want to accomplish something that is very essential for him. If I were to think that it rests with me, well, he couldn't need anything from me, since he is so extremely noble and I am so lowly; therefore it cannot rest with me. Yet who knows? There are things that a great person can accomplish through a small one, so I wonder if it might rest with me after all! Then again, if I think it might rest with my lady, well, that would be impossible, since she is not someone whom people point out and speak about; but again, who knows? Yet as this man is as noble as she, it is possible that it rests with her. And it is doubtful that it rests with any of our friends." She will not decide upon anything immediately, since she possesses great discernment.

"Next," she thinks, "it is impossible that he might be bringing this leaf-skirt and wreath out of pure graciousness, since he seems so anguished. This, too, makes me wonder." We shall present some poems on that theme under the verse that begins, "Understanding through pondering..."[214]

---

[213] And their good qualities depend on their fate, which itself derives from their past karma.

[214] *The Study of Stolen Love*, 7. The poems are *Pāṇṭi-k-Kōvai*, 75–76.

Still, how does he know that she is more excellent than her friend, when there was nobody around to tell him, you ask? He just knew, didn't he? After he had joined her in natural union, when he was standing nearby and watching her, where she could not see him, he witnessed the others giving her their worship, as well as the particular worship that she performed, the graciousness that she showed to all the others, and especially the graciousness they showed her. He realized, "She is more excellent than her, and that also will help me." Since he realized that, he will go only to her.

But won't the girls who go around with her suspect something, you ask? How could they suspect anything? He comes to her when she is off alone somewhere looking for things to make into leaf skirts and wreaths. Does he know she will be standing alone like that when he goes to her, you ask? He does not; fate takes him there and makes him come upon her.

Next, why did he add "accomplishing" instead of saying just "entreating exists for the hero," you ask? "Entreating" means doing what one does when he needs to accomplish something. "Accomplishing" entails behaving affectionately in such a way that its accomplishment appears essential.

Yet why did he add the word "even" in "even accomplishing through entreaty," you ask? It would be excellent if he simply decided to marry her; but if he is not convinced, this is how he will behave: he said "even" in order to imply this.

Next, one school of thought claims that "after uniting" means "after natural union," that "not behaving in that manner" means "not meeting her through his friend, nor coming upon her alone," and that he tries entreating her friend first; but it is inappropriate. What is the reason, you ask? Because his friend is such a great help to him, is he not? Is there any way her friend could be such a help? At such a moment he would think of his own friend first, never of hers.

* * *

Verse 6.

> **Entreating without accomplishment, looking for**
> **the opportune moment when the heroine and her friend are together,**
> **asking place, name, and other things,**
> **approaching and speaking as a stranger,**
> **even for the reconciliation of knowledge, he is fit, they say.**

What does this declare, you ask? It presents a way to reconcile knowledge. And what is its relation to the above verse, you ask? In the above verse it was stated that he will follow her friend, entreating her with deferential speech. Yet she does not understand, does she? Rather, she wonders, "What sort of thing does he wish to accomplish?" Now, because of her lack of understanding, he engages in these pursuits, thinking, "I shall follow her and let her know what I wish to accomplish." That is the connection.

Its meaning:

Entreating without accomplishment—the entreaty occurs, but not the accomplishment.

the heroine and her friend—the heroine is the female protagonist, and her friend is her foster mother's daughter. Why? Because he said,

> Her friend is the daughter of the foster mother.[215]

when ... are together—when those two are together in the same place.

looking for the opportune moment—it must be proper for him to look for that sort of situation, and to go and stand there, when he speaks to her friend.

asking place, name, and other things—asking the place is asking what town; asking the name is asking what names they have; asking other things is asking things like, "Have some wild beasts run past here?" or, "Did my attendants come along here?" or, "Have any elephants passed through here?" Here are some poems for that:

Asking The Place And The Name

Girls!
You, guarding
these green, ripening
terraced fields,
rainfed and rich,
on Mount Potiyil
of the king
  who wrested strength
  and armies of victory
  from his enemies
  at Nelvēli,
  King Neṭumāṟaṉ
  filled with virtue,
  whose lance
  is righteous!

Please,
may I know
the name of your town,
and your own
names?[216]

---

215 *Tolkāppiyam: Kaḷaviyal*, 34.

216 *Pāṇṭi-k-Kōvai*, 53.

You, with gorgeous jewels—
You, guarding ripening
terraced fields
on this resplendent
Mount Potiyil
    of him who seized
    his enemies' elephants
    and fast-gaited horses
    at Nelvēli,
    the husband
    of the earth goddess,
    the lord of
    wealth!

Please, may I know
the name of your town,
and your own names?[217]

You with your bangles—
you are like
feminine ambrosia!
Your dainty foreheads
are like crescent moons
in the sky!
You, who guard
these rainfed
terraced fields
    on Mount Kolli
    of the king
    who took up
    his blood-stained lance
    so other kings,
    their warrior's anklets clanging,
    just dropped dead
    at the Battle of Āṟṟukkuṭi!

Please, tell me,
don't hide!
Tell me your names,
and where you live.[218]

You, innocent girls,
your eyes are so wide
and tranquil,
your dainty foreheads

---

[217] *Pāṇṭi-k-Kōvai*, 54.

[218] *Pāṇṭi-k-Kōvai*, 55.

far prettier
than the crescent moon!
You are like cool Pukār City
of the Lion to His Enemies
    with jangling warrior's anklets,
    who vanquished Kaṭaiyal
    in the South,
    with his blood-red,
    righteous lance!

Please, may I know
where you live,
and what your
names are?[219]

By the phrase "other things" it indicates that he speaks these poems as well, as he stands there:

Asking About An Elephant

You, with perfect jewels
and pretty, little feet!
You're like Vañci City
of Tirumāl[220]
    who measured the earth, the
    Gift of the Gods, with horses
    harnessed to his chariots,
    whose munificent hands
    are like dark rainclouds
    rising![221]

Did a huge,
warring elephant
with red eyes, white
tusks, a black trunk,
and the shape of a great,
dark mountain pass
by your terraced field?[222]

You innocent girls,
with your sharp,
lance-like, wide eyes!

---

[219] *Pāṇṭi-k-Kōvai*, 56.

[220] The God Vishnu, an appellation of the Pāṇṭiyaṉ king.

[221] In the semi-arid Tamil country, rain is the bestower of all blessings.

[222] *Pāṇṭi-k-Kōvai*, 57.

You are like Pukār City
of him who conquered
    Pūlantai in the South,
    where crowned kings with
    three rutting elephants
    fell in the dust
    of the fierce
    battle!

Did a huge bull elephant
pass through your vast
terraced fields,
followed by his
mate?[223]

Asking About A Stag

You girls,
your arms
covered with conch bracelets—
your breasts heavy,
excellent, and pretty—
you are like
the Vaiyai River lands
    of the king who grabbed
    his sharp lance
    to make the Cēraṉ king
    and his powerful, raging navy
    perish at Naṟaiyāṟu
    in the south, and forfeit
    all his valor!

Has a herd of deer
run into your terraced fields?
Tell me![224]

You with conch
bracelets—
you are like
the watered lands
in the South
    of the king
    whose lance excels
    in killing,

---

[223] *Pāṇṭi-k-Kōvai*, 58.

[224] *Pāṇṭi-k-Kōvai*, 59.

the king who warred
to make other kings
with excellent archers
flee a reddened
battlefield!

Has a stag, hit
with a fine-tipped arrow and
separated from his herd,
come into your rainfed,
terraced fields?
Tell me![225]

You good girls,
doll-like with your
musical, honeyed words—
you are like
the broad Potiyil Mountains
of the king who held
a crashing thunderbolt
from the sky
in his pennant,
so that enemy kings
who faced him
at Kaṭaiyal
died!

Has a deer
pierced by a wounding arrow
come near your terraced
fields?[226]

Asking The Way

You with your soft hair,
standing beneath
the young kino tree
in this grove
dripping with honey
on the slopes of Mount Kolli
of the king who grabbed
his blood-red lance,
that the smithy knows
so well, and made those

---

[225] *Pāṇṭi-k-Kōvai*, 60.

[226] *Pāṇṭi-k-Kōvai*, 61.

who opposed him at Viḻiñam,
thinking they might win,
journey up to
heaven!

I do not know the way
to your village:
tell me![227]

Speaking, But Getting No Reply

You with that face
as bright as moonrays
shining in the groves
around Mount Kolli
of the king
who holds in his flag,
fluttering in front
of his armies,
the thunder of the clouds
which even resembles him!

If you were to answer
my questions,
would those ever-bright
pearls drop right out
of your mouth?[228]

Take the above as the poems.

as a stranger—like someone who has never been to that place, nor seen them before.

approaching and speaking—saying such things as are appropriate to that place, and for inquiring of them.

even for the reconciliation of knowledge, he is fit, they say—knowledge means understanding; it means that he is fit to reconcile someone's understanding.

Whose knowledge, you ask? Take it to be her friend's knowledge. Since it says that he reconciles her knowledge, take it that her knowledge had been split earlier. How was it split, you ask?

From the very moment of their joining in natural union, the heroine's eyes appeared reddened and her brow altered. Therefore, her friend wondered, "Have these changes overcome her through acts of the gods, or through humans?"

[227] *Pāṇṭi-k-Kōvai*, 62.

[228] *Pāṇṭi-k-Kōvai*, 63.

Also, she noted, "From that same point in time, he began bringing these leaf skirts and wreaths and following me unabashed, entreating me; whom does he need to help him in accomplishing his purpose?" In her confusion she concentrates, analyzes, and understands: "It would seem that the changes overcoming her have come about because of him, and that he is following me and entreating me because of her." Here are some poems for that:

Sensing, In A Way, The Thoughts Of Those Two

Guarding terraced fields
in the Kolli Mountains
that dip into the sky,
mountains of the Scholar,
    the king, with his fragrant wreath,
and the movements
of deer—

that's not
what's on her mind,
this girl with flowing hair,
nor is it on his!

They're speaking to each other
with their eyes:
something else
is on their
minds.[229]

In this vast grove
in the Potiyil Mountains
    of him who wore great
    victory wreaths
    on his golden crown
    at Pūlantai,
    while those who came at him,
    wearing their battle wreaths,
    died,
the eyes of this lord
of the mountains,
who came oh, so close,
and the black eyes
of this girl whose brow
is so bright,
mingled:

---

229 *Pāṇṭi-k-Kōvai*, 64.

there must be some
reason here![230]

Take examples like these.

But then, why is the word "together" necessary? Would it not have been appropriate if he had said simply, "Entreating without accomplishment, looking for the opportune moment when the heroine and her friend are there?" He put it in there to say that it is proper for the hero to come together with his chariot, during the period of Stolen Love. Why? Because there are poems of the ancients that follow that pattern, such as this one:

Ocean tide,
long life to you!

You rolled across wheel ruts
from our dear lover's
tall, strong chariot,
and erased them,
you rolled over them,
and they disintegrated!
Yes, you may stay
here with us
like a member
of the family,
but you are not
one of us!

Ocean tide,
long life
to you![231]

Note poems such as that one.

What is the word "even" for in the phrase, "even for the reconciliation of knowledge," you ask? He said that to bring out that attaining her through marriage is still the best.

* * *

Verse 7.

Understanding through pondering, understanding through the entreaty,
and understanding through his coming to where they both are:
those three are her friend's understandings, they say.

---

230 *Pāṇṭi-k-Kōvai*, 65.

231 *Cilappatikāram: Kāṉalvari*, 36.

What does this declare, you ask? It declares the names, manners, and number of her friend's means of understanding.
Its meaning:
Understanding through pondering—she sees the reddened eyes and altered brow of the heroine following natural union and seeks out what the heroine conceals; then she understands, it says.

How does she manage to understand, you ask? She poses this question: "This change was not part of your old nature, my lady. How did it come about? Tell me." The heroine answers, "Yesterday when I left you, I saw a superb mountain pool and bathed in it. This change came about because I stayed there, bathing, for such a long time. That reddens your eyes and alters your brow, doesn't it?" To that, her friend replies, "If everyone who bathes in that mountain pool attains such exquisite, feminine beauty, I shall try bathing there, too!" Here are some poems for that:

Speaking In Amazement Of The Mountain Pool

If you can get
such swelling beauty,
like the peacocks
in the Potiyil Mountains
  of the famous king
  from the South,
  who waged war to make
  swordsmen, and grand
  chariots, flee the
  reddened battle grounds,
girl with perfect jewels—

I too will bathe
in that great, blue
mountain pool,
like you![232]

If it will make me
as beautiful as you,
like a peacock
in the Potiyil Mountains
  of him who witnessed
  the confederacy
  of garlanded kings
  wage war at Pūlantai
  in the South,

[232] *Pāṇṭi-k-Kōvai*, 66.

suffer wounds
in their precious chests,
and reach heaven
right there,
woman!

I too will bathe
in that bright
mountain pool,
like you![233]

The stately she-elephant,
her cheeks hollow,
distressed, and feeling worse
and worse, hugged her calf,
whose folded ears
look like the strong wings
of a bat flying
in distress,
searching for fruit
trees, one miserable
evening—

her hard-eyed bull,
terrified of a lion's
fierce strength, jabbed
the rough barked trunk
of a sandalwood tree,
then pressed against it
with his feet
to draw out his shapely,
lustrous white tusk,
and the sandalwood tree
crashed into the deep,
cool water of a mountain pool:
it makes it very fragrant.

Friend, I shall bathe, too,
like you, and let
my conch bracelets jingle,
to see if I can gain
your eye-snatching beauty,
like a brightly spotted peacock
that thrills to see black
thunderheads come
to the woodlands
fragrant with flowers

---

233 *Pāṇṭi-k-Kōvai*, 67.

near Alaivāy with its sweet
waters, that place
of Lord Murukaṉ
whose jewels glisten,
and whose gleaming lance
ripped the insides out
of a mountain![234]

The heroine will bow her head and scratch in the earth with her big toe when she hears this; then her friend will understand that union has actually occurred.

Moreover, she wonders at other changes in the heroine. Note, for example, when she spies the happy little baby moon, red in its tips, nestled in the belly of the sunset sky: she worships it and says to the heroine, "Look, you worship it, too!" Here are some poems for that:

Saying, "Worship The Crescent Moon"

Look with your wide,
black, flower-like eyes!
look there, in the belly
of the sky, red like
Vishnu's painted chest,
see the tender bud
of the crescent moon,
progenitor of the lord
of the sweet Tamil people
    of the South,
    him who fought
    on the red battlefield
    where great, warring,
    enemy kings fell!

It has come there
for us to
worship.[235]

You with thorn-sharp teeth,
look: it has appeared before
for us to worship,
and here it comes now,
in the same direction,
for us to worship.
This is the crescent moon,

---

[234] Unidentified verse.

[235] *Pāṇṭi-k-Kōvai*, 68.

excellent because its light swells
like that of the jewels
of the famous Cōḻa king
    whose great,
    rutting elephants
    fight forever![236]

But the heroine does not worship the moon, even though she hears this, because to do so would mean infidelity to the hero; and when her friend sees this, she understands the truth of her union.

Alternatively, she may speak of the heroine as a bewitching goddess of the mountains. Here are some poems for that:

Equating Her With A Bewitching Goddess

O, you bewitching
mountain goddess!
She took her bath
in that deep pool
in the Kolli Mountains
    of him who wears a cool garland
    of coral tree blossoms,
    Māṟaṉ, whose fame
    fills the earth!
Her face is like
a bright lotus,
her figure
equals your own,
and bees swarm
about her hair,

but whenever she comes,
you move away![237]

Speaking In Amazement Of The Mountain Pool

In those tall, distant
Potiyil Mountains
of the king
    who conquered
    a great army
    of soldiers
    at Āṟṟukkuṭi,

---

[236] Unidentified verse.

[237] *Pāṇṭi-k-Kōvai*, 69.

that cascade never touched
your feet!

Could a pretty mountain pool
turn your wide, bright eyes
red, and your red mouth white?
or pin long-stemmed
flower blossoms,
swarming with bees,
all over
you?[238]

These are called "probings for modesty."

Next, here is how she "probes for trembling:" she says, "There is a bull elephant lumbering around in our terraced fields—its tusks are stained with blood." Here are some poems for that:

Girl, your mouth
is like a red
silk-cotton blossom,
and you are like Kūṭal City
of King Neṭumāṟaṉ,
    who loosed arrows
    from his murderous bow
    and enemy warriors died
    at Kaḷattūr!
Today, in our cool,
terraced fields
I saw a fighting elephant—
his ferocious tusks
were tangled in blood
and flesh.[239]

In those green terraced fields
on the Kolli Mountains
    of the Goad to His Enemies,
    with his long lance
    that strikes like the sun,
    the king who conquered Kaṭaiyal
    and sent to heaven
    the precious souls of all who
    wished for war, hoping
    to snatch this world from others
    to build their glory—

---

[238] *Pāṇṭi-k-Kōvai*, 70.

[239] *Pāṇṭi-k-Kōvai*, 71.

girl, I saw an elephant there,
today, its white tusk
was smeared with
blood.[240]

Girl with eyes dark
as the blue lotus blooms
in Pal̲aiyan̲ūr
    of Katiran̲
    with his tiṇṭi drums,
I know this elephant!
I have seen it before,
in our millet patch
in the terraced fields,
in broad daylight!

Its tusks
have blood on them.[241]

The heroine will tremble when she hears that; she will think, "My lord comes to that place often! Has this bull elephant done him some harm?" When her friend sees that, she will realize the truth of their union.

Probings For Modesty And Trembling Are Not Defined Within The Modes Of Love

This type of understanding is inappropriate, because probing for modesty or trembling is not characteristic of the modes of love. Why? Because he has said,

> Her friend does not probe for modesty or trembling
> in the heroine, when one investigates.[242]

Moreover, her friend would also worry about harm that might come to the heroine through such probings, as she could even die through excessive modesty or fear. Moreover, these probings would indicate a lack of respect for the heroine; and since she would have to speak without properly understanding the heroine's intent, it would mean that she does not have good manners. All these faults persist in people who insist that she engage in these probings.

---

[240] *Pāṇṭi-k-Kōvai*, 72.

[241] Unidentified verse.

[242] Unidentified verse.

Realizing By Pondering

What, then, is the correct commentary, you ask? The Realization Through Pondering occurs while she is in a quandary: she has noted changes in the heroine following natural union, and wonders, "Did these changes occur through a god, or something else?" Here are some poems for that:

Researching Through Her Appearance

Dark-haired girl, why
has your brilliant
brow faded—
did you hurt your waist
while you played
with your pretty, soft
flowery gameball
with your friends
in that grove
where blossoms dance
in bunches, that
grove of Neṭumāṟaṉ
  with his warrior's anklets
  and rutting elephants
  that tug at their
  leg-posts—

or did you hurt your feet
when you came to play
on these white sands?[243]

Why would this
bright browed
girl grieve
like foes
of the Goad to His Enemies,
  on whose victorious lance
  vultures ride,
  who devastated Cēvūr
  in war—
is it because
she played there
in those fine, cool
flower-strewn waters—

[243] *Pāṇṭi-k-Kōvai*, 73.

or is it because
she went to swing
on that perfect swing,
with ropes of gold?[244]

Understanding Through The Entreaty

Next, **understanding through the entreaty**—when he stands shamelessly behind her friend, bearing a wreath and a leaf skirt, she realizes, "All right, then: this beseeching and standing around behind me seem to be due to her!"

But that interpretation is inappropriate. Why? Because it would contradict the heroine's greatness. It would mean her friend thought disrespectfully of her: she would find herself thinking that anyone who approached her to get something accomplished would be doing so because of the heroine. Then how does Understanding Through the Entreaty come about, you ask? She wonders, "He's following me about and beseeching me, but what is it all about?" Here are some poems for that:

Searching For What Is On The Minds Of These Two People

On cloud-clad Mount Potiyil
of great King Māṟaṉ
    whose munificent hand
    is like the very clouds,
he brings twin-petaled gamboge,
a leaf skirt rich with long,
pretty, aromatic sandalwood leaves,
and a lovely wreath—
he cannot seem to leave
the very area
of these cool,
terraced fields!

I do not understand
what is on his mind.[245]

He never leaves!
He keeps coming
to these terraced fields
in the mountains

[244] *Pāṇṭi-k-Kōvai*, 74.

[245] *Pāṇṭi-k-Kōvai*, 75.

of him who owns
    rich, glimmering Mount Nēri,
    the king who wore
    the flowers of war
    upon his crown
    to make enemy kings
    with their long,
    sharpened javelins
    die at Cēvūr!
And he's offering us
a brilliant flower skirt!

I do not understand
what is on his mind.[246]

Both of these poems are spoken with a feeling of doubt, not a sense of determination.

Understanding Through His Coming To Where They Both Are

understanding through his coming to where they both are—take it that she has been harboring these suspicions, but that she understands and determines the truth when he comes to a place where she and the heroine are together and inquires about their names, home town, and other things. Here are some poems for that:

I know all that's going on
between her and him,
with his curly,
aromatic hair,
him who came here
to the slopes of
the Kolli Mountains
    of the king who felt shame
    when he saw the backs of kings
    fleeing the red field of war,
    the King of the South,
    with tight, black
    warrior's anklets!
what's the use
in imagining
all sorts of things:

---

[246] *Pāṇṭi-k-Kōvai*, 76.

these two have but one
dear soul![247]

What's the use in making up
all sorts of thoughts and deeds
for him and for her,
whose voice sounds
even as music, who
is like the ocean lands
    of him who conquered Kaṭaiyal
    as the sharp edge
    of his lance head,
    and his eyes, reddened,
    the Great Māṟaṉ,
    with his garland
    of colorful flowers—

There is only one dear soul
between these two people![248]

She is not guarding
her millet,
and he is not stalking
his deer—
he with his wreath
of aromatic grasses,
and she with her
stealthy mind—
they're thinking
of other things!
Before me they seem bashful
enough, but in their hearts
they thrill to the pleasures
of secret drinkers!

And they hold their own counsel
with their eyes.[249]

We take it that her earlier understanding was split, since this is termed the reconciliation of knowledge; we do not take it in the sense of a determination. But since he collected all three "understandings" together and said, **those three are her friend's understandings**, a sense of determination would be most appropriate, you think? It is true that an understanding gained through deter-

[247] *Pāṇṭi-k-Kōvai*, 77.

[248] *Pāṇṭi-k-Kōvai*, 78.

[249] Unidentified poem.

mination can be called "understanding," but so can an understanding gained through wondering, when we look at understanding in general: it is like calling both sandalwood and *nux vomica*, "trees." In this way, her friend's inquiry, decorum, worry about possible harm, and respect for the heroine all are evident.

But if he were determined to say "all three," he would have used the word "all," saying, "*all* three are her friend's understandings," because it is said,

> Expressions for parts and wholes, when the total number is known,
> require "all" when they take a verb as an aggregate.[250]

That is true, but then again, he elides the word "all" here, since there is a grammatical rule for such an elision.

But it should read, "his going," instead of "his coming to where they both are," you say? And why? Because he has said,

> The two words "give" and "come"
> occur in the first and second persons.[251]

> The other two occur in the other person.[252]

You do not know what you are talking about; his usage is proper, since it is all to be concluded through the technique of interpreting superfluous words,[253] utilizing the verse beginning with,

> Of the words, "go," "come," "give," and "bestow,"...[254]

Is it not for this very reason that the ancient author wrote,

> (The fish) did not come
> when the fisherman
> reeled in (his line)...?[255]

* * *

---

[250] *Tolkāppiyam: Kiḷaviyal*, 33.

[251] *Tolkāppiyam: Kiḷaviyal*, 29.

[252] *Tolkāppiyam: Kiḷaviyal*, 30. This is a sticky point in Tamil grammar that is impossible to put across in English. There are three different verb stems for "give," and two different stems for "go" and "come," whose usage may depend on the social situation or the grammatical person involved. At first glance it may seem inappropriate for the verse to say, "*coming* to where they both are." Despite seeming support from *Tolkāppiyam* to the contrary, however, Nakkīraṉār shows that it really is the appropriate verb.

[253] See footnote 212 on page 80.

[254] *Tolkāppiyam: Kaḷaviyal*, 28.

[255] From *Akanāṉūṟu*, 36.

Verse 8.

> **Other than understanding in that way with the heroine,**
> **her friend herself has no accomplishment.**

What does this declare, you ask? This verse also declares a characteristic of her friend.

Its meaning:

Other than understanding in that way—other than after having understood in that fashion.

with the heroine—with the female protagonist there.

her friend herself has no accomplishment—her friend has no occasion to say, "I shall accomplish something."

What does this verse mean to say, you ask? It refutes those who want there to be a probing into the concealed.

Would it not be enough to say, "her friend has no accomplishment?" What is the word "herself" for, you ask? Later she will speak of a desire for accomplishment, but not as herself; she will be considered then to have actually become the hero, because she will take his anguish upon herself.

* * *

Verse 9.

> **Even if she has understood through pondering**
> **speaking does not occur except after he beseeches.**

What does this declare, you ask? It declares a situation in which her friend stands before the hero and converses with him.

Its meaning:

Even if she has understood through pondering—even if she has understood the truth of their union through the reconciliation of knowledge.

except after he beseeches—except after he follows her and entreats her; we shall describe the manner in which he does this when we comment upon the verse that begins,

> Her friend, who understands the entreating hero,...[256]

speaking does not occur—she does not say, "I will accomplish something."

This is how it works: After the hero causes the reconciliation of knowledge and informs her of his intent, he continues to follow her friend, still carrying the leaf skirt and wreath. She thinks along with him of future unions and teases him about trysts, until her modesty disappears. His anguish increases day by day as

---

[256] *The Study of Stolen Love*, 12, page 118.

she teases him, and her modesty decreases as she observes his anguish increase, until the two rest equal in the scales. His anguish has reached its limit; it can increase no further. And so has her modesty reached its limit; it can decrease no further.

At this point the hero says something. What does he say, you ask? He says, "I have followed you all these days and suffered. I thought you could do this thing for me; but since I realize now that you cannot, I will turn to doing even debased things to accomplish my end. It is absolutely essential to me!" Doing debased things means riding a rough palmyra-leaf horse, or leaping off a mountain. Here are some poems for that:

Riding The Palmyra Horse

When love ravages
them, and swells
greater than the ocean,
men will grow thin
as the foes of the king
  whose lance does more
  than just kill, the king
  who conquered Pāḻi,
  the Pāṇṭiyaṉ whose triple
  fortress bastions
  are crowded,

and then men will ride
horses of black palmyra,
and they will do things
that are not to be done
in this world![257]

You, who seem like
the southern lands
of Neṭumāṟaṉ, with his
  bright red lance,
  which has seen long
  wars, who destroyed
  enemies with grand,
  warring armies at the
  Battle of Pūlantai!

---

[257] *Pāṇṭi-k-Kōvai*, 79.

when their vast, precious love swells,
men will think of riding red stems
from tall, black palmyra trees![258]

They ride palmyras
and call them horses,
they tie on wreaths
of tight erukkam buds
and call them flowers,
they suffer jeers
in the streets,
and they turn
to worse things, too,

when love
turns hard.[259]

If one claims the hero says this, he does not; it is the anguish born within him that speaks.

Now she had felt modesty in her contemplation of helping him, had she not? That dissolves when she hears this; and as it goes, she takes his anguish upon herself and says something to console the hero. What does she say, you ask? "It is the gift of the great," she says, "to be able to bear difficulties, is it not? Don't act like this! I, too, shall see what I can do." His anguish departs as she says this, and she examines the hero and decides he is not going to die. Then she speaks. What does she say, you ask? She says, "You said you would ride the palmyra-leaf horse: but you are a gracious man! Would it be proper for you to do such a thing?" Here are some poems for that:

Speaking On The Nature of Graciousness

Lord,
your shoulders
are strong as a rock!
The palmyra grows
with burgeoning
clusters of fruit
at Cape Kaṉṉi
of the king in the lunar dynasty,
  Māṟaṉ, Nēriyaṉ,the king
  of this land,
  surrounded by roaring waves,

---

258 *Pāṇṭi-k-Kōvai*, 80.

259 *Kuṟuntokai*, 17.

the king who fought
at Neṭuṅkuḷam!
You will not cut
its rich fronds
to ride on,
I trust:

that would destroy flocks of birds,
their young, and their eggs.[260]

Many are the young
of the white heron,
but even more are the baby
black crows, and more yet
are the eggs in weaver-bird nests
hung high in the clustered fronds
of the tall palmyra tree.[261]

"Not only that," she adds, "but when a man rides a palmyra-leaf horse, he paints a picture of his love before he climbs on, doesn't he: can you do that?" Here are some poems for that:

Declaring That Her Speech And Gait Are Hard To Paint

She is like the wide world
of the Lion to His Enemies,
the king with grand,
tall chariots!
Just suppose you could,
somehow, paint her form—
still, are there images to paint
for the fragrance
of her cool, black hair,
like a cascade of sapphires,
or for her walk,
or for her musical
voice?[262]

Did you ask me?
Is it so easy to paint
the fragrance of her black hair,

---

[260] *Pāṇṭi-k-Kōvai*, 81.

[261] Unidentified poem.

[262] *Pāṇṭi-k-Kōvai*, 82.

or her voice, like a parakeet's?
She is like the southern lands
of the king with the white canopy
of lustrous pearls
who conquered Kaṭaiyal,
Neṭumāṟaṉ with his warrior's anklet,
and his rutting elephants:
paint her first!

Then ride that pretty
palmyra hobbyhorse.[263]

"Moreover," she says, "is this how you intend to paint her?" Here is a poem for that:

She is like Kūṭal City
of the southern king
who conquered Cennilam
as his enemies died
in the thick of the battle!
And you painted a bow
and called it her eyebrow,
you painted a tender lotus bud
and called it her breast!

For her voice
have you chosen to paint
a parakeet?[264]

The hero becomes anguished all over again when he hears that, but since she figures he ought not to die at this point she says, "Don't be like that—I'll do it for you. The girl you want is very close to me." Here are some poems for that:

Making Him Desist By Agreeing With Him

Even if I float along
on a raft in the cool,
flowery waters in the midst
of the full River Vaiyai
of the king
who defeated
and routed Saturn,
the Supreme One
with his righteous scepter
and his growing, great

---

[263] *Pāṇṭi-k-Kōvai*, 83.

[264] *Pāṇṭi-k-Kōvai*, 84.

renown,
still she will come to me—

these days that's how
her sweet grace is.[265]

She is like Kūṭal City
in the South, the city
of King Neṭumā<u>r</u>a<u>n</u>, who fought
to send his enemies
into the black mountains,
full of forests, and on
to the heaven
of the celestials,
that day at Kaṭaiyal—
wherever she may be
with flowers in her hair,
she won't play in the water,
nor swing on her soft swing
without me:

this is her
precious grace.[266]

If her friend takes the first raft,
so will she!
If her friend takes the last one,
so will she!
And if her friend were to let go
of the raft
and drift with the current,
so, it seems, would she!
Her eyes are dewy cananga buds,
swollen, streaked
with red filament lines,
ready to burst,

and she is like a tiny leaf
with a raindrop at its
tip.[267]

---

265 *Pāṇṭi-k-Kōvai*, 85.

266 *Pāṇṭi-k-Kōvai*, 86.

267 *Ku<u>r</u>untokai*, 222.

The Speech Of Bearing Up

When the hero hears this he thinks, "Now she will do it for me." His anguish departs, and he cools down. Why? When a man of this world worries because he thinks something is impossible, he will rejoice when he finds a way to accomplish it. And the hero returns home, feeling as though he has already accomplished what he wanted to. That is what they call the speech of bearing up. Why? Because it bears the hero up when he is about to die. After she consoles the hero by saying this, she will return to the heroine and look for ways to accomplish what he wants.

* * *

Verse 10.

> **Hiding her inner understanding and not letting it become clear,**
> **there are also entreatings of the heroine**
> **at the time of knowing the signs.**

What does this declare, you ask? It declares how her friend, having agreed to help the hero, causes the heroine to accept him.

Its meaning:

Hiding her inner understanding and not letting it become clear—hiding the emotion in her heart, so it is not openly known.

of the heroine—to the heroine.

there are also entreatings—there are also requests for fulfillment.

at the time of knowing the signs—when she makes known the indicators of the hero's anguish.

What is "inner understanding," you ask? It is her understanding of the truth of their union. Alternatively, it could mean her understanding that it is essential to him to accomplish this, or it could mean the concern, "Can she bear it if I entreat her?" It could also mean the conviction, "I must make her accept him, because if I cannot, he will die!"

The clause, "not letting it become clear, there are also entreatings of the heroine" also implies that she hides her feelings well when she entreats the heroine; she does not let on that she realizes the truth of their union. That is how she entreats the heroine when she causes her to accept the hero.

Why does he use the plural verb "are" instead of the singular form "is," you ask? It is put in that manner because there are multiple occasions of entreaty. What are they, you ask? They are: causing the effect through gentle words, and causing it through strong words.

Of those, this is how she causes it through gentle words: "Here is a hero," she says, "who seems to want to accomplish something through me. He is not the sort of person who has others accomplish things for him; rather, he does things for them: therefore this must be particularly essential to him. I represented myself as someone who could accomplish things on his behalf, since it seemed so essential to him, and thus I told a lie. I knew I was lying, but I went ahead and lied. Why, you ask? I just lied: I figured that by now he would have accomplished it himself somehow or other. Why? Because I thought nothing was really impossible in this life. He took my lie as the truth, since he has never known a lie in his life! He left, but he will come back today; and then if I haven't accomplished it, he'll realize I lied, won't he?" Here are some poems for that:

O, girl, your hair filled
with fine flowers—
If that lord
with his splendid bow
and arrows
comes here
in this rich
terraced field,
and brings his wreath
and leaf skirt for you,
from a sweet mango tree
blooming fresh
in the Kolli Mountains
    of the Goad to His Enemies,
    the King of Tamil,
    with its excellent poetry,

I can't think of a lie
to tell him today,
as I did yesterday.[268]

Moreover,

I see a man every day
by a terraced field
filled with fragrance
near the Potiyil Mountains
    of the king
    who took Kōṭṭāṟu Castle,
    with its massive walls
    crowded with banners!
His qualities seem noble
and he wears a warrior's anklet;
his pretty garland sways,
but he will not tell me
what he wants—

---

[268] *Pāṇṭi-k-Kōvai*, 87.

Is he the son of the Tall One
who measured the earth?
I do not know.[269]

You who are like
the Vaiyai lands
    of the Gift of the Gods,
    the king whose righteous scepter
    bridles the earth,
    who waged war in Naṭṭāṟu
    to make the warring kings
    who came at him there
    go on up to heaven!
A man keeps bringing these
beautiful, cool
leaf skirts;
he wears a warrior's
anklet, and holds
a swift bow—
what does he
want?

He never leaves
these vast terraced fields.[270]

Girl, with your golden
jewelry!
Will they ever wither?—
these flowers
in the skirt he gave you,
the mountain-country lord
who quartered that elephant
that came to raze and devour
our vast terraced field
in the Kolli Mountains
    of the king
    with eternal splendor,
    who conquered Pāḻi,
    the Goad to His Enemies,
    the Emperor

---

[269] *Pāṇṭi-k-Kōvai*, 88. The god referred to is the God of Love, son of Vishnu, who stepped the measure of the world in three strides.

[270] *Pāṇṭi-k-Kōvai*, 89.

of exalted, sweet,
Tamil poetry![271]

You, so like a swan,
with your jeweled sash
about your waist!
There is a stranger
who never leaves
this vast terraced field
in the grand, gleaming
Potiyil Mountains
of the Supreme One,
he who heard exalted,
sweet Tamil poems
from the lips
of Akattiyaṉ
in days of yore!
He comes and asks me
about lost quarry—
who is he?

His garland is, oh,
so fragrant![272]

You with your big, serene eyes,
and black hair, swarming with bees!
He even brings you
skirts made of flower buds
from Mount Potiyil
of the king
who roasted the world's
warring kings
at Pūlantai!
He never leaves!
He took that lie I told him
to be true—
he'll probably come
again today—
and if he does,

I do not know what
to say to him next.[273]

---

[271] *Pāṇṭi-k-Kōvai*, 90.

[272] *Pāṇṭi-k-Kōvai*, 91.

[273] *Pāṇṭi-k-Kōvai*, 92.

You, your nature as delicate,
as the southern lands
    of the Emperor
    who pressed into service
    fierce beasts from his foes
    that day at the Battle of Cēvūr,
    so his enemies lost
    their splendor,
    and drowned
    in red flames!
He brought you this skirt
made of mango leaves,
and his pretty garland swayed—
who is he?
He comes and asks me
about a stray elephant,

but he never leaves
our guarded terraced fields![274]

He never leaves
this grand terraced field:
his misery is long and harsh,
    like that
    of those who will not honor
    the feet of Neṭumāṟaṉ, him
    with his pointed lance:
    they waged their war,
    and that Cēraṉ king perished
    with his bow
    at Cēvūr!

You, with your thick tresses—
this is where those
who bestow their breasts
do so![275]

In his mountains,
where a mountain girl
with big eyes, murderous
as spears, dries her hair
in the moist, cool north breeze
that opened the fiery buds
of a glory lily,
wrapped in sepals,

---

[274] *Pāṇṭi-k-Kōvai*, 93.

[275] *Pāṇṭi-k-Kōvai*, 94.

the lord suffers
in awesome anguish—
aah!

This is where women
who bestow their breasts
do so![276]

The heroine feels secure when she hears these things; she muses, "Our lord told me, 'I will not leave you; I would die if I did!' But he has not died, since he followed her and entreated her!"

Next, here is how she causes the heroine to accept him through strong words: "Here is a hero," she says, "who seems to want to accomplish something through me. He is not the sort of person who has others accomplish things for him; rather, he does things for them. But I behaved falsely: I told him I would do it for him, since it seemed so essential to him. Then yesterday he came into this seaside grove and met me; as we were watching a crab protect its mate, he said, 'Now there is wisdom and manliness, is it not!' He esteemed it well. Then that anguished man looked at me, and at the crab, and left. But he left his emotions behind, in his understanding of that crab, and of me! What has become of him? He did not come back today." Here are some poems for that:

There was a man of noble mien
who stood lost in thought
for a long time yesterday,
until he left:
he praised a crab
that played there
with its mate
in the seaside grove
at Cape Kaṉṉi
    of the king who watched
    as enemy kings fled from Pāḻi,
    where the winged songs of bees
    sound through
    the groves!

But he was looking
at me.[277]

It was on grand Cape Kaṉṉi
    of him who prevailed
    when the Cēraṉ king perished

[276] *Pāṇṭi-k-Kōvai*, 95.

[277] *Pāṇṭi-k-Kōvai*, 96.

in the Battle of Pūlantai,
the Cēraṉ king of undying,
widespread renown,
there it was
that a swan protected
his mate's delicate body:
He said that was a good deed,
and melted in desire,
as he looked at me,
and then he left!

He has never been back
to this rich terraced field.[278]

You with your curly hair
tied up tight![279]
The lord of the ocean front
with its roaring waves
watched a spotted crab
play with its mate:
he looked at me
in that seaside grove
brimming with clusters
of screwpine blossoms—

then he left,
his feelings numbed,
and I can't make him out.[280]

Only after he had softened up
my good heart
with all those
humble words
he used so many
times—not one
day, not two days,
but day after day!
that's when he left me:
like honey ripened
in the mountains,
he went away.
Where is he now,

---

[278] *Pāṇṭi-k-Kōvai*, 97.

[279] Literally, in five braids. This way of fixing hair was characteristic of women in ancient Tamil poems.

[280] *Cilappatikāram: Kāṉalvari*, 31.

a father to me,
my staff to lean on?

Like rain thundering down
on good land, far away,
my heart weeps.[281]

Why didn't the heroine die when she heard these poems, you ask? She thought to herself, "If I were to die, he would die, too—what else would he do?"

* * *

Verse 11.

To her friend, who has expressed her inner intent,
there also exists an expression, due to the union of meeting,

What does this declare, you ask? It declares the character of the heroine after she has been asked to accept him in that fashion.

Its meaning:

To her friend, who has expressed—to her friend, who has lent her support.

her inner intent—the intention in the mind of her friend.

there also exists an expression—the heroine expresses her own character.

due to the union of meeting—because of their natural union: did he not say, "I will not leave you; if I did I would languish?"

What does this amount to, you ask? It amounts to saying that she both understands and misunderstands the situation.

If her friend makes her accept him through gentle words, the heroine would worry that the hero may have behaved in a degraded way, would she not? Yet she will not let that anxiety show. If, however, she uses strong words to make the heroine accept him, her anguish is even greater: she fears that he might have died, since he did not show up yesterday. Then she does let it show.

Next, here is a school of thought: they want her to have speech, and also to refrain from speaking. Here is how that is to come about: The heroine has been languishing in the thought that he may already have died. Then when her friend uses gentle words to get her to accept him, she realizes that he is alive, and her anguish departs. Her modesty returns, and she does not want to stand before her friend any longer, so she will make some pretext to leave. "Let's pick kino flowers!" she says, "Let's watch some peacocks dance! Let's play in the waterfalls!" Here are some poems for that:

Let's pick flowers,
golden ones,

---

[281] *Ku<u>r</u>untokai*, 176.

from the kino trees!
Let's watch the dancing
of a dark, sapphire colored peacock,
with its tail spread wide!
Let's play in the cascades
with their pure water
in those gorgeous, grand
colorful Potiyil Mountains,
where the sun dips,
Potiyil of the king
  of the southerners,
  the lord
  with the reddened lance,
  who vanquished
  at Vallam![282]

You with your glistening
forehead!
Let's pick kino and glory lily blooms
bursting with fragrance!
Let's watch dark peacocks dance,
row upon row, on wide rocks!
Let's bathe in the full waters
of cascades
in the Kolli Mountains
  of the southern king
  who fought to make those
  who joined battle against him
  die at Cēvūr
  with its gorgeous waters,
  full of waves![283]

So go the poems to be spoken.

If her friend gets her to accept him through the use of strong words, take it that she becomes so anxious thinking he must have died that no speech is born; that is particularly so because he did not show up yesterday.

Next, another school of thought holds that this verse declares how the heroine stands with honor to her friend;[284] it happens, they say, after the heroine has been shut up in her home immediately following natural union. This is how they develop their interpretation:

---

[282] *Pāṇṭi-k-Kōvai*, 98.

[283] *Pāṇṭi-k-Kōvai*, 99.

[284] See the Commentary on later verses, particularly verses 14 and 28, for detailed descriptions of "standing with honor."

To her friend, who has expressed her inner intent—to her friend, who has come to understand the changes in the heroine.
there also exists an expression, due to the union of meeting—the expression itself exists because of the union of meeting. Why? Because of the meaning of the verse,

> The heroine, who is shut up due to the union of meeting,
> gets to speak in the manner of adducing reasons, united with subtlety,
> with a view to protecting her fidelity,
> to her friend, who manifests the emotion of sorrow,[285]

they claim that the heroine stands with honor to her friend. We shall put off our description of her standing with honor until we comment upon the verse that ends,

> ...
> in all four of these, shedding her bodily modesty,
> standing with honor also belongs to her friend.[286]

When someone addresses another, we must describe the nature of the addressee, must we not? In the previous verse he said that her friend entreats the heroine, so in this verse he must relate the heroine's nature. Therefore, the above is the only correct commentary.

There are also some who say that the heroine is to see the hero when she is made to accept him; her friend understands her intent and lets the hero know that the heroine is willing. Here are some poems for that:

Saying That She Likes The Leaf Skirt

Lord!
She who is like Vañci City
    of the Gift of the Gods,
    the lord who carved
    the tiger and the carp
    above the bow
    on the pure, tall
    mountain of gold[287]—
she held to her breast
the leaf skirt you sent,

---

[285] Unidentified verse.

[286] *The Study of Stolen Love*, 29.

[287] The reference is to the Pāṇṭiyaṉ king's successful military expedition to the Himalaya Mountains. While he was there, he is said to have carved images of the tiger, the carp, and the bow into the rock. Those three things are the emblems of the three Tamil kingdoms: Cōḻa, Pāṇṭiya, and Cēraṉ, respectively.

pushed it past
her soft shoulders,
and placed it on her head,
right in her thick, soft
hair—

she took it.[288]

Lord
with your fragrant
garland of flowers
where beetles and bees
suck honey!
She who is like
Kūṭal City, with its cool waters,
    of the king whose long lance
    drips with the fat
    of enemies, the king
    who conquered Kaṭaiyal,
    watered all around,
    who let ghouls wallow
    in blood,
she adored
the leaf skirt you picked
and gave her—

she took it and placed it
upon her head.[289]

* * *

Verse 12.

Her friend, who understands the entreating hero,
accedes but sends him away, saying the heroine is shut up;
she says, 'why are you hiding it from me?'
and narrates the ways in which the union of meeting took place;
she laughs with him about illusory union,
says, 'Go tell her yourself,' and leaves;
she acts as one who does not know; she speaks nonchalantly;
she speaks words of invention; she takes intentions differently;
and other things that express the desire to bring them together:
these belong to the union of meeting, they say.

---

[288] *Pāṇṭi-k-Kōvai*, 100. Note that placing it on her head is a mark of the respect she feels for the hero.

[289] *Pāṇṭi-k-Kōvai*, 101.

What does this declare, you ask? Once her friend has caused her to accept him, she understands the heroine's intentions and arranges trysts for them herself. This verse declares that she will say all these things to the hero and send him away, in order to make him decide to attain the heroine through marriage.

It can also be taken as a declaration that she lets the hero know he can continue having trysts until the heroine's modesty perishes; she thinks of arranging these meetings for them when he entreats her to, and when she understands the heroine's mind.

Its meaning:

Her friend, who understands the entreating hero—her friend, who correctly understands the mind of the hero who comes entreating her: it means that, though there had been a period when she did not understand him completely, that no longer applies; moreover, it also means that she understands his anguish; moreover, it also means that her friend has understood directly from the hero that as he begs and entreats her, and departs in anguish, he will suffer as long as she cannot arrange a rendezvous.

accedes but sends him away, saying the heroine is shut up—being shut up means being under heavy guard; "saying" means telling; "sends him away" implies that she agrees with him, yet sends him away: it means she will tell him about the heavy guard in order to make him leave; the word "accedes" means "agrees" in his state of anguish; therefore we derive that she will speak a few words of consolation that sound as though they would upset him; note that there are also some who say that this word "accedes" does not mean "agrees," but is part of a compound word that simply means "removed him, sent him away, got rid of him."

This is how she tells him that the guard is heavy: "This place has a heavy guard," she says, "It would be improper for you to come here." Here are some poems for that:

Refusing Him, Saying, "It is Guarded"

Please don't come
to these mountains,
cool and beautiful,
that capture the eye,
these Potiyil Mountains
that brush the sky,
these mountains
    of the Emperor
    born as a Gift of the Gods,
    whose righteous scepter
    bridles the earth
    who brought to his enemies

the blessing of riding
up into heaven
at Vallam—

our green terraced field surrounded by groves
where the sound of the bees surpasses music
is watched![290]

Go on, don't stop here
on the rich, beautiful slopes
of these Kolli Mountains
that belong to him who stood
for all the people
in this wide world
to worship,
the king with the canopy
of glistening pearls,
whose bow engaged
and destroyed commandants
who would not embrace him
at Naṟaiyāṟu—

This vast terraced field
is watched.[291]

Here in the sapphire-hued
Kolli Mountains
that belong to him
who was born the Gift of the Gods,
whose army of beasts
annihilated those kings
who wouldn't embrace him
at Pūlantai
where flowers bloom
in cool groves,
my cousins
will not leave:
they have strong bows,
and plenty of arrows—
they stand guard day
and night—

---

290 *Pāṇṭi-k-Kōvai*, 102.

291 *Pāṇṭi-k-Kōvai*, 103.

please, don't come
into this guarded
terraced field![292]

How can all this console the hero, you ask? That very speech consoles him, because it makes him think, "Isn't she telling me this because she cares about me, and she wants me to know exactly what's going on? She has so much sympathy for me that there's no way she'll fail me in what I want!" A further implication is that he may attain the heroine through marriage if it should prove too difficult for her friend to arrange trysts. Why does she say all this to the hero, you ask? She says it in order to make him feel, in the midst of his anguish, that it will be easy for her, yet still to have him realize that it is not. Next, how does that speech console him, you ask? Because if he feared it impossible, he might die. Introduce this thought throughout this verse as you continue your commentary.

she says, 'why are you hiding it from me?'—her friend fears that the languishing hero might die if his anguish were to increase.

"Why," she asks, "are you undergoing all these changes?"

He thinks, "She doesn't comprehend my anguish! If I tell her all about it, she might refuse me, since she doesn't understand! But if I keep on softening her up, she'll eventually realize it on her own; then she'll do it for me." And so he does not tell her what his anguish is all about.

She says, "What do you gain by hiding your anguish from me?" Here are some poems for that:

Describing The Concealment

Lord
of your cool and beautiful
ocean front, where the tender
aroma of screwpine drowns
the stench of seawater
the River Vaiyai longs to join,
the Vaiyai of our king
    who drowned
    the king of his enemies
    at Viḻiñam
    with the victory
    of his reddened lance
    that drowns out
    the very lightning!

[292] *Pāṇṭi-k-Kōvai*, 104.

Will you get what you want
if you hide it from me?
I wonder.[293]

So you've come
to this dark terraced field
in the Kolli Mountains
    of our king who sheathed
    his shining lance
    when he watched
    able kings
    with strong chariots
    die in the Battle of Cēvūr!
You came here to accomplish
something, you brought along
a fragrant honeyed wreath,
swarming with bees—

do you really think you'll manage it
just between yourselves,
if you hide it from me?[294]

In saying that, she implies that they will succeed if they don't conceal it from her.

and narrates the ways in which the union of meeting took place—the union of meeting is natural union; the ways are the trysts arranged by his friend and by her friend.

It implies that she says, "I will accomplish this for you if you don't hide it from me." Therefore it further implies that he feels consoled, thinking, "She doesn't know what I want; but when she figures it out, she will do it for me."

she laughs with him about illusory union, says, 'Go tell her yourself,' and leaves—she laughs with him and tells him that his following her around and saying all those imaginary things are common enough occurrences in the world.

She says, "Who knows whether or not it will happen? I cannot speak for her without knowing what she has in mind—I'm just her errand girl. You go to her yourself and tell her what you want." Here are some poems for that:

Refusal By Saying, "Tell Her Your Troubles Yourself"

Sir, with your noble qualities
and your garlands brimming with fragrance,
tell her yourself about this misery

---

[293] *Pāṇṭi-k-Kōvai*, 105.

[294] *Pāṇṭi-k-Kōvai*, 106.

that has made you grow so thin!
Tell her,
with her delicate shoulders
like shoots of bamboo
in the Potiyil Mountains, so
flowery and cool,
    of the king, the southern king,
    who stood like the God of Beauty[295]
    himself, yet fought so well
    that foes who took him on
    at Cennilam
    went up to heaven
    and walked right in![296]

Lord
of your great ocean front!
Would it be too much
for you to go, yourself,
and speak straight to her
of the softening of your heart,
to her with her soft, dark hair,
prettied with flower wreaths?
to her who is like
the figurine
in the Kolli Mountains
    of the king who watched
    the flood rage, the
    flood of blood
    from dissenting kings
    who perished at Pūlantai
    as they waged their war,
    riddled with faults?[297]

He feels upset when she says this. Why? Because if you beg someone to do something saying, "You must do this for me," and the other person replies, "I cannot; go and do it yourself," you feel utterly miserable, don't you! It is like that. But then he grabs hold of something in consolation. What, you ask? He thinks to himself, "She laughed while she said that, didn't she? That laugh must mean something." And so he is consoled.

Next, **she acts as one who does not know**—while the hero follows her around with his wreath and leaf skirt, she says, "I don't know who it is you're talking about!" Here are some poems for that:

---

[295] "The God of Beauty," in this stanza, means Murukaṉ.

[296] *Pāṇṭi-k-Kōvai*, 107.

[297] *Pāṇṭi-k-Kōvai*, 108.

Acting As One Who Doesn't Know, And Asking For A Reminder

There are so many girls
with thick hair, playing games
in these seaside groves filled
with fragrant flowers
at Cape Kaṉṉi
    of King Neṭumāṟaṉ
    who vanquished Nelvēli
    and wields his righteous scepter
    in the one path
    over all the world,
    who carved the carp,
    so beautiful,
    into the mountains
    of the north!

On whom do this lord's
thoughts rest?[298]

There are so many young girls
with big, red-lined eyes,
with bracelets, and with
pretty breasts, playing
at housekeeping here
on the beaches by Toṇṭi,
Toṇṭi that belongs
    to him who rode
    his elephant—
    with little eyes
    and a huge, black trunk
    with a hole in it—
    as enemies who reveled
    in opposing him
    died at Cēvūr!

On whom do this lord's
thoughts rest?[299]

He is upset when he hears this, but then he feels consoled, thinking, "She really does not know who is troubling me. When she realizes, she'll fix it up for me." **she speaks nonchalantly**—she doesn't accept his offerings, though he praises them, saying, "This is a good leaf skirt, a good wreath; they are fit for you to

---

[298] *Pāṇṭi-k-Kōvai*, 109.

[299] *Pāṇṭi-k-Kōvai*, 110.

receive;" instead, she changes the subject, and leaves. Here are some poems for that:

> Beautiful golden pollen spilled
> from fragrant mastwood trees
> near glistening bright coral
> the waves have piled up here
> in this lovely seaside grove
> at Cape Kumari
> of the southern king,
> Tirumāl, the Gift of the Gods,
> who granted his foes heaven
> at Vallam,
>
> and this pretty beach
> looks like a rainbow![300]

> On this beach in the South,
> at Cape Kaṉṉi
> of the king
> who smashed the disciplined armies
> and the chariots of those
> who opposed him in anger
> at Kaṭaiyal, with its groves
> decorated in clouds,
>
> ocean waves smash our cute playhouses
> of glistening white pearls,
> built on vast sands.[301]

He feels upset when he hears this, thinking, "She will not do this for me! I have suffered in vain, and now she's saying any old thing in answer to me." But his anguish grabs onto something in consolation. What consoles him, you ask? He hopes, "I must have come at a time when she is worried about something else; otherwise she wouldn't withhold her reply. I'll come back when she is not preoccupied."

she speaks words of invention—he praises his offerings; he says, "This leaf skirt is good, and so is this wreath, and these pearls are, too. They are fit for you to receive," and then she replies; what does she say, you ask? "My father and her father come around here often," she says, "and if they were to see you, they would do you harm—their anger is harsher than the God of Death! If you really have a problem, it would be better attended to from a distance." Here are some poems for that:

---

[300] *Pāṇṭi-k-Kōvai*, 111.

[301] *Pāṇṭi-k-Kōvai*, 112.

Refusal Through Words Of Invention

You, your jewels
eclipse the lightning!
But don't come here
with that skirt
of kino blossoms
that eclipse
the glow of gold:
Lord of the mountains,
her father often comes
here!
She is like
beautiful Māntai City
    of the Emperor
    who took up his
    honed lance
    to make an impertinent king
    weaken at Viḻiñam!

But please, don't come near
this cool terraced field![302]

In the high Potiyil Mountains
    of the Supreme One
    who drove his strong chariot
    to make kings with tall chariots
    and well harnessed horses
    perish in the land
    of Pūlantai,
mountain men carry javelins,
they have dogs along with them
and they whistle,
they have their arrows ready
and their bows are always
strung!

Please, don't come near
this terraced field,
ripe for the harvest![303]

You ask how this can be "speaking words of invention?" When speaking of great people, the masculine should not interfere in what is properly feminine nor the feminine in what is properly masculine; so, take it that these are words of

302 *Pāṇṭi-k-Kōvai*, 113.

303 *Pāṇṭi-k-Kōvai*, 114.

invention because she invents non-existent things as she speaks. Yet he feels anguish when he hears it. Why? He thinks, "She is just saying this to get rid of me." But his anguish, as usual, grabs something in consolation. What does it grab, you ask? He cools down as he thinks, "She is worried now about harm I might suffer in this way, so she might also worry about harm that will come to me if I do not attain the heroine!"

she takes intentions differently—although she really does want a tryst, she appears not to, since she does not speak. He becomes upset the moment he notices that. Why? He thinks, "She cannot do what I want her to, and all my suffering is in vain!" But isn't this also the very reason for his consolation? "Okay," he thinks, "I must have come at a time when she is worried about something else; she will give me a reply some other time, when she is not preoccupied." That cools him down, and he returns home.

But then, aren't all the things described above "taking intentions differently?" Why is this one singled out to be designated in that way, you ask? Those other situations do not exhibit subtle intentions, since she speaks openly. Here her disinclination to a tryst is exhibited without words.

Next, this is how others interpret "taking the intentions differently:" She says, "What shall I say to her before I leave? She is not herself!" Here are some poems for that:

Saying The Heroine Is Not Aware Of Herself

You, with your garland
loaded down with flower petals,
she is like southern Kūṭal City
  of Neṭumāṟaṉ, the king
  who strung his strong bow
  to make other kings
  in tall chariots
  with murderous horses
  perish at Āṟṟukkuṭi!
Yet she wears no blue lotus
in her long, thick hair,
she just stands around,
thinking—

I don't know how to approach her,
or what to say.[304]

---

[304] *Pāṇṭi-k-Kōvai*, 115.

Lord of this cool ocean front,
where waves are tossed about—
she wears no blue lotus
from your dark
backwater canals—
she won't even play games
with the polka-dot crabs,
nor with ones
with fine stripes—
she just stands around,
thinking, and sweat
beads up
on her little brow—

What could I say
if I went up to her now?[305]

He becomes upset when she says that, but her speech itself is the crutch he grabs for consolation. How, you ask? He cools down as he thinks, "She said that the heroine is not aware of herself; she will speak to her when she is herself again." **and other things that express the desire to bring them together: these belong to the union of meeting, they say**—she thinks, "I shall bring them together, as in the union of meeting," and so on; take it that these are things for her to say; the author began to recite them all and found them multiplying, so he recited a few and left a few out, since there is a stylistic rule for doing that.

By saying, "and other things," he means such things as these: Her friend says, "You do not realize her preciousness and nobility, do you, since you are a newcomer;" or, "Her relatives guard her whenever she goes out, just as inner petals guard the center of a lotus blossom;" or, "She is the greatest in this land, a goddess who has made herself visible to us, is she not? We may look at her, join our palms and worship her with bowed heads, but how else can the likes of us let her know what he wants?" Some poems on these themes:

Declaring The Difficulty In Expression

Lord of the mountains
fragrant with flowers!
She is a goddess
who moves where we can
see her—
do you see?
She is like Uṟaiyūr City
of the Emperor

---

305 Unidentified poem.

who fought
and made the King of Pūḻi
leave with a melancholy heart
from the Battle of Pūlantai,
where birds lament
upon the waters!

How could I be so immodest
as to speak to her
of these changes?[306]

You ask my help,
you ask me to remove
the anguish of your dear soul
that my friend caused,
my friend
with her perfected jewelry,
and her armletted shoulders—
and just yesterday
and the day before,
I myself was too shy
to speak with you,
a stranger,
after all!

She won't fall easily
for our words—
she's a goddess,
my lord, visible
though she is
to our eyes,
is she not?

Daughter of the king
of sapphire mountains,
engulfed in clouds,
where rich, pretty,
long mountain-pepper
vines thrive,
she strokes
the striped backs
of sleeping tigers.[307]

Next, she also says this: "You are great, and we are small; it is not right for us to be talking together." Here are some poems for that:

---

[306] *Pāṇṭi-k-Kōvai*, 116.

[307] Unidentified poem.

Refusal By Stating Family Rank

Don't mix with us,
don't think we're
of your mold!
Your people are rich,
settled in a land
fertile with water—
ours are mountain folk
from the slopes
of the Kolli Mountains
    of the king with a canopy
    of cool and glistening pearls,
    a canopy like the great moon,
    his own ancestor,
    the king who demolished
    his foes at Pāḻi
    with his armies![308]

Need I mention
that your people
in their countryside
of brilliant waterways
are very wealthy?
But when it comes to us,
we are mountain folk:
we live in the Kolli Mountains
in the West, mountains
    of King Māṟaṉ,
    the victorious king
    of the dynasty of the moon,
    who fought the Battle of Cēvūr
    and saw the back
    of the Cēraṉ king,
    much to the chagrin
    of that king's queen![309]

Lord, rich in jewels!
You are lord
of a countryside
with cool waterways,
but our people
are mountain folk

---

[308] *Pāṇṭi-k-Kōvai*, 117.

[309] *Pāṇṭi-k-Kōvai*, 118.

from the pretty slopes
of cool and splendid Potiyil
with its waterfalls
and sandalwood trees,
rich in foliage,
    Potiyil of the Emperor
    with three massive wreaths
    of flowers and leaves,
    who conquered Kaṭaiyal
    of the great waters,
    as he rode his famous
    thundercloud
    of an elephant![310]

She is a fisherman's daughter,
her people stir up
the great blue sea
to catch their catch,
and live in their quaint
little village
by the sea grove,
But you!
you are the pampered son
of a rich man, you have
a racing chariot, and you live
in that ancient city
where long banners flap
in all the bazaars!
What do we care
if you're so
handsome?

We drive off hordes
of gulls who want fillets
from fat sharks we cut up
and set out to dry—
we stink
of dead fish, go
on, get out
of here!

Our little village
and our good life
from the yield
of these great waters

---

310 *Pāṇṭi-k-Kōvai*, 119.

are not like
yours—

and we have our heroes here,
among our own kind.[311]

He becomes upset when she says that, but he cools down as he thinks, "What she actually said was, 'You are great, and we are small,' wasn't it? That means I can attain her yet, doesn't it!"

Next, she also speaks verses like these:

Lord,
here you come
every day,
to this sea grove
of grand waters,
and bring us
your pearls!

But we have no lack
of pearls—
Our home is
splendid Koṟkai,
with its white
sand dunes:
we use glistening pearls
in our play houses
when we play jacks,
or when we put on
our clever magic
tricks, or
whatever game
we're playing![312]

When their sandcastles sank
beneath the sea's roaring waves,
they shouted, "Watch out,
ocean: I'm telling
my mom on you!"
and they ran back home—
pearls they spilled
as they ran
looked like buds
of mastwood blossoms

---

[311] *Naṟṟiṇai*, 45.

[312] Unidentified poem.

from the nearby seaside grove,
and confused passers-by:

Such is Pukār,
our home.[313]

Also, there are such verses as these for themes that are acceptable because the author said, "other things:"

Accepting A Leaf Skirt

In this cool terraced field
on the Kolli Mountains
    of the king,
    the southern king
    who vanquished the Cōḻa
    and the Cēraṉ
    and took their shining crowns,
    who wields the stormcloud's thunderbolt
    to make unattached kings
    bow low,
you ask us
about an elephant,
you bring us a delicate
leaf skirt,
and wait around:
you look like a man
of profound accomplishment!

And you come near us,
but you will not leave![314]

Our terraced field
is ready to harvest
here on the slopes
of the Kolli Mountains
    of the Goad to His Enemies,
    the Emperor of sweet Tamil poetry,
    who witnessed
    the misery
    of unloving kings
    at Pāḻi,
Lord of moist
mountainsides!
You asked if an elephant

[313] Unidentified poem.

[314] *Pāṇṭi-k-Kōvai*, 120.

with an arrow wound happened
by here—

is that full leaf skirt in your hands
supposed to be medicine
for the poor beast's wound?[315]

You, sir,
with your grand wreath
buzzing with bees
and full of honey—
even she
whose long eyes
mock javelins
likes it!
Still, I have
a few things
to tell you:
in these great Kolli Mountains
    of him who triumphed
    and sent his foes to heaven
    at Vallam

even us forest folk
have already seen leaf skirts
as fragrant as that![316]

You, sir,
with your fragrant wreath,
you who protect the whole world:
On these beautiful slopes
of the Kolli Mountains,
wrapped in clouds,
    of the king with the gleaming,
    sharp tipped lance
    and the victorious
    thunderbolt banner,
    who triumphed at Kaḷattūr,
I would accept this skirt
of plucked flowers
for that girl
with eyes like
sharp tipped javelins,
and a waist
like a tiny drum,

[315] *Pāṇṭi-k-Kōvai*, 121.

[316] *Pāṇṭi-k-Kōvai*, 122.

if I knew
what she would say.[317]

You, sir,
with your wreath
prettied up with flowers:
Even if you gave us
this sweet skirt
of tender mastwood leaves
and red flowers
from Mount Potiyil,
dipping into the sky,
    that mountain of him
    who snatched up victory
    with his glistening lance
    on the fortified walls
    of his enemies,

would it be proper
for our fair-skinned darling?[318]

Lord,
with your thick garland
laden with honey!
You are a newcomer here:
If our poor girl adorns
her soft, bulging breasts
with this dress of mango leaves
from the mountain
with sapphire-blue waters
    of the king
    who just rode
    upon his horse
    to cause emperors
    with their armies
    already fanned out
    to run onto the battlefield
    to die,

it will turn out
absolutely awful![319]

---

[317] *Pāṇṭi-k-Kōvai*, 123.

[318] *Pāṇṭi-k-Kōvai*, 124.

[319] *Pāṇṭi-k-Kōvai*, 125.

You, sir,
with your fine
fragrant wreath,
with flowers
where nectars linger!
That poor girl,
with a forehead
like a bow and fine arrows
will accept your skirt,
but there is one thing—
it stands out, and
I must let you know:
this sweet skirt
does not exist,
save here
in this fine grove
brimming with honey
in the cool Kolli Mountains
    of the Goad to His Enemies,
    the king of fine Tamil poems,
    the king of the lands of Pūḻi![320]

Lord of grand,
cool mountainsides!
This skirt of sandalwood leaves
comes from mountains
in our own land—
it comes from this mountain
in the land of cool,
luxuriant Mount Potiyil
    of the king who angered,
    and that made his angry foes
    shower arrows
    from the bows in their hands,
    yet die at Cennilam!

That is not right.[321]

Interpret all these suitably and take them as examples, like those given above.

But why would she grieve him thus if she really wants to help him, you ask? She continues the trysts until her modesty wears out; then she will speak of her own intentions.

Then again, did her friend realize the truth of their union, since he said, "bring them together ... (as)... in the union of meeting," you ask? She did not.

---

[320] *Pāṇṭi-k-Kōvai*, 126.

[321] *Pāṇṭi-k-Kōvai*, 127.

She thinks, "I will bring them together in order to regulate their meetings." It was only the author who compared that thought to the union of meeting.

* * *

Verse 13.

> **Union through entreaty by her friend**
> **does not exist for the heroine, in bringing them together.**

What does this declare, you ask? It declares a characteristic of the heroine.
Its meaning:
Union through entreaty—union that is caused by entreating.
by her friend—through her friend.
does not exist for the heroine—the heroine does not have.
in bringing them together—in the definition of bringing them together.

It means that the heroine never meets him through the entreaties of her friend. What does that mean, you ask? Suppose her friend were to say, "Here comes this hero who seems to want my help in something—something very important to him. If you don't agree to meet him and grant his wish, I'll never serve you again!" The heroine does not agree to meet the hero and grant his wishes through fear of such a loss: tradition comprises no such union.

Is it not enough that he said earlier,

> Other than of that nature, union that is caused
> at no point exists in Stolen Love,[322]

you ask? He did say that, but he also said,

> Hiding her inner understanding and not letting it become clear,
> there are also entreatings of the heroine
> at the time of knowing the signs,[323]

and so he needed a verse to emphasize his point, as otherwise one might doubt whether or not he actually can accomplish a union in this way through her friend.

Next, here is another school of thought: Isn't it enough to say, "Union through entreaty by her friend does not exist for the heroine;" what is the phrase, "in bringing them together" for, you ask? Meetings arranged by her friend fall into three types: first, middle, and last. In the first of those types they do not realize, "We are uniting with each other because she set up our tryst," but they do in the middle and last types. Otherwise, could this poem have been written?

---

[322] *The Study of Stolen Love*, 4.

[323] *The Study of Stolen Love*, 10.

With his gracious heart,
he came, and leaned upon his lance,
but never was he
wicked!

And you it was
who brought him here,
yet you did
no wrong!

Friend!
I gave to you
endless, unbearable misery:
It was I who did
wrong.[324]

Place here the rest of the poems that come in this vein as well.

* * *

Verse 14.

> **Those fit for her friend to the foster mother**
> **are speeches also, with no contradiction.**

What does this declare, you ask? It declares how one goes and stands with honor.

Its meaning:

Those fit for her friend—poems her friend may speak.

to the foster mother—to the heroine's foster mother.

are speeches also, with no contradiction—are also poems spoken with no discrepancies.

With what is there no contradiction, you ask? Take it that there is to be no contradiction with the mother's knowledge, the heroine's greatness, her fidelity, her friend's chaperoning, modesty, nor the world. By what rule, you ask? There are variations in all four places mentioned in the verse beginning,

> If desire increases when guarding becomes excessive...[325]

and her friend recognizes them the moment they occur. Why? Because she and her friend are not different.

Her friend then realizes, "Since it is clear to me, it will be clear to my mother as well—and she won't keep quiet: she'll ask the pundits. They will reply that God caused it all." Why? Gods are not such that people can point them out and

---

[324] *Akanāṉūṟu*, 72.

[325] *The Study of Stolen Love*, 29. The variations noted here refer to physical changes in the heroine, such as lackluster eyes, a worried brow, and so forth.

understand them; yet pundits will do just that, even though they don't know what they're talking about: it's their job! When they have made their pronouncement, she will cause the heroine to worship a god, and that will spoil her fidelity to the hero. Why? Because faithful women worship no god but their husbands.

The heroine will suffer with the thought of losing her fidelity through worshipping a god, and she will grieve even further thinking, "Our ancient family has always eschewed blemishes of character, but when I come along I'm like a scratch on a piece of jewelry! Our family has never known the dance of frenzy, but now they will have to accept it, all because of me!" And she will be afraid, thinking "To soothe my sufferings, and through the power of the priest's frenzied dancing, might they even bring my lord to the frenzy field?" She will worry, thinking, "Shall I conceal these changes that have come over me so no outsiders will recognize them, to keep my lord from being brought to the frenzy field? But if I do, my lord might think it looks like something else can undo those changes he himself caused in me." Her friend grieves, too.

But her friend's anguish grabs hold of something in consolation. Why, you ask? Because nothing else can console her. She thinks, "Before mother asks the pundits, she will check with me—she'll only go to them if I say I don't know what is wrong with the heroine. Now, then, what shall I say when she asks me?" She does not look to facilitate any more rendezvous, but examines these things in her mind.

While she is steeped in these thoughts, her mother[326] comes in, carrying a mirror. She looks her daughter over from head to toe and says, "Dear, my daughter is not her old self. Do you know what has caused these changes in her?"

"I do know a little something from a long time ago: do you want to know what it is? One day back in our childhood, when we still did our hair up in bunches, you fixed us up in our day-time make up and told us to go out and play with the rest of the pretty, innocent, little girls. So we went off to play in this grove with white sand and cool flowers all around. A hero came by, carrying a lotus blossom from a mountain pool, and your daughter looked up at him and said, 'Please may I have that lotus blossom for my doll?' He thought nothing of it and gave it to her; then he left. This all happened back when we were so innocent!" Here are some poems for that:

---

[326] And hence, by definition, the heroine's foster mother.

Standing With Honor

On the vast ocean front
at Cape Kaṉṉi
    of the king
    who took up his sharp lance
    so that angry foes
    riding thick necked elephants
    died at Cennilam,
this girl,
with her big eyes,
whose fingers are forever
playing with her gameballs,
asked fresh flowers
for her doll,
and a man
gave her some.

She accepted them
and decorated her doll.[327]

She is like
the good Vaiyai lands
    of the king
    with his righteous scepter
    who protects that land
    of good waters,
    the southern king
    who destroyed other kings
    in solid war at Cēvūr!
This girl,
with her big eyes,
saw in the hands
of a young man there
some lotus blossoms
as pretty as eyes,
and begged for them—

he gave her those cool flowers,
and she put them on.[328]

"All this happened," continues her friend, "at a time when she did not know what she should have known. Now she does know what she needs to know: she realizes that he was an eligible young man when he gave her those flowers, and

[327] *Pāṇṭi-k-Kōvai*, 128.

[328] *Pāṇṭi-k-Kōvai*, 129.

that she accepted them. She feels that if something were to happen to her and she did not worship him, it would be a blight on the family, since young girls with golden bracelets like herself belong to their families. That is why your daughter has changed."

This formulation does not contradict the mother's knowledge, since she had told them to go out and play.

Next, it does not contradict her greatness since she still remembers a good deed done to her long ago.

Next, it does not contradict her fidelity since she feared a blight on the family if it were to happen any other way.

Next, it does not contradict her friend's chaperoning, since it happened when they both were present.

Next, it does not contradict her modesty because it happened at a stage in her life when she did not know what she now needs to know.

Next, it does not contradict the ways of the world, since she noted that girls with golden bracelets belong to their families.

This is what is meant by saying that her speech is without contradiction.

This formulation is called the Union Bestowed Through Flowers.

Next, here are some poems on the Union Bestowed Through An Elephant:

This innocent girl,
in her great fidelity,
thinks of nothing but
a mountain lord
who dispelled our distress:
he killed
a small-eyed elephant
that had charged
right up to us,
and had already
ruined our terraced field
nestled among the boulders
in the grand Kolli Mountains
    of the king,
    the Supreme One
    who raised the strong thunderbolt
    so his enemies reeled![329]

Even now this young girl
with her breasts so heavy
can think of nothing
but the mountain-country lord

---

[329] *Pāṇṭi-k-Kōvai*, 130.

who dispelled our distress
when he killed
an angry elephant
that stood
square in our path
and stole millet
from our terraced field—
there in the Potiyil Mountains
where clouds settle,
mountains of Māṟaṉ
    who vanquished the Cēraṉ
    and watched grief grow
    in the hearts of his foes
    at Kaṭaiyal![330]

Comment in the same way upon such poems as these as well.
Next, here are some poems for the Union Bestowed Through A Flood:

We were in the cool,
swelling currents
of the Vaiyai River
    of the Supreme One
    with his rising,
    white canopy,
    his warrior's anklet
    of pure gold,
    and his righteous
    scepter,
and we were playing
and bathing,
when your girl
with immaculate jewelry
started to drown,
caught in the river's clear,
full waves!

But then a man of noble character appeared,
and performed his most gracious deed![331]

Never have we forgotten,
not even for a few days,
the precious grace
granted by one
who is like the Chief

---

[330] *Pāṇṭi-k-Kōvai*, 131.

[331] *Pāṇṭi-k-Kōvai*, 132.

with his flowery arrows,[332]
who came to us there
when the golden current
caught us up
at the bathing-steps
on the River Vaiyai
 of Māṟaṉ,
 who vanquished the Cēraṉ,
 whose fighting
 ended the days
 of that king
 who waged war against him
 at Cēvūr, in the South.[333]

Comment in the same way upon such poems as these as well.

She was just wading
with us there in the
beautiful, swift rapids,
when she covered
her lotus eyes—
she weakened, and
fainted!

But as she was
being swept away
he leaped in with grace—
his garland of flowers,
fresh and fragrant, from
tall mastwood trees
glistened!
When he brought her back
he was hugging her jeweled breast
close to his:
Since that day,
when his broad chest hugged
her budding breasts,
my friend can bring rain
whenever it's needed:[334]

that's how great
she is.[335]

---

[332] The God of Love.

[333] *Pāṇṭi-k-Kōvai*, 133.

[334] Tradition declares that faithful women can bring rains to the semi-arid Tamil country.

[335] *Kalittokai, Kuriñci-k-Kali*, 3.

Next, the word "also" is a further indicator of the lack of contradictions. This is how that works: If the heroine's foster mother asks the pundits instead of her daughter, they will tell her, "It happened through God," and she will call a priest so the heroine can perform divine worship. Her friend then addresses the priest as he dances in his frenzy; here are some poems for that:

Eschewing The Frenzy

Priest!
You killed a goat
to feed a god,
    just like the bodies
    of foes who rose
    against the southern King
    at Vallam
    with its grand groves
    filled with bees,
and on you dance
in your frenzy!
Yes, you will give us
Lord Murukaṉ,
with his cool garlands:

but will the bright, garlanded chest
of the lord of these cool, flowery mountains
also eat of your grand sacrifice?[336]

O, priest, wise
in words, you who came
here praying and praising
Lord Murukaṉ, hold back your ire,
for I have something
to ask of you:

When you perform
your rites of sacrifice
with all those colored grains
of cooked rice,
when you kill a little goat kid
and daub her[337] pretty brow
with earth muddied in its blood,
will the chest
that really torments her,
the chest of our lord

[336] *Pāṇṭi-k-Kōvai*, 134.

[337] "Her" refers to the heroine (not the goat kid).

of the mountains
dipping in the sky,
his broad chest,
adorned with its gleaming
garlands—

will it also eat
of the sacrament?[338]

What do these speeches mean? They mean, "What you are doing will work only if the cool, garlanded chest of our lord of the mountains also eats of your offerings."

In order to fathom her intent, her mother says, "What do you mean?" and then her friend stands with honor as described above.

Next, when she observes the priest's divine possession, her friend may speak as though she is addressing some bystanders; here are a few poems for that:

Telling Others That Murukaṉ Is Ignorant

The girl
is like rich Kūṭal City
    of Māṟaṉ
    who conquered the Cēraṉ
    and wears his long, tormenting
    warrior's anklets—
and well enough did he know
that it is the garlanded chest
of the lord
of these vast, cool mountains
that torments her,
with her tender, young,
tormentingly pretty breasts!
Yet he came on and kept dancing
in his frenzy:

this Lord Murukaṉ may be a great tormentor,
but he certainly is stupid![339]

Out in front
of all these people
from the grand lands
    of the Southern King
    whose gleaming lance
    torments the lightning,

[338] *Kuṟuntokai*, 362.

[339] *Pāṇṭi-k-Kōvai*, 135.

who played
with the flesh of his foes
at Pūlantai,
with its freshets
that torment
pure gold,
he not only came
to dance,
but still he's
dancing—
And he knows
he has never been
her tormentor!

He may be the king of tormentors,
but this Lord Murukaṉ
sure is stupid![340]

Long life to you,
Sir Lord Murukaṉ!

Yes, you knew
her brooding,
incurable heartaches
grew from the chest
of the lord of that land
where a water nymph
wears unpicked lotus flowers
opening over their lilypads
in a divine mountain pool—
she ties them ever so cleverly in
with blood-red lily blooms,
as she dances to the beat
of a sweet waterfall drumming
till these great hills
ring with splendor!
Yes, you knew
it was not due
to you—

Yet here you come,
into this hall of frenzy,
wearing your fragrant,
fresh cadamba wreath,
and gawking upwards,
because some priest

[340] *Pāṇṭi-k-Kōvai*, 136.

said he wanted you
to!

You may be a god—
but for sure
you're a fool![341]

In order to fathom her intent, the mother then says, "What do you mean?" and then her friend stands with honor as described above.

* * *

Verse 15.

As there is no speech before uniting,
what is known as Marital Love follows Stolen Love.

What does this declare, you ask? It declares the definition of Marital Love.
Its meaning:
As there is no speech before uniting—this is a verse in which the word order is switched; take it as I have presented it.[342]
what is known as Marital Love follows Stolen Love—that which has the eminence of being called "Marital Love" follows Stolen Love.

That is, since speaking does not precede their union, the conduct known as Marital Love follows that known as Stolen Love.

In saying there is no speech before their union in Stolen Love, he refutes those who would have conversation. Additionally, he implies that there is conversation both during and following their union; nevertheless, speaking during their union is not to be explicit unless they find in it a source of strength.

Next, there are explicit speeches following their union. On what themes, you ask? Take it that they are his Expression of Love, the Fear of Separation, and the Reassurance.

Following the path of such a Stolen Love as that, Marital Love occurs when he attains her through her relatives. By all this, then, there is the further implication that this is not Stolen Love as it exists in the world. Why? Because speech precedes union in worldly Stolen Love.

Why does he add "What is known as," instead of saying simply, "Marital Love follows Stolen Love," you ask? In the world, Marital Love may occur without following Stolen Love; he added that phrase to indicate that Marital

---

341 *Naṟṟiṇai*, 34.

342 The commentary here presents the verse with the order of two of the words switched. In either case, the translation would have to read as given; hence the summary statement, "Take it as I have presented it," which follows the sense of the commentary.

Love is not all that eminent. Thus, this verse fundamentally connects Stolen Love with Marital Love.

* * *

Verse 16.

> **There is a breach in Stolen Love if guarding increases when there is a delay in marriage.**

What does this declare, you ask? It declares the obstacles that trouble the hero during Stolen Love.

Its meaning:

There is a breach in Stolen Love—there are intervals during which the heroine does not unite with him during the period of Stolen Love; one may also say that there are days when the hero does not attain the heroine.

if guarding increases—when guarding is increased.

when there is a delay in marriage—it also occurs when their marriage is delayed.

It means that the breach occurs either when guarding is increased or when marriage is delayed.

"Guarding" means these things: her mother not sleeping, the dog not sleeping, the town not sleeping, watchmen hastening, the moon coming out, an owl hooting, and a cock crowing.

"Increasing" means multiplying, and it occurs in these ways: one of those occurring on many days, many of them occurring jumbled together, or many of them occurring in regular order.

Of those, here is what "mother not sleeping" means: One night during a period when the hero visits her at night trysts, her mother does not close her eyes: she means to teach her daughter about wisdom and propriety. It is an obstacle when that occurs.

"The dog not sleeping" means this: Neither is it conducive when a dog who knows the path always barks at everything he sees, because there will be an investigation into why he is barking so much at this one place. Thus this also becomes an obstacle.

"The town not sleeping" means that it is an obstacle when the town does not sleep because it is celebrating a festival. It alludes to festivals such as these: Āvaṇi Aviṭṭam in Madurai, Paṅkuṉi Uttiram in Uṟaiyūr, and Uḷḷi Viḻā in Karuvūr. All others of that sort are obstacles as well.

"Watchmen hastening" means this: Watchmen are guards: they roam around with their lanterns thinking, "We shall be vigilant in guarding the town, the place, and so on...," don't they? It is, of course, an obstacle when they are about.

"The moon coming out" means this: When the moon takes upon itself the nature of daylight, rising as the sun sets and shining until it rises, it also becomes an obstacle.

There are other obstacles as well, similar to these; we shall adduce poems for all of them in commenting upon the verse that begins,

> The speech out of much brooding over increased desire...[343]

Do you think it incorrect to say that obstacles occur both when there is a delay in marriage and when guarding increases? Do you think that because he said, "when there is a delay in marriage," one should interpret it to mean, "there is a breach in Stolen Love when there is a delay in marriage, if guarding increases?" Yes, but there is an "and" that has been elided from the phrase, "and when there is a delay in marriage," leaving the verse as it stands, worded only "when there is a delay in marriage." Since "and" is a clitic, it elides when it is placed at the end. How come? Grammar says,

> ...
> Elision of their endings and other particles occurring there:
> all such things are proper, they say.[344]

* * *

Verse 17.

> **False signs also belong there**
> **as signs for knowing of his coming.**

What does this declare, you ask? This also declares how obstacles develop in Stolen Love.

Its meaning:

False signs also—thinking things are signs also when they are not; we shall discuss how they come about later on.

belong there—this also pertains to the development of obstacles in Stolen Love.

as signs for knowing of his coming—signs that are supposed to let her know of his arrival, when they are caused by something else.

This is how it happens: One night, during a period when the hero is conducting night trysts, signs that he usually makes are brought out on their own, without his coming. They are: a mastwood fruit dropping into the water and the flushing of a covey of birds.

---

343 *The Study of Stolen Love*, 30.

344 *Tolkāppiyam: Iṭaiyiyal*, 3.

Here is how they come about without him: mastwood fruit falls when its stem ripens, when the breeze blows, or when birds shake its limb; and birds may be flushed out if they are startled, or when other birds fly in.

If she sees these things and thinks that he caused them, she goes to keep their rendezvous; when she realizes that he did not cause them after all, she returns to her house. Then when he actually does come, and does make his signs, she cannot go out a second time, can she? Why not? Her family would think, "They just went out a little while ago, didn't they? And here they go again!"[345] And they would follow to investigate.

Then again, if she does manage to leave the house, she speaks to him, but as though she were just addressing the moon, or perhaps a swan. She tells him, "We have already been here once, when we noticed some signals that you never caused." Here are some poems for that:

Informing The Hero Of The False Signs

You with pretty bangles
on your wrists!
At Cape Kaṉṉi of the king
    whose pointed lance
    glistens with blood,
    who destroyed enemy emperors
    with their clanging
    warrior's anklets
    at Āṟṟukkuṭi,
here in this pretty grove
by the shore,

not a single aṉṉam bird in the mastwood tree
has been able to sleep.
How come?[346]

My good girl!
You are like
sweet Tamil,
its poetry settled,
    that the king knows,
    the king who is the god of death
    upon the battlefield,
    whose lance and angry bow
    annihilated the machinations
    of another king

---

[345] The family notes the sortie of two people: the heroine and her friend.

[346] *Pāṇṭi-k-Kōvai*, 137.

with a sharp-tipped javelin,
and sent him off to heaven
from Pūlantai!
Here in our fresh
shore grove,

not one aṉṉam bird,
with pure, delicate feathers,
has slept a wink tonight.[347]

Long may you live,
you waves,
in your ocean!

Just don't wet
these aṉṉam birds,
whether they prefer
to roost in mastwoods
or settle in flowering branches—
they walk
just as my friend does,
with her dark hair
in braids.[348]

O, moon,
you with your
soothing rays!
He told her
he'd never cheat her,
yet he has left,
and her tender shoulders
bearing her cut conch armlets
have withered—

you have not glimpsed him yet
though you've been standing there,
all night long.[349]

When she speaks under any of these pretexts he returns home in grief. "It seems," he thinks to himself, "that they have waited up for me all night long: only someone who hasn't been asleep could know that other creatures have not slept. I guess they woke up thinking it was a signal from me: poor me! They came, but they went back home!" Nevertheless, he does not die. Why not, you

[347] *Pāṇṭi-k-Kōvai*, 138.

[348] Unidentified poem.

[349] Unidentified poem.

ask? He does not die because he thinks, "If I die, so will she!" Isn't that so? Here are some poems on his colloquy with his heart as he returns:

Conversing With His Heart, After Receiving
No Answer To His Signs

O, my heart,
you pitiful thing!
You hurt me profoundly
and eternally
when you thought
that girl
with her brilliant,
pretty brow
would be easy
to get to!
Now, like confused soldiers
    fighting Neṭumāṟaṉ
    on a battlefield,
    King Neṭumāṟaṉ
    with rutting elephants
    and a warrior's anklet,
    who vanquished Viḻiñam,

now you're going
to wear out.[350]

O, my heart,
you pitiful thing!
You hurt me eternally
when you thought
this girl
with her fragrant hair
would be easy
to get to!
Now, just like enemy soldiers
    and kings with their
    warrior's anklets
    and elephants
    that look like storm clouds
    when they set to war at Cēvūr,
    and would not honor
    the feet of Māṟaṉ,
    the Southern King,

---

[350] *Pāṇṭi-k-Kōvai*, 139.

now you're going
to wear out.[351]

Just like a mangy heron
standing in the breakers
on a seashore in the east,
craning its neck
to stare at ayirai fish
in Toṇṭi City's harbor,[352]
    that city of Poṟaiyaṉ
    with his strong chariots,
you search for
your impossible girl—that's
your disease:

O, my heart!
it looks like
that's your fate.[353]

Note these.

* * *

Verse 18.

> **That which is called a tryst, at night and in the day,**
> **is a place specifically mentioned, they say.**

What does this declare, you ask? It declares how trysts occur.
Its meaning:
That which is called a tryst—that which is said to be a tryst.
Although he said, **at night and in the day**, take it reversed; read "in the day and at night." Why? Because the night-tryst occurs after the day-tryst; this verse is to be commented upon with respect to the proper order of their conduct, which requires reversal of the word-order.

But then would he not have said, "That which is called a tryst, in the day and at night," you ask? That is the question; its answer is that the night tryst was mentioned first in the verse because it is ornamented with the fact of hiding, which is not as appropriate to a day-tryst as to a night-tryst.
is a place specifically mentioned, they say—a place that was named in such a way as to be clearly understood, say the professors.

---

[351] *Pāṇṭi-k-Kōvai*, 140.

[352] Toṇṭi is on a seashore in the west, all the way across Tamil Nadu.

[353] *Kuṟuntokai*, 128.

Who mentions this place, and to whom, you ask? Her friend names the place to the hero; here is how it works: When the hero followed her, entreating her to help him in his task, she spoke a few words to him to cool him down, and got the heroine to accept him. Now, when he encounters her friend again, she speaks to him with hidden implications, saying, "Come to such and such a place..." Here are some poems for that:

Naming The Trysting Place So The Hero Understands

Bees sing
with chimerical wings,
rich, dark shade spreads
on vast moonlike sands:
the place is as sweet
as the meanings
in really sweet
Tamil poems
are to literati—
it is as cool
as the grace
of the Potiyil Mountains
    of the famous
    King Māṟaṉ,
and swans flock there!

That's what it's like,
there where we play.[354]

The place
is surrounded by pools,
cool and pretty,
where lotus flowers bloom,
its white sands
are sprinkled with
immaculate mastwood blossoms,
swarming with bees
at Toṇṭi City
    of him who showered arrows
    on enemies at Kaṭaiyal!
It is just as sweet
as the soul of cool Tamil poems
is to literati.

---

[354] *Pāṇṭi-k-Kōvai*, 141.

That's what it's like,
there where we play.[355]

When he hears her say that, he understands that she has told him to go there, so he does. Her friend knows that he has gone, and brings the heroine to the trysting place. When they get there, she just says, "I'll go pick some red water lily blossoms: but there's a spirit over there, and you shouldn't come. Just wait here in this grove for a little while." So she makes the heroine wait as she leaves her. Here are some poems for that:

What She Says As She Hides Herself After Bringing The Heroine To The Trysting Place

You with cotton-soft feet!
I'll go and get
some pretty water lily blossoms
with bees, on pretty wings—
but, no—it's not a place
for you to go:
spirits mingle there
and live in those groves
where clouds settle
in the high Nēri Mountains
    of the king who used
    his enemy's chest
    as a sheath
    for his lance,
    at Pāḻi![356]

You with your fragrant garlands,
wait right here!
I'll go and get us
some glory lilies
that look like fire,
spreading,
but it wouldn't be good
for you to come—
there are spirits there,
in those hills
surrounded by the Kolli Mountains
    of our king
    with his army
    and grand cavalry,

[355] *Pāṇṭi-k-Kōvai*, 142.

[356] *Pāṇṭi-k-Kōvai*, 143.

who razed the lands
of the Cēraṉ at Pūlantai,
with its grand groves
where flowers
blossom![357]

Here, on this Red Hill
of him who sports
a warrior's anklet
and armlets,
who slaughtered
demons and reddened
the battleground,
the master
of red-shafted arrows
and elephants
with reddened
tusks,

glory lilies bloom in bouquets,
red as blood.[358]

She leaves when she has said this. But the heroine stays behind in the grove, where the hero meets her and unites with her. Her friend returns after their union and says, "Here—I've brought you some glory lilies that look like your hands, my lady! Please, be gracious enough to show no anger at my delay!" Then she takes the heroine away and reunites her with the flood of their friends. That, then, is how a daytime tryst comes about.

Yet the heroine languishes during a period when the hero comes to daytime trysts, because the amount of time that she does not see the hero is much greater than the amount of time she does see him; her heart hurts severely. So she addresses the sea, or the grove, or some birds, or her heart, like a baby crying in vain. Here is a poem in which she speaks like that:

Lamenting With The Heart

My heart left
with the grand chariot,
bedecked with beautiful gems,
of the seacoast lord
who came to this seaside grove
where precious jewels gleam,

---

[357] *Pāṇṭi-k-Kōvai*, 144.

[358] *Kuṟuntokai*, 1.

near the ocean at Cape Kaṉṉi
    of King Neṭumāṟaṉ,
    the great, sapphire-hued king
    who destroyed grand
    jewel-crowned kings
    warring at Pūlantai—

it left me![359]

If the hero overhears the heroine say that, he will decide to marry her; if her friend hears it, she will demand that the hero marry her. But she will even feel better just for having said it, even if no one overhears her: her anguish will diminish a bit from its previous level, just as some heat leaves a covered saucepan with the steam that escapes when you lift the lid.

Next, her friend sympathizes with the heroine as she languishes during this period of daytime trysts, when the intervals of not seeing him are longer than her occasions to see him. She muses, "Watching nearby birds used to make her feel better, but now they're gone. How can I console her?" While she speaks to herself, the hero is standing nearby; here are some poems for that:

Informing Him Of The Departure
Of Things That Console

When the sun set
behind that gorgeous
golden mountain
we call the Setting Mountain,
herons quit feeding
and left the dark backwaters
of Cape Kaṉṉi
    of the king
    whose scepter is
    perfect righteousness,
    Neṭumāṟaṉ
    with his warrior's anklet,
    Tirumāl, the Southern King!

She who walks like a swan
is hurt.[360]

At Toṇṭi City
    of our king,
    Māṟaṉ with his

[359] *Pāṇṭi-k-Kōvai*, 145.

[360] *Pāṇṭi-k-Kōvai*, 146.

warring anklets,
who watched enemy kings
drown in the glistening
pools of blood
that gathered
around Pūlantai,
there is a sea grove
where white storks stood feeding
on red legs in the dark water.

But with the setting of the sun
they lost their love for the grand backwaters—
they left her.[361]

A flock of birds in the sea grove
and their army of friends
betrayed our tender natured girl
to a fiery, spreading sunset—
they left her,
just as the foes
of the Lion to His Enemies,
whose fame spreads across the earth,
lost that day
on the seashore,
and left![362]

If the hero hears her say this, he thinks to himself, "My coming and acting like this must have caused her this anguish." He then decides to marry her, instead of prolonging this period. Take it that all of these things come under the rubric of the daytime tryst.

Next, here is how a nighttime tryst develops: Her friend is upset; she keeps thinking that the hero, who has been coming to daytime trysts, will see the light "today or tomorrow." But he doesn't, and continues his visiting for a long time. She is afraid that the heroine might die if her conduct became known to outsiders, and that he would then die as well. As a way to demand their marriage, she will first of all tell the hero that the heroine is shut up at home. She says that when the heroine's family suddenly shut the heroine up in her home, "mine kept me in my house, too!" At that, he too feels anguished. This is why she will tell him right away of the heroine's being kept in her house. Why? Because then when he is anguished, she can clarify matters by saying to him, "I just told you clearly what I had to!"

---

361 *Pāṇṭi-k-Kōvai*, 147.

362 *Pāṇṭi-k-Kōvai*, 148.

Next, when her friend demands their marriage, she has two ways of doing it: through suggestion, and openly.

Of those, here is how her demand for marriage develops through suggestion: She simply says, "My mother looked so pointedly at us!"

When she says that, the hero thinks to himself, "If she looked at them that way, it must mean that she's thinking of keeping her shut up in the house: then they won't be able to come out and play." He sees the light and attains her through marriage. Here are some poems on her mother looking pointedly at her:

Saying That Her Mother Knows

The girl
is like the Kāviri River country
  of him whose complexion
  is like that of the god
  colored as a stormcloud,
  the King of Pūḻi,
  who annihilated the battle skills
  of his enemies at Nelvēli,
  who cut down
  their cool, flowering lime tree,
  the Emperor
  the color of the waters,
  who stood upon white waves!

Our mother looked her beauty over,
then turned to me.[363]

She is like that ocean
of an army
  of him who vanquished
  angry foes
  who controlled their own
  faint-heartedness
  and rose up to fight,
  yet could not
  as they entered
  the Kaṭaiyal battlegrounds!
And her splendid smile
is like lush jasmine!

---

[363] *Pāṇṭi-k-Kōvai*, 149.

Mother looked at her young breasts,
budding in her chest,
then she looked at me.[364]

Or, she might use this method of informing him of the heroine's being shut up in her house:

Speaking Words Of Suggestion Using
Terraced Fields

Our field is ripe
on the slopes
of the sapphire mountain
where clouds settle
on peaks that rub
the handsome sky,
but it's dying,
it's being picked away
like the foreign kings
 on the battlefront
 of Māṟaṉ the Protector
 with his carp insignium,
 who conquered Pāḻi
 in the South!

Lord of these mountains,
tell us what to do.[365]

If the terraced field
gleams like gold
among the boulders
on the slopes
of the sapphire mountain,
it's because rain
poured down in sheets
with handsome flashes of lightning—
but now it's dying,
it's being plucked
 like the battlefield
 he conquered, as kings
 on the flanks
 perished before him!

---

[364] *Pāṇṭi-k-Kōvai*, 150.

[365] *Pāṇṭi-k-Kōvai*, 151.

Lord of these mountains,
how is she to keep
her beauty alive?[366]

Next, her friend may also speak directly to the hero, indicating that he is not to come there any more.

Next, she may also utter this theme as a colloquy with a kino tree; if she does, she must know that the hero is there and will overhear. Here are some poems for that:

Her Friend Using Humble Words In Addressing A Kino Tree

They have set the proper day
to harvest our millet field
on pretty, bright Mount Potiyil
    of the Supreme One
    with his righteous scepter
    and widely heralded
    grand renown,
    who triumphed
    that day at Cennilam,
    when enemy kings drowned
    in pools of blood
    filled with
    waves!

You, young kino tree,
with blossoms filled with fragrance,
no more will we take leave of you![367]

You, kino tree
in the Kolli Mountains
    of him who carved his carp
    into the golden mountains,
    the destroyer of enemies,
    the Southern King,
    who took the victory
    when he caused the destruction
    of an invincible army
    of the King of Vañci
    at Kōṭṭāṟu,
    and hurled his mace
    upon the crown

[366] *Pāṇṭi-k-Kōvai*, 152.

[367] *Pāṇṭi-k-Kōvai*, 153.

of the king
of the gods!

No more will we
be taking leave of you.[368]

She may also speak like this:

If we had plucked tender buds
from the kino tree
that day
in the Kolli Mountains
of him who built a mountain
with the corpses
of long-trunked elephants
as they floated by,
elephants of those
who waged wicked war
at Naṟaiyāṟu,
our grand terraced field
would have survived,
wouldn't it?

You, with your fine forehead:
you did not do so well.[369]

She may also speak like this:

When our lord
of the mountains
reaches the slopes
of these Kolli Mountains
of him who crushed kings
with shoulders like round rocks
and made them flee,
who saw the misery
of their titled women
in their finely woven
garlands—
when he sees the stubble
in this terraced field,
when he stands here
in sorrow, clutching
his victorious bow,

[368] *Pāṇṭi-k-Kōvai*, 154.

[369] *Pāṇṭi-k-Kōvai*, 155.

will the lush kino grove say,
"There, there, don't feel so bad!"[370]

She may also speak like this:

Great astrologers they were
who set the right day
to harvest this beautiful
terraced field
in the cool Kolli Mountains
    of our king
    who donned the grand wreath
    of victory
    upon his golden crown
    when those who came
    with wreaths of war
    died at Pūlantai!
But it is our girl
with her dark eyes
who guards
that field—

how can we still call them "golden,"
those kinos?[371]

She may also speak like this:

They live on the slopes,
where clouds settle,
of those Potiyil Mountains
that dip into the sky,
    mountains of him
    to whom victory
    is just a way of life,
    whose righteous scepter
    is set in truth,
and there they felled
the sandalwood trees—
but they missed
the kino that settled the day
for her to leave,

---

370 *Pāṇṭi-k-Kōvai*, 156.

371 *Pāṇṭi-k-Kōvai*, 157. The word used here for astrologer also means "kino tree."

this girl whose mound of love
seems like the fresh hood
of a dancing snake![372]

If the hero understands clearly what is going on when he is told of the heroine's being shut up at home, he will hold her friend's hand and say, "I will marry her on such and such a day. Comfort her until then: I entrust her to you."

But as he takes her hand, her friend thinks he is swearing a vow: she thinks so because people in the world solemnify vows by touching Brahmins, cows, or women. "Wouldn't it be enough for you just to say you will marry her? Do you need to take a vow?" she asks, "Isn't it only liars and opportunists who take such vows? Is swearing really called for among people who never speak anything but the truth? And if even you lie, how can truth ever take root in this world?" Here are some poems for that:

Her Friend Addressing The Hero When He Takes A Vow

Lord of these beautiful mountains!
If falsehood appears in you,
and your righteousness fails
concerning this girl
with her immaculate jewelry,
and her shining, collyrium eyes,
who is like the southern lands
    of Neṭumāṟaṉ
    with his well-oiled lance,

then is truth to disappear
from this wide world,
leaving not a trace?[373]

You with your rich,
fragrant wreath,
swarming with bees!
If you lie to her
who is like the Vaiyai River
    of him who simply spoke
    to make the Cēraṉ king

[372] *Pāṇṭi-k-Kōvai*, 158. See the note to the previous poem, *Pāṇṭi-k-Kōvai* 157, on the dual meaning of the kino tree.

[373] *Pāṇṭi-k-Kōvai*, 159.

head for the mountains[374]
from Cēvūr
with its dark
ocean waters,

who will be left in this world
to speak truth?[375]

Lord of this city
by cool lakes
where a little kingfisher sleeps
on the low hanging branch
of a murdah tree
after a meal
of crayfish,
while girls from the city
pound white sand,
heaped up like fish eggs,
with swift,
silver capped pestles,
their thin waists swaying
from side to side
like vines,
as they sing
of the wealth
of their families
under the shade
of river portia boughs!

Really noble men will accomplish
what they want—
they know their nobility,
and seek unswerving righteousness
and wealth:
should even their hearts,
which know no desire,
want for something,
they control their desire,
using wisdom they have learned
as their goad—
such is the conduct
of the great.
Examine the lives
of these people:

---

374 The reference is to the practice of defeated kings starving themselves to death in mountain forests to absolve their dynasty of disgrace.

375 *Pāṇṭi-k-Kōvai*, 160.

if falsehood appears
mingled with these qualities
even in people like yourself,

then where is there truth
in this world?[376]

When she says that, he will think to himself, "I must not delay, since she took it as a vow when I held her hand and said that I entrusted the heroine to her." Later on, he will marry the heroine.

But on the other hand, if he does not understand clearly what is going on, he will say, "I shall come to nighttime trysts as well; then I will marry her." Her friend points out the dangers in nighttime trysting, and rejects the idea. How does she reject it, you ask? She says, "There are all these dangers: snakes, thunder, tigers, bears, and white-tusked elephants! How could she stand to have you come through the ups and downs of those difficult mountain trails in the pitch dark of midnight with nothing but your javelin to protect you?" She thinks to herself that if this cools the hero down, he will most likely attain her through marriage.

In the end, she agrees to the nighttime tryst because she fears that otherwise he might die in his anguish. Once she has agreed, she asks the hero, "What kinds of flowers do they have in your country? And what kinds of sandal paste? What kinds of trees do they play under?"

When he hears this, he thinks to himself, "She has always refused me before, but now she's speaking with a purpose." He also replies, "And what kinds of flowers do they have in your country? What kinds of sandal paste? And what trees do they play under?"

When he asks these things, her friend replies, "We wear lotus and kino blossoms, and we use sandalwood paste in our make up. We play beneath mastwood trees." Here are some poems for that:

Naming The Trysting Place

In these cloud capped
Potiyil Mountains
    of the king
    with a warrior's anklet
    and elephants that pay
    no heed to their hitching posts,
    who raised his thunderbolt banner
    to rub out kings
    who did not agree with him

---

[376] *Akanāṉūṟu*, 286.

one day in the past,
we use sandalwood paste,
our flowers are pretty glory lilies,
and the cool grove where we play
is filled with divinely pleasant
mastwood trees,
with flowers
blooming in bunches,
like fire.[377]

The flowers we put
in our dark hair
are pretty glory lilies—
our make up
is sandalwood paste
from the cool and beautiful
Potiyil Mountains
of the Emperor
who took up his sharp lance
to weaken his foes,
who fled from Kaṭaiyal!

And we play in a grove
where mastwood buds burst their fetters
and bloom like fire.[378]

She names these things because this theme occurs in the mountain country mode; she will name the appropriate things for other modes as well.

When she utters that poem, he realizes, "All right: she seems to be telling me to come and do those things." Later, he puts on those flowers and that sandal paste, and sets a date to play beneath that tree. Her friend gathers that he is coming, and she speaks; here are some poems for that:

Her Friend Realizes His Coming, And She Speaks

Here in this grove
by the slopes of the Kolli Mountains
of the king
who took up
his bright, splitting lance,
to make those
who rode in upon

[377] *Pāṇṭi-k-Kōvai*, 161.

[378] *Pāṇṭi-k-Kōvai*, 162.

beautiful black elephants
die on that day
at Vallam,
great, sapphire colored peacocks
cannot sleep in the memorable,
colorful kino tree
filled with golden
blossoms!

They are perturbed,
but why?[379]

In these precious Kolli Mountains
of the Lion to His Enemies,
the king with reddened eyes,
who but grasped his lance
to make warring kings
wearing long, clasped
warrior's anklets
flee Kaṭaiyal,
here in this green grove
where talented beetles and bees
sound like music,
the peacocks
and their mates
haven't slept
a wink—

what were they
doing?[380]

When she realizes through all this that the hero is coming, her friend brings the heroine: she just says to her, "Let's see if the lotus has bloomed! Let's see if the spreading jasmine has budded!" Here are some poems for that:

Taking Her To The Trysting Place

You good girl,
like a peacock
from the town of Pūḻi!
Come along to the green,
flowering forest lands
by Vañci City
of the Pāṇṭiyaṉ

---

[379] *Pāṇṭi-k-Kōvai*, 163.

[380] *Pāṇṭi-k-Kōvai*, 164.

who vanquished his enemies
at Pāḻi,
the Lion to His Enemies,
the king who protects
the world girt by the seas!
We can pick huge blooms
from potted water lilies there,

that blossom
like your eyes![381]

You, there, with bracelets
on your wrists!
You, you're like
the sweet Tamil
of him who destroyed
the kings who reveled
in openly opposing him
at Cēvūr,
the Scholar,
the Emperor
who cultivates
so many glories!

Let's go and pick jasmine buds,
pretty, like the sharp teeth
you've sprouted in your mouth![382]

She says these things as she brings the heroine to the trysting place, where she leaves her just as she had done for the daytime tryst, standing all by herself. The hero meets her there and unites with her. After their union, her friend returns and takes her away. That is how the night tryst develops.

Why did he go to the trouble of saying "That which is called a tryst, at night and in the day," instead of simply "a tryst, at night and in the day," you ask? It is a signal of the importance attached to the tryst; he put it that way to indicate that the trysting place is such that

...
beetles, dragon flies, and bees
with lines upon their tails,
sound like lute strings
plucked in harmony
...[383]

---

[381] *Pāṇṭi-k-Kōvai*, 165.

[382] *Pāṇṭi-k-Kōvai*, 166.

[383] Unidentified fragment.

He said it to intimate that the tryst encompasses within itself experiences of all the five senses; that it is set in a beautiful place, amid many types of trees; that people outside that place can hardly see in, yet people on the inside can easily see out; and that it is of such a nature as to kindle desire even in the hearts of those noble ones who have renounced desire.

But then, he said simply "a place mentioned," instead of "a place mentioned for someone to understand." Why, you ask? That was done to explain that there are four verb-phrase forms. What are they, you ask? They are those of the agent, the causal agent, the instrumental agent, and the patient agent.

Of those:

Agent: the house that the carpenter built; the sword that the blacksmith made

Causal Agent—making the commander the agent: the reservoir that the king excavated; the temple that the king built; and so forth

Instrumental Agent: the sword cuts; the dagger pricks; this cauldron will cook four measures of rice; and so forth

Patient Agent: the porch was mopped; the vessel was washed; the tree was cut

The phrase "a place specifically mentioned" functions as a patient agent. But is there a rule for calling something of this sort a patient agent, you ask? There is:

> Taking something that was done and calling it something that did,
> thus giving it agency, is a tradition common in usage.[384]

But still should he not have constructed the verse to read "those which are called trysts," since it describes two types of trysts, daytime and nighttime? Not so: he said, "That which is called a tryst" in consideration of the unity of the location.

* * *

Verse 19.

Night tryst does not transgress the limits of the home.

What does this declare, you ask? In the above verse he noted that there are two types of trysts; of those two, he here declares where nighttime trysts occur.

Its meaning:

Night tryst—the location of a tryst at night.

does not transgress the limits of the home—does not leave the home.

In saying this, he means that it does not occur outside.

Note that others also have said,

---

[384] *Tolkāppiyam: Vinaiyiyal*, 49.

Nighttime tryst does not transgress the limits of the home,
by the sayings that make one understand.[385]

When he says that nighttime trysts do not transgress the limits of the home, he implies that daytime trysts do. Why? Because the statement "A nightbird does not eat" clinches the fact that a daybird does eat.

Next "nighttime tryst" becomes "night tryst" here, simply because of prosodic rules. Why? Because he has said,

When part of the ending after a short syllable elides,
it is proper in poetry for a short 'u' to become evident.[386]

* * *

Verse 20.

Even if a day tryst transgresses, they do not object.

What does this declare, you ask? It declares the location of the daytime tryst.
Its meaning:
a day tryst—the location of the daytime tryst.
Even if (it) **transgresses, they do not object**—even if it should transgress, they find no fault with it.

Transgression means exceeding something: whether you say transgressing or exceeding, it is all the same thing—to exceed unity is to become many.

At one time it may occur in a kino grove, and at another time it may occur in a cottonwood grove, if it is in the mountain-country mode.

If it is in the seaside mode, it may occur one time in a sea grove of mastwood trees, and at another time in a sea grove of screwpine.

Keep this in mind when you comment upon the other modes as well, since he has said,

Daytime tryst unions are many[387]

By the word "even" in "Even if a day tryst transgresses," he emphasizes that daytime trysts also must be unitary. Why, you ask? Because even the girls who take her to the grove are on his side: they go off and play, thus leaving them to do as they please.

---

[385] Unidentified verse.

[386] *Tolkāppiyam: Eḻuttatikāram, Uyirmayaṅkiyal*, 32.

[387] Unidentified verse.

Next, in response to people who think, “Who knows, unlike last time maybe this season she will take her into a sea grove,” note that there must be many groves, because she wittingly goes into many types of groves.

* * *

Verse 21.

> **Other than the place of the tryst that transgresses the home at night, there is no meeting the hero for the heroine.**

What does this declare, you ask? It finds various places established for nighttime trysts and declares their differences. Above, when he said, “Night tryst does not transgress the limits of the home,” he meant that the hero will not meet her if their meeting place does not lie within the limits of her home. He implied that that trysts could be assigned to those other places as well, and this verse removes some such previous implications.

Its meaning:

that transgresses the home at night—which leaves the home during nighttime.

Other than the place of the tryst—other than the place that was mentioned.

there is no meeting the hero for the heroine—the heroine does not meet the hero.

Thus it is to occur within the limits of her home, but not within the limits of her house. It means that the tryst can take place on a handmade playhill, in a park, in a flowery arbor, on a playground, in similar places near these, or other places, but not in the kitchen, the granary, the storehouse, the upstairs salon, a bedroom, the queen’s apartments, or the dance hall. Thus it means, “Let the nighttime trysting places not be as varied as they are for daytime trysts.”

So what would be lost if the tryst were to occur inside the house, you ask? The house is to be thought of as a sort of temple, since it is where the parents live. Moreover, it is not suited to trysts because it is difficult to enter or leave secretly. But to support those who would say it can occur there, you cite the poem,

> ...
> the hero reached
> the inside
> of her pure home
> ...[388]

do you? Well, such poems are not properly interior poems; they come under the “interior-exterior” classification. Note that others also have said,

---

388 Unidentified fragment.

There is one night tryst that comes up:
It occurs in a place where the speech of people in the house can be heard,
but where the activities of coming and going do not exist,
in the boundary areas beyond the house—it is excellent;
If it is interior-exterior, it shall be reversed.[389]

* * *

Verse 22.

Gesturing and gossiping are Stolen Love.

What does this declare, you ask? It declares that such and such are affairs of the heart that happen to them during a long course of the conduct called Stolen Love.

Its meaning:

Gesturing and gossiping are Stolen Love—no one else thinks these things have occurred; that is why it is called Stolen Love: it is stolen because those who engage in it are the only people who know about it.

Gesturing means the sprouting of buds,
gossiping means the occurrence of words;
Gesturing means the occurrence of words,
gossiping means the household knows;
Gesturing means the household knows,
gossiping means the neighborhood knows;
Gesturing means the neighborhood knows,
gossiping means the quarter knows;
Gesturing means the quarter knows,
gossiping means the city knows;
Gesturing means the city knows,
gossiping means the province knows;
Gesturing means the province knows,
gossiping means the nation knows.

That is inappropriate. Why? What they called gesturing turns into gossiping, and vice versa: they do not demonstrate the difference between the two, showing how this is gesturing and that gossiping; yet those two terms were employed precisely because of some differentiation between them.

What, then, is the correct commentary, you ask? What he called gesturing is an expression just budding out, without any words: one cannot know what it is about. But what he called gossiping is spoken clearly, in order to say that something of a certain nature occurred between such and such a man and such and such a woman. The tiny bud of expression grows into a full bud and

[389] Unidentified verse.

eventually blossoms. Gossiping is distinguished by noting that it is the state into which the full bud opens, exposing the stamen and the ovary of the blossom.

When they have been continuing this conduct for a long time, they consider other people, who have been keeping aloof from them. They think, "It seems as though they will look into our behavior!" It is the way of the world for people with things on their consciences to have such thoughts. Yet since it comes from God, no other people will ever really know about their conduct, will they?

When do "gesturing and gossiping" occur, you ask? They occur when there is excessive guarding, since that is when the protagonists suspect, "Won't our conduct become openly known as we prolong the course of our Stolen Love?"

"But," a student asks, "if I took this situation, in which the actual conduct of Stolen Love disappears because of such suspicions, as belonging to Marital Love, that wouldn't be correct, since he has not married her yet; and if I make it an activity of Stolen Love, that would not be correct either, since nobody does anything. How should I categorize it?" Take the state of gesturing and gossiping as belonging to Stolen Love. This is inappropriate. Why? Since he has said,

> Exposure indeed, when explained,
> is the effect when such people know
> as father, mother, and brothers.[390]

he implies that as long as such people do not know about it, it is called Stolen Love.

* * *

Verse 23.

> **Even after it is exposed, there is speech.**

What does this declare, you ask? It declares what happens after the occurrence of gesturing and gossiping appears in their minds.

Its meaning:

Even after it is exposed, there is speech—take it inverted, like this: "After it is exposed, there is still speech;" speech here means marriage negotiations.

Saying that speech is still appropriate means that there is yet something else to be said. What is that, you ask? Her elopement with him is also an appropriate poetic theme.

We shall describe how it can be appropriate. It concerns the heroine and her friend: they figure there must be many people who know about her conduct, since they think, "Both of us know what's happening." So her friend goes to the

---

[390] *The Study of Stolen Love*, 26.

place where he has been meeting the heroine, and says to herself, "Even if he shows up suddenly now, I will not have him come any more."

Then she does meet the hero; she circumambulates him saying, "The graciousness you have bestowed upon her has become gossip; many people know about it." Here are some poems for that:

Informing Him Of Gossip

Lord!
She is like Vañci City
    of the Gift of the Gods,
    who has horses and chariots,
    who wears palmyra and neem blossoms
    upon his jewel encrusted crown,
    the king
    who muddied his lance
    with the fresh, wet fat
    of soldiers who fought him
    in multitudes
    only to die
    at Pāḻi!

But the precious grace you granted her
has ripened into gossip.[391]

Lord,
with your cool garland
where bees sing
just like maruḷ songs!
In this cool grove
at Cape Kaṉṉi
    of him who triumphed
    and made his foes climb
    dense, dark mountains
    at Pūlantai,
    the Mind-Born King,
    who stands as the Ultimate,

the grace you granted to this girl
with her choice jewels
has ripened into gossip.[392]

---

[391] *Pāṇṭi-k-Kōvai*, 165.

[392] *Pāṇṭi-k-Kōvai*, 166. See also footnote 374, on page 165, on enemy kings starving themselves to death.

Lord!
Your graciousness
toward my friend,
with her dark braids
who came to your trysts
in that seaside grove
of mastwood trees—
your graciousness has ripened
into gossip.

It's as noisy
as the boulevards
where chariots clatter,
where bees buzz endlessly
at the mouths of wine jars,
there in the town of Ārkkāṭu
where fluttering banners
line the avenues,
the Cōḻa town
with pure gold jewels,
and elephants,
their bells clanging—

These gossips say
this wise young pair
is not righteous—
and it's spreading!

If she lost her sweet, young life now,
it would, for sure, be terribly bitter.[393]

She invents more things after she says this, going on to say further, "You have been behaving this way because you just don't understand virtue: if you did, you would have married her and kept all this from coming up. Besides, there are other men who have come with her breast price—they're just waiting to adorn her in gold and attain her through marriage!" Here are some poems for that:

Telling Him Of Marriage Negotiations

She, you know,
is like Cape Kaṉṉi
  of the king whose lance
  excels in war—
  it played
  with his enemies' fat

---

[393] *Naṟṟiṇai*, 227.

at Neṭuṅkaḷam,
fenced round
by beautiful waters!
Lord, with your great,
gleaming warrior's anklet,
other men have come, you know:
their grand drums
sound like thunder—
they want to adorn her
in gold!

What do you think
about that?[394]

Lord of those mountains
with groves that rub the heavens!
Here in rich Kūṭal City
of Neṭumāṟaṉ,
the king with a sword
and a canopy with strings
of shining pearls,
wedding drums will sound
this morning
in the courtyard
of her elegant home—
they have already decided the future
of this innocent girl
whose eyes surpass javelins![395]

She is like Pukār City
of him who crushed foes
skilled in the arts of war
at Pūlantai:
her breasts
are filling out
her bodice.
But others have come,
beating their drums—
it sounds like thunder:
they're thinking of marrying her
to somebody else!

---

[394] *Pāṇṭi-k-Kōvai*, 167.

[395] *Pāṇṭi-k-Kōvai*, 168.

Lord, you in your handsome garland—
what do you think of that?[396]

Lord of your mountains
dipping sky!
In great Kūṭal City
of the Lion to His Enemies,
the patron of Tamil,
which scholars study
in ancient texts,
there in the courtyard
of her elegant home,
they will beat
upon booming kettledrums:
they'll make their decision
by the end of the day

about the girl whose tender shoulders
are even as shoots of bamboo![397]

She also speaks like this:

Speaking Of The Adornment In Gold

Mountain country lord,
decide today
what you're going to do!
You know what it means
to the innocent girl
who wears bunches of delicate flowers
in her hair,
she who is like
Kūṭal City in the South,
the city of Neṭumāṟaṉ
with his elephants
like mountains,
and his righteous scepter!

Will wedding drums sound all day tomorrow
in our town hall if you don't?
I wonder.[398]

What shall we do,
O, you who are so like a kind god!

---

396 *Pāṇṭi-k-Kōvai*, 169.

397 *Pāṇṭi-k-Kōvai*, 170.

398 *Pāṇṭi-k-Kōvai*, 171.

They have tied
the engagement thread
on our girl of fine family!
They agreed to a man
from the lands of waters
in the South,
    lands of the king
    whose shoulders
    are like round rocks,
    the king who triumphed
    at Nar̲aiyār̲u!

Will wedding drums and right-whorled conches
sound in the courtyard of her many-storied home, lined with pennants?
I wonder.[399]

When the hero is told this he exclaims, "What have I done!"

"Don't ask me," replies her friend, "You are supposed to know what's right: do it! There is no way I can discern these things as well as you, since it is written,

Even if they are of sharp intellect, and familiar with the texts,
women's knowledge is mostly ignorance.[400]

Besides, I am an errand girl; I'm supposed to do what you tell me. It would never do for me to tell you what to do."

Here is a poem for that:

Relating The Offer Of Breast Price

Her family won't even take
those southern lands
with swollen, resounding waters
    of the Scholar
    with his flashing lance
    who won the Battle of Pāl̲i
as price for the budding breasts
of this innocent girl
whose eyes bees mistake
for fresh flowers before them,
as they draw near!

How can I tell you
what to do?[401]

---

[399] *Pāṇṭi-k-Kōvai*, 172.

[400] Unidentified verse.

[401] *Pāṇṭi-k-Kōvai*, 173.

When the hero hears this, he says, "But if I should decide to elope, could she stand the fiery desert, without water or shade? I wonder."

"Even if the desert burns so badly," replies her friend, "my lady would find it sweet, if she's with you." Here are some poems for that:

Declaring The Heroine's Love

Hot though they be, hot
as the lance of the King of the South,
    that lance that vanquished
    crowned monarchs
    on the battlefield,
    the lance of the king
    whose milkwhite canopy
    covers the earth
    and grants it shade,
    the lance of Māraṉ
    with his jewel encrusted crown,
    whose elephants
    are like storm clouds,
deserts would feel cool,
cool as his righteous scepter

to that girl who is like a liana,
if she is traveling with you![402]

Even if they're fiery hot,
    hot as the battlefields of him
    who drives off his foes,
    the king with the warrior's anklet
    and fiery lance, the king
    who vanquished and caused the deaths
    of embattled kings with their
    anklets of war,
    there at Kaṭaiyal,
    rich with the waters
    of irrigation canals,
deserts would feel cool, very cool
like the shade from his canopy,

to our girl with her perfect jewels,
if she's traveling with you![403]

---

[402] *Pāṇṭi-k-Kōvai*, 174.

[403] *Pāṇṭi-k-Kōvai*, 175.

When he hears this, he says, "Then I have decided to elope: you must tell her."

"Good!" she returns, "I shall let our lady know what our lord has so graciously done." Circling the hero, she goes then to the heroine and divines what is in her heart.

"Our lady," she says, "Our lord is thinking of eloping with you! What do you think?"

Now there are only two alternatives for the heroine, when she hears this: approval or denial of his wish. If she honors him and elopes, she loses her modesty; yet if she declines, she loses fidelity. Of those two, which type of woman will she be, you ask? She has both modesty and fidelity, does she not? Of the two, fidelity is the stronger. Why is it stronger, you ask? Since he has said,

> Modesty is more important than life; fidelity
> with faultless perception is even more important than modesty,[404]

she would never think of letting her fidelity go to ruin, even if it meant her modesty were ruined. So she agrees to elope, as she inclines her head and stands scratching the earth with her big toe: standing like that amounts to agreeing. Here are some poems for that:

Lamenting The Ruination Of Modesty

On this wide earth
protected forever
    by the righteous scepter
    of Neṭumāṟaṉ
    whose warrior's anklet
    all enemy kings see
    as they bow down,
    their strength
    and enmity
    sapped,
here, my modesty
which never forsook me
wherever I went,
my modesty,
that played when I played,
and always tagged along with me—
it's gone!

---

[404] *Tolkāppiyam: Kaḷaviyal*, 23.

Fidelity has overtaken it,
and my modesty groans yet again.[405]

Ah, how my modesty sat still
and suffered all with me—
now, as when sweet currents
wear away a bright little
sandy riverbank
rife with white blossoms
of sugar cane,
until it crumbles,
she has born
all she can:

Love has worn her out,
she can no longer stay.[406]

It is like saying this, as well:

In little groups
and in crowds, leering
at me out of the corners
of their eyes, and touching
their fingers to their noses
in contempt, my neighbors
are whispering!
And mother! She
struck me!

But tonight
he's coming
in his fine chariot
he's forcing fast horses
to fly even faster,
horses whose beautiful backs
have the smells of the flowers
they brushed in the backwaters,

and I have decided

to go with him.

This stupid village
can just sit here
and gossip![407]

---

405 *Pāṇṭi-k-Kōvai*, 176.

406 *Kuṟuntokai*, 149.

407 *Naṟṟiṇai*, 149.

And so she agrees. Her friend understands and goes off to see her mother. Her mother, it happens, had also noticed the changes affecting her daughter, but she could not figure out what was going on—her luck must have deserted her just then! She says, "Dear, how did this change come over my daughter? Tell me."

To that, her friend replies, "There is a little something that even I know about," and she stands with honor as we have already noted in commenting upon the verse that begins,

> Those fit for her friend to the foster mother...[408]

And so she stands with honor.

The foster mother exclaims with a joyous heart, "Look! My daughter surely is wise!" She then stands with honor to the heroine's real mother, who in turn stands with honor to her father and elder brothers, her own heart content. When they hear of her wisdom and decorum, they incline their heads silently, and their hearts rejoice.

Would she really phrase it in such glorious terms, you ask? She certainly would describe it in an extremely glorious way. Moreover, she also makes the hero postpone the elopement: she says to him, "Why would she want to go and suffer along those waterless desert trails?" Here are some poems for speaking like that:

Causing The Departing Hero To Tarry

She does have shoulders
like shoots of bamboo
from the cool, sweet
Potiyil Mountains
    of the King of the South
    who strung his bow
    to rub out those
    who came riding
    high-stepping horses
    and battled in enmity
    at Pāḻi!
And she does want
to go with you

but when she thought of her friends here,
her eyes rolled, and filled with tears![409]

---

[408] *The Study of Stolen Love*, 14.

[409] *Pāṇṭi-k-Kōvai*, 177.

At dawn
when the dark
was dissipating,
and the noise of the butter churn
sounded through the stable yard,
its worn-out rod, eaten up
by the old rope,
rattling in the cream pot,
belly full, filled
with the aroma of woodapple,
she hid her body
and slipped off
her anklets
with their
rattling stones;
she put up
her pretty little
striped gameballs.
"Oh my," she thought,
"if my friends see
these things, they'll feel awful!"

Yes, she does want to elope with you,
yet her eyes cried, out of control.[410]

The hero puts off the elopement when he hears this, and her friend says to him, "Decide to marry her tomorrow. Marriage would be splendid for you!" Then she leaves him and returns to the heroine.

Or, she may postpone their elopement if she says, "We can elope, but only if the desert is shady and cool, and if there's enough water!" In that case, the hero will decide that very day to hurry on with their marriage.

That is how it can be appropriate to speak even after their conduct has been exposed.

Next, here is an interpretation of the word "even" in the verse, bringing out their elopement: If standing with honor fails, then her friend will glory in bringing her to him and getting them to elope, just as she used to bring them together for nighttime trysts. In this case, her friend speaks poems on the theme of entrusting the heroine to him. Here are some poems for that:

Entrusting

Lord, she is like
the Vaiyai River lands
  of the joyful God of Love,

---

[410] *Naṟṟiṇai*, 12.

the husband of the River Ganga,
the king who fought the battle
of great, well defended Maṇaṟṟimaṅkai!
Think of her as a trust
in the palm of your hand
and be gracious to her,

even when her hair turns gray,
and her breasts sag.[411]

Lord of the land
where great mountains
dip into the sky!
This innocent girl,
you see, like a vine,
has a pair of large eyes
that excel in killing,
like javelins
of the Emperor of Emperors
the Scholar
with his grand chariots
and his army of archers
who vanquished his foes
at Naṟaiyāṟu!

Never despise her, sir,
even when her hair grays
and her delicate breasts
droop.[412]

She took you at your word,
and good words they were, and true,
just as the victorious Colas—
they deck out their grand chariots
with jewels, and oh their sweet wine
cuts hard—just as they trusted
to the lances they captured
from Paḻaiyaṉ, Lord of Pēr,
with his painted elephants,
when they pacified
the people of Koṅku...

My lord of this town
dazzling with flowers,
take good care of her!

---

[411] *Pāṇṭi-k-Kōvai*, 178.

[412] *Pāṇṭi-k-Kōvai*, 179.

May you never forsake her,
even when her pretty,
highset breasts begin to sag,
or when her fine,
long hair, cascading
like sapphires down
her golden body,
is braided in with gray.[413]

Is there anyone
who doesn't appreciate
fine, grand deeds?
Yet though she
has done but one
good work with you,
let your love grow,
and forget your irritations,
care for her and value her:
Sir! You, from
the good mountains where
deer with delicate steps
hunt young leaves on
tall bamboo stalks
and lie down to sleep
on those cool,
fragrant slopes—

without you
she'd have
no one.[414]

Sir, you from the seashore,
where winter winds whip
the water and make it look
like scattered screwpine buds,
like roe sprayed on a dark
water lily blossom—
a baby still opens its mouth
and wails, "Mommy!"
even when its mother
turns cross and slaps it,
and so it is with you
and my friend:
whether you hurt her

---

413 *Naṟṟiṇai*, 10.

414 *Kuṟuntokai*, 115.

or caress her in kindness,
it's your bounds
she lives within,

she has no one else
to weed out her sufferings.[415]

Without you she has no one,
and without her
with those mascara eyes,
my mother has no one,
nor would I!

Lord of the land of grand mountains!
Please, don't forget.[416]

She will leave him then, once she has spoken this sort of Entrustment.

But it is really right for her to leave? Wouldn't she rather stay, you ask? She is not one to hang around and worry about her problems; she leaves in order to have expressed all of this in a cultured manner. But she has told the foster mother, and wouldn't she be able to express it all in a cultured manner, you ask? One would not be as convinced by what the foster mother says as by what the heroine's friend says. Why? Because she is known to have been their constant companion.

Next, here are some poems for the hero to speak as he comforts the heroine and leads her away:

Gently Leading Her Away

You whose words sound
like music,
walk softly!
People love coming
to the groves humming
with bees,
and to the rivers
with sand as black
as sapphires,
in the woodlands
we shall travel through,
like the grand lands
of the Vaiyai River
    of the king who fought

415 *Kuṟuntokai*, 397.

416 Unidentified poem.

to make his foes perish
in the battlefield.[417]

My girl with your pretty brow
walk on, it won't hurt—
The green, fragrant
forest, where bees sing
on fresh blossoms
surrounded by leaf buds,
breathes beauty
like the grand
Vaiyai River lands
of the King of the South
who took up his sharp lance
and mounted his elephant
with small and tender eyes
just to fold up
those who opposed him
and fought at Pāḻi
in the South.[418]

We took your pretty shoulders,
tender like shoots of bamboo,
and banished from them
misery and bewilderment,
just as zealots see
the gods they entreat
when they tackle their tasks,
and show no faintness
of heart.

In the woodlands
there are cool, fragrant groves
where cuckoos coo
in joy and feed on mango buds,
and on our path
we shall pass through many
a little town, so rub
some pretty, glistening
leaf buds from a puṉku tree,
with blossoms like puffed rice,
upon your golden spotted breasts,
where the goddess of pride resides—
stay on where you find shade,

[417] *Pāṇṭi-k-Kōvai*, 180.

[418] *Pāṇṭi-k-Kōvai*, 181.

and build yourself a playhouse
when you find some sand:

you can walk with me,
it won't hurt.[419]

He leads the heroine away while he is saying this, as though she were bringing all her friends with her.

Now here are some poems that people speak when they meet them along the way:

Voicing A Dissuasion From Traveling

Lord
with shoulders
like rocks!
The hot sun has disappeared
behind the mountains,
    like kings who opposed
    him whose pearl canopy
    is decked out with
    garlands of flowers
    and the buds of leaves,
    full of bees,
    him who is the
    Lion to His Enemies,
    him who wields
    the righteous scepter,
    him who wears
    the beautiful, trembling
    warrior's anklet,
and the girl is suffering—
her body is weak,

Stay here in our little town—
you can press on later.[420]

Young man
with your sharp javelin—
the girl
is like Kūṭal City
    of the Scholar
    who destroyed all
    who opposed him,

---

[419] *Naṟṟiṇai*, 9.

[420] *Pāṇṭi-k-Kōvai*, 182.

until they drowned
in blood
at Neṭuṅkaḷam,
but she has grown very thin,
and the brilliant sun
has already disappeared
behind the mountains:
Our little town
is quite close.

What would you lose if you stayed
in our little village
for a while before you press on?[421]

You, with your flower garland
upon your chest!
There is no town but ours
anywhere close by,
and the hot, angry sun
has dropped his rays;
the mountain rivers
are hard to cross
and very far away,
and your girl is young
and tender natured,

please, stay a while
before you go.[422]

People who see them along the road may also speak thus:

Declaring The Proximity Of A City

Keep going, you can make it today
to the fields where carp leap
like eyes jumping from pretty
lotus ponds,
where bloom the faces
and the mouths
of youths,
in that land of waters
in the South
of the King of the South
who fought at Nelvēli,
and rubbed his enemies out—

---

[421] *Pāṇṭi-k-Kōvai*, 183.

[422] *Aiṅkuṟunūṟu, Iṇaippu*, 5.

you'll make it there today,
with her![423]

Later, when the foster mother realizes that her ward has eloped, she feels confused and terribly worried. "She must have had this in mind," she says, "when she spoke to me yesterday!"

Here are some poems for that:

Speaking In Worry

Her long hair hangs
so low, and she is so
very like the Tamil lands
    of him whose white canopy
    is decked with cool pearls,
    of him who crushed his foes
    at Viḻiñam!
She gave into my hands
her long ankle strings
of bright pearls,
she kissed me right
upon my old, dry breasts,
empty of milk—
she hugged me, too!

Was all that just her way of preparing to go
into that endless wasteland,
where dry bamboos kiss the sky?[424]

"I'm sweating too much!"
she said,
when I turned her around
for her goodnight hug,
and now I know why
she hated it so.
Oh, her fragrance
is that of the kino
and the glory lily
blossoming upon Mount Potiyil,
where clouds crawl,
the mountain
    of Āy,
    whose armlets
    are jingling

423 *Pāṇṭi-k-Kōvai*, 184.

424 *Pāṇṭi-k-Kōvai*, 185.

and she is ever so much cooler
than any lotus blossom![425]

She finds no consolation in saying this, and she worries even more; she continues, "How can a girl like her travel through such a wilderness?" Here is a poem for that:

Sorrowing In Thoughts Of The Desert

My precious, bewitching girl,
she has never even left
her own golden rooftop terrace,
here in Kūṭal City,
in the South,
    that city of Neṭumāṟaṉ,
    the king whose grand crown
    has such ornamental curves,
    him who destroyed his foes
    at Pāḻi!
How can she stand
her own anklets
slapping at
her tender feet
as she traipses along
after that young man

through hot wastelands
where hunter tribes put up
their hovels?[426]

"How can such tender feet travel," she asks, "through so hot a desert?" Here is a poem for that:

Sorrowing In Thoughts Of Her Feet

She is like Uṟaiyūr City
    of the Supreme One
    whose scepter is righteous,
    whose white canopy
    is decked with pearls
    and fine colors!
But the ankletted feet
of that little girl
with her bright,
pearly smile—

[425] *Kuṟuntokai*, 84.

[426] *Pāṇṭi-k-Kōvai*, 186.

they tremble
just on the sands,
white like hills
of pearls:

Have they really walked across
that burnt wasteland, following her lover?[427]

Next, here are some poems for the foster mother to speak as she follows them; she addresses her lament to a bottle-flower bush:

Speaking In Sorrow To A Bottle-Flower Bush

She is like Kūṭal City
    of King Māṟaṉ,
    who defeated the Cēraṉ,
    whose munificent hands
    are like dark clouds
    filled with rain,
my little girl with jewels
upon her breasts.
Yet even as she crossed
this mountain, dense
with stalks of bamboo,
eloping with a strange man,
you stood there and
watched her go,
you cool
bottle-flower bush!

And yes, you have even raised oh,
so many of your own flower-dolls,
smothered in your leaves![428]

I once bore a doll—
she shone in our home
in the grand land of him
    who vanquished his foes
    at Neṭuṅkaḷam,
    astride his great elephant
    resplendent in action,
but I grieved.
Yet you, you have borne
oh, so many dolls
here in the woods,

---

[427] *Pāṇṭi-k-Kōvai*, 187.

[428] *Pāṇṭi-k-Kōvai*, 188.

yet you suffer none
of this unbearable grief:

Bottle-flower bush, you are lucky
beyond belief![429]

Now suppose I said
to the bottle-flower bush,
"How could she?
Tell me: how could my girl
with her bright forehead
traipse after him
through those wastes
so like the battlefronts
  of our King Māṟaṉ,
  who proved strong enough
  to vanquish the army
  of the archer king
  and make it crumble
  and climb up into heaven
  at Naṟaiyāṟu?"
Would it tell me,
even though it has brought up
its own tender leaves,
and raised its own flower dolls?[430]

As they travel through the wastelands, the hero and heroine meet other people who say, "Who are these people coming toward us like that?" Here are some poems for them to speak:

Subtle Sayings of People Who See Them
In The Wastelands

A golden warrior's anklet shows
upon the strong feet
of this young archer,
and there are anklets, too,
upon the twin feet
of this girl,
with teeth like pearls—
Here they are,
like enemies
  of the Pañcavaṉ
  who fought that day

---

429 *Pāṇṭi-k-Kōvai*, 189.

430 *Pāṇṭi-k-Kōvai*, 190.

in Neṭuṅkaḷam,
filled with fields
of rice—
they, too have come
to these harsh
wastelands!

But who are they?[431]

This archer
wears the warrior's anklet
upon his foot,
and the girl,
with bracelets
on her arms,
wears her anklets,
too, on her delicate feet—
they are well bred.
Poor things, alone,
they chose this bamboo jungle,
where white sirissa seeds
rattle like drumbeats for the antics
of tightrope dancers!

But who are they?[432]

Next, here are some poems for the foster mother to speak as she inquires of Brahmins she meets along the way:

Asking The Brahmins

You Brahmins, coming here
through this harsh desert,
toting your umbrellas
for shade, and dangling
your waterjars
just so:
did a girl
with dark hair
follow a man
with a warrior's anklet
through these mountains,
just like enemies
of the God of Love
in this degenerate age,

431 *Pāṇṭi-k-Kōvai*, 191.

432 *Kuṟuntokai*, 7.

him who holds
the righteous scepter?

Tell me![433]

You, Brahmins
trudging, tired
through these mountains,
toting your umbrellas
for shade, with your waterjars
dangling from your yokes!
Did you see a girl—
her waist is like
the bright, sweet Tamil
of Kūṭal City in the South,
the city of the Supreme One
who claims the whole world
with his gleaming lance?

And was she following a young man
through this monstrous desert?[434]

Here are some poems for the foster mother to speak when she notices a spot where the heroine stood, and sees an elephant that the hero killed:

Speaking In Wonder

So here she stood,
her garland exuding fragrance,
here in this wasteland
that is like
the battlefronts
of Neṭumāṟaṉ,
the king who holds
to the path,
who surpassed
those emperors
with their tight
warrior's anklets
in the Battle
of Cēvūr!

---

433 *Pāṇṭi-k-Kōvai*, 192. The God of Love is a title used for the Pāṇṭiyaṉ monarch.

434 *Pāṇṭi-k-Kōvai*, 193.

And her young man shot this raging elephant
with an arrow from his bow, strong and shining![435]

So this
is where she stood,
her eyebrows looking
like ornamented bows,
    here outside Nēri
    in the southern lands
    of our King Neṭumāṟaṉ,
    with his broad hands
    and long bow, who loosed
    arrows to cripple kings
    with their armies
    and cruel bows
    at Kōṭṭāṟu!

And that is the angry elephant her lord shot
with an arrow from his own swift bow![436]

In pursuit, her foster mother inquires about them from people coming toward her along the way. Here are some poems in which they tell her that the hero and the heroine must by now have reached such and such a place:

Speaking To The Distressed Mother

That young man
and the girl
must have crossed
these woods
    like the enemies
    of the Lion to His Enemies,
    whose elephants are always angry
    even with men—
today they will see fields
where white vāḷai fish[437]
and the red-eyed varāl
rejoice in drinking
the clear wine

---

[435] *Pāṇṭi-k-Kōvai*, 194.

[436] *Pāṇṭi-k-Kōvai*, 195.

[437] Since rice fields are flooded with irrigation water, they contain fish at certain times of the year. Fish leaping in such flooded fields is a metaphor for abundance.

that spills from the fronds
of a coconut palm.[438]

As soon as they leave
these mountains,
with their stream-fed pools,
these mountains as high
as the mind of him
    who defeated his foes
    at Naṭṭāṟu,
    when he rode his rutting,
    slobbering elephant,
    looking like
    an awesome mountain,
    when the ghouls
    all laughed and danced,

then they will reach fields
full of vāḷai fish, leaping, with
mouths agape.[439]

Here are some poems for people to speak when they meet the foster mother lamenting in the wastelands; they speak to clarify things for her:

Relating The Nature Of The World

The grand mountains
    of King Māṟaṉ
    who defeated the Cēraṉ
    and carved his carp
    into the northern mountains
    in days of yore,
hold sandalwood trees,
but never have they known
its cool paste
to be rubbed upon
someone's body—
Don't fret so for your girl
with her carp-like wide eyes,
and her mound of love
like the hood
of a snake!

---

[438] *Pāṇṭi-k-Kōvai*, 196.

[439] *Pāṇṭi-k-Kōvai*, 197.

She traveled these wasteland trails
with her lover, you know.[440]

On cool Cape Kumari
    of Him Who Drives Off His Foes,
    who caused the nature
    of enemy kings
    to perish at Naṟaiyāṟu,
when the ocean
bears pearls,
it is for others
to wear them,
we are told!
Now, don't fret so
for your tender natured girl,

she followed her own young man
into these hot, hard wastelands.[441]

Nowhere in this great,
ocean-girt world
    of him who vanquished
    that day at Neṭuṅkaḷam
    with the lance
    that pursues and kills,
are those people
born as girls
of any use to their parents—
parents are like white conches
in the dark sea,
with its three waters:
they bear cool
radiant pearls,
but never wear
them!

Don't take on such grief,
huge as the sea![442]

"You, sirs,
you Brahmins
who carry your waterjars
hung just so

---

[440] *Pāṇṭi-k-Kōvai*, 198.

[441] *Pāṇṭi-k-Kōvai*, 199.

[442] *Pāṇṭi-k-Kōvai*, 200.

from your staffs
on your shoulders,
who shade your famous tridents
from the burning sun
with your umbrellas,
who keep your minds concentrated,
who have your principles,
who control your senses naturally,
and who travel this hot trail!
Did you see those two here,
a daughter of mine,
and the son
of another woman?

Once, their union
was known only to themselves,
but now it is the talk of the town!"

"We cannot say
we did not see them: we did.
And you look to be the mother
of that girl with her fine jewels
who chose to come
through these wastelands
in the forests
with her lord,
who has all
the beauty
a man can!

Though the mountains
bear the aromatic sandal
that goes into many perfumes,
what good does it do them
without someone else to rub it on?
Your daughter, too
is like that to you,
when you come
to think of it!

Though the sea
bears fine white pearls,
what good are they
without someone else
to put them on?
Your daughter, too,
is like that to you,
when you come
to examine it!

Though the lute
bears sweet notes
from its seven strings,
what good are they to it
without someone else
to sing them?
Your daughter, too,
is like that to you,
when you come to ponder
over it!

Don't imagine harm
could come to any girl
with such extreme fidelity—
she followed an excellent man,
she worships him!

Her path is not divorced
from virtue."[443]

There are also those who say that the foster mother does not actually go into the wasteland, that she speaks from within her own home. Understand it in whichever way seems appropriate.

Moreover, a few days after they have eloped in that manner,

Ever-excellent wise ones console,
in appropriate ways, both her parents,
who are like gods of eminent nature,
and who came to know of it through standing with honor,
and her brothers of incomparable strength.
They realize clearly, through fate, that it is natural.
Then he returns and attains her through marriage
in a worthy and excellent manner, to the liking of the large city, they say.[444]

When the heroine returns in that way, she requests those who go ahead of her in the wastelands, "Tell my friends that I'm coming home!" Here are some poems for that:

Saying To Those Who Go Along The Path, "Tell Of My Coming"

You who travel
so fast!
Please tell my pretty,
large eyed friends

---

[443] *Kalittokai: Pālai*, 9.

[444] Unidentified verse.

that I am coming back
through these wastelands
as hot as the battlefronts
of Him Who Drives Off His Foes,
who saw the backs
of those who fought him
in the Battle of Cēvūr,
the strong king
with his unique scepter
of righteousness![445]

You who travel
so fast!
Please tell my friends
with their bright eyes
where red lines run,
that I am coming back
through these hot wastelands,
the home of hunter tribes,
a land as hot
as the lance
in the hand
of the king
who fought
to make emperors leave
the fort at Kōṭṭāṟu,
with walls as high
as mountain peaks,
and head for the mountains
like jungle people![446]

You who rush on ahead!
Please tell my friends,
with their sweet smiles,
that I am crossing
the wasteland
where a red dog
with its full,
drooping mane,
found a wild sow
and her piglet,
but did not attack!

---

[445] *Pāṇṭi-k-Kōvai*, 201.

[446] *Pāṇṭi-k-Kōvai*, 202.

Tell them I'm coming
close![447]

Moreover, when her mother hears that the heroine is coming home, she says, "Will he bring her here, to our great house; or will he take her home to his own fortified mansion?" She calls a priest to divine the hero's intention. Here are some poems for that:

Asking The Priest

Tell me, priest!
He is returning now,
that young man,
through vast wastelands,
hot as the lance
of the King of the Southerners,
the Lion to His Enemies,
with his beautiful
garland of flowers—
Will he let her come straight
to our home, this house
of impeccable excellence?

Or will he take her right to their
munificent home?[448]

That young man
is coming home
through wastelands
as hot as the battlefronts
of our king,
the Supreme One
with his righteous scepter
and the thunderbolt
upon his banner—
Tell me:
Will he permit my innocent girl
to come home
to our beautiful house
of untainted wealth?

---

[447] *Aiṅkuṟunūṟu*, 397.

[448] *Pāṇṭi-k-Kōvai*, 203.

Or if not, will he take her
to that grand house of theirs?[449]

"My little daughter,"
her mother thinks,
"with her wide shoulders,
who traveled through
the harsh wastelands,
is coming home with her young man,
his lance renewed!"

So she paints
her mansion's outer wall
with red clay in fine designs,
she spreads fresh sand
in the courtyard,
hangs out garlands,
and decks her home
with sweet pleasantness,
we hear!

"But what if he doesn't
honor and love me
for giving birth
to that good young girl
with eyes like those of a doe—
it's still to my credit
that I helped her through
so many days:
I combed her hair,
I took good care of her,
I carried her on my hip,
I adorned her with jewels,
my innocent girl,
with her sweet,
smiling teeth—
it might be best if he knew
that I wish
nothing more!

You, wise priest,
with your cloth
tied into your topknot,
with your staff of many heads,
from which hangs your little sack:
you know the future,
tell me

449 *Pāṇṭi-k-Kōvai*, 204.

what the molucca beans
portend.

Will he bring her first
to our house,
so my eyes
can sleep soundly?
They have grieved incessantly
in the dark, they
have cried unending tears!
Or will he take her
to his house?

What are his
intentions?"[450]

When the hero returns, the heroine's mother hears that he has decided to perform the wedding rites in his own home. She says, "Might she who bore that young man agree to let the wedding rites be performed in our house, if all the other rituals are performed in hers?" Here are some poems for that:

The Real Mother Speaking With The Foster Mother, With A Desire To Conduct The Wedding

That woman has a good heart,
she knows her duties,
the one who bore the young man.
Would she let the marriage ceremony
be performed in our home tomorrow,
so all the people
in this world
    of King Māṟaṉ,
    who took up his sword
    in his right hand,
    so those who did not
    worship his feet
    died at Caṅkamaṅkai,

can rejoice?[451]

That woman
with her heavy earrings,
who bore the young man
whose shoulders are thick

---

[450] *Akanāṉūṟu*, 195.

[451] *Pāṇṭi-k-Kōvai*, 205.

and hard as rock—
would she let them
wed in our house tomorrow,
so good people can rejoice,
as they do at the festival
in Kūṭal City
    of the Scholar
    who strung his bow
    to make enemy kings
    enter into heaven
    at Pūlantai?[452]

That woman with golden earrings
who bore the young man
who practices nothing
but falsehood—
Would she let our girl,
with her hair anointed
in fine oils,
celebrate her marriage
in our house,
just like the festival
in the truly excellent
city of Madurai,
    the city of him
    who defeated kings
    and made them flee
    from Kaṭaiyal,
    with its dark waters,
    and groves
    where clouds climb?[453]

Where is the harm
in suggesting to the mother
who bore that young man
with his victorious lance,
his feet adorned
with faultless
warrior's anklets,
who is oh, so skilled
in lying—
"You hold
the ritual removal
of the anklets

[452] *Pāṇṭi-k-Kōvai*, 206.

[453] *Pāṇṭi-k-Kōvai*, 207.

in your house,
but pray,

let's perform the wedding itself
in ours."[454]

* * *

Verse 24.

Marriage before Stolen Love is exposed, and
marriage after Stolen Love has been exposed:
they say these are the two types of marriage.

What does this declare, you ask? For a student who takes it that since he said, "Even after it is exposed, there is speech,"[455] there is no marriage other than that which follows, in order, the exposure of Stolen Love, this declares that there is another type of marriage.

Its meaning:

Marriage before Stolen Love is exposed—marriage before they have the thought that their conduct must be known to large and small groups of people.

He is quite likely to see the light and marry her after they unite in natural union. If he doesn't see the light then, he is likely to see the light and marry her after uniting with her through the help of his friend. And if he doesn't see the light then, he is likely to see the light when her friend makes her unavailable to him, as he follows and entreats her; then he is likely to marry her. If he doesn't see the light even then, he does when her friend divines their union through her knowledge and puts him off as he follows and entreats her; then he is likely to marry her. If he still does not see the light, he will when he unites with her through the help of her friend, or when he learns that she is shut up in the house, or when she points out the dangers of nighttime trysts, or when she demands marriage; then he is likely to marry her.

Take all these as the variations of marriage before Stolen Love is exposed.

Next, take it that there are no variations in marriage after Stolen Love has been exposed.

Of the two, marriage before Stolen Love is exposed is the more praiseworthy; take it that the other is not as praiseworthy since he is forced to marry her.

This is not an exposure of Stolen Love and refutes those who say it is; and it implies that any marriage before the exposure of Stolen Love also occurs before the standing with honor.

marriage after Stolen Love has been exposed—marriage after the standing with honor has taken place.

---

[454] *Aiṅkuṟunūṟu*, 399.

[455] *The Study of Stolen Love*, 23, page 174.

We described above how marriage occurs both before and after Stolen Love has been exposed; comment here as we did there.

they say these are the two types of marriage—they say that these are the two sorts of marriages.

* * *

Verse 25.

> **A hero who does not marry after it happens,**
> **leaving for a long interval for wealth,**
> **and, not leaving for wealth, staying in some place**
> **is proper, they say, to Married Love.**

What does this declare, you ask? It declares one of the variations that can succeed her standing with honor.

In the previous verse he set forth the contexts of marriage; in this one he declares obstacles that come in its way.

Next, for a student who wonders, "He did not marry the heroine; when her friend stood with honor, he left her: is such a heroine in Married Love or Stolen Love?" It states that she is in Married Love.

Its meaning:

A hero who does not marry after it happens—a hero who does not attain the heroine through marriage after she has stood with honor.

leaving for a long interval for wealth—his departure in search of wealth, leaving countries, forests, and many leagues between them.

and, not leaving for wealth, staying in some place—leaving not for wealth, yet remaining in some other place.

is proper, they say, to Married Love—these are appropriate for her entering into Married Love.

How does the hero know that she has stood with honor, you ask? Her friend informs him.

The idea of this verse is that during these two obstacles, it is in accord with Married Love for her friend to console the heroine while she is languishing, or to speak in response to her reply to such consolation, and all such things.

Does the heroine know when he leaves, you ask? Yes, he leaves with her knowledge; he makes everything known to both her and her friend.

The heroine underwent some changes when he left like that, and her friend said, "Our lord has gone to do good works; you shouldn't be so grieved!" Then the heroine replies to her friend, "I'm not grieving because he has left me. I'm worried when I think about the sort of country he's going through: that's why I'm so upset. People just don't understand that." Thus, she blames the town. Here is a poem for that:

The Heroine Describing The Nature Of The Townspeople

If my conch bracelets fall off
as soon as my lover leaves
for the wastelands,
where they kill
and waylay,
  as on the battlefield
  of Māṟaṉ, Lord of Nēri,
  the King of the World,
  who stood upon the foaming waves
  with his lance shining
  like the very lightning,

these townspeople keep thinking
it's something it isn't![456]

Discussing His Qualities

Her friend might scorn the hero, thinking that to be the only way to console the distraught and languishing heroine. If so, the heroine's reply is to praise the hero to her friend. Here is a poem for that:

You, my dear,
long may you live!

So what if he did
withhold his pleasure, so what
if he left us, and we lost
what beauty we had, and
the beauty of our shoulders
spoiled—

So what if he left
and let gossip grow
louder than the battle barrage
  when our King Cempiyaṉ demolished,
  pulverized Kuṭṭuvaṉ's
  castle walls, and set fire
  to his city,
  that very same day—

So what if he did
take off to the woodlands
of Pulli of Swift Horses,

---

456 *Pāṇṭi-k-Kōvai*, 208.

those forests where the she-elephant
trumpets forever in grief,
echoing down the valleys
when her bull with his huge,
dangling trunk is seized
in the mouth of a monstrous snake,
there on those slopes,
high in the mountains
where lily petals open
as the flower bends over—

he will yet give us joy—
he loves me.[457]

Scorning His Nature

Still, her friend does scorn the qualities of the hero when he has been away for a long time in search of wealth, if she sees the heroine in anguish. How does she scorn him, you ask? She says, "These immodest birds are even crueler than that man who left her to languish: they see her anguish, yet do nothing about it. Instead, they shamelessly go about their search for food, in broad daylight!" Here is a poem for that:

She is like the lands
at Cape Kaṉṉi
  of him who vanquished
  hostile emperors
  as they stood there before him
  reveling in the fight—
  they took their refuge
  in heaven
  at Iruñciṟai!
And these birds,
they see her swollen anguish
today in her loneliness,
yet off they go,
seeking their prey
in these wide backwaters
now, in broad daylight—

they have no shame.[458]

When the heroine hears this she thinks, "She wouldn't speak like that if she hadn't noticed my anguish," and the result is that she discards her anguish.

457 *Naṟṟiṇai*, 14.

458 *Pāṇṭi-k-Kōvai*, 209.

Next, if the heroine is distraught because the hero has stayed off somewhere, her friend can say, "Our lord would never desert us in such a land: why are you so upset?" Here are some poems for that:

You are like Vañci City
of the king
with the righteous scepter
unblemished in this world, the
Lion to His Enemies,
whose rutting elephants
seem like mountains at war!
And he is lord
of the high mountains
where bees sing
songs of the hills,
and feast on fresh honey
in red glory-lilies!

Can you think
he could desert you?[459]

He is lord of good lands
and shady hills—
waterfalls in his hills
feel moved in their hearts
to sprinkle water
like the tears
monkeys shed
when they think, "Oh,
poor things, they fell
in the fire!" when they see
swarms of bees, buzzing
like flutes,
leap into clusters
of red glory-lilies,
with their grand leaves!

Would he desert you?
Never.[460]

* * *

[459] *Pāṇṭi-k-Kōvai*, 210.

[460] Unidentified poem.

Verse 26.

> **Exposure indeed, when explained,**
> **is the effect when such people know**
> **as father, mother, and brothers.**

What does this declare, you ask? Earlier he spoke only about exposure in itself. This verse declares what the various types of exposure are.

Its meaning:

Exposure indeed—the exposure of Stolen Love indeed.

when explained—when one expands upon it and makes it known.

is the effect when such people know as father, mother, and brothers—happens when these people know about it: father, mother, and brothers.

Effect, definition, and nature all mean the same thing, and exposure means standing with honor. Whether one says exposure or standing with honor, both rest upon the same meaning, although they do have different thrusts. Stolen Love is known by no one; when it happens that her father, mother, or brothers do know about it, it is to be called an Exposure of Stolen Love. On the other hand, it is called standing with honor because the heroine does not lose her virtue.

* * *

Verse 27.

> **Among them,**
> **the others know because the mother knows.**

What does this declare, you ask? It declares that these people know about it only if the mother tells them; they do not find out on their own.

Its meaning:

Among them—among the three people mentioned above.

the others know because the mother knows—her father and brothers know because her mother tells them.

That is, when her friend stands with honor to the foster mother, she stands with honor to the real mother. In turn, her real mother stands with honor to her father and brothers.

How do we get that the foster mother stands with honor to the real mother, you ask? We get it through the literary device of adding things in the commentary.[461]

* * *

---

[461] This device is an approved commentarial practice, provided all things added can be shown to serve useful purposes and to fit harmoniously with the rest of the work.

Verse 28.

> **Father and brothers, to these two classes,**
> **she has no speech other than by suggestion there.**

What does this declare, you ask? It declares how the real mother stands with honor to the father and brothers.

Its meaning:

Father and brothers, to these two classes—to the two categories of people called her father and her brothers.

she has no speech other than by suggestion there—she will not tell them straight, but will use suggestive speech.

Here is how it works: When the real mother stands with honor to the father and brothers, she says, "It is like this: What is it like, you ask me? There is this man; he is from a grand family, with quality and wealth, whom everybody approaches to get things done, but who is not so small that he would ever approach anybody else to accomplish anything for him. He has begun making worship of us his very life! Would there be anything amiss if we were to establish relations with him?"

They listen as she speaks; and what do they think, you ask? They realize, "This sounds like a suggestion that she has thought about a good deal; could it have something to do with her daughter?"

We can interpolate, through the extraneous word "there," the idea that she sometimes speaks through words that are like suggestions, and not exclusively through suggestion alone.

Here is how it comes about: When the hero sends a Brahmin on ahead with precious jewels to ask for her in marriage, her father and brothers refuse him. They will make themselves inaccessible and consult together over the proposal. After all, a hundred-year deed is to be done only after consulting a hundred people.

Additionally, they will make themselves inaccessible so people will think, "See, they must already have received men asking for their daughter; we are the hundredth in this deed for a hundred; who will get their girl?" or, "She must be hard to get."

Additionally, they will make themselves inaccessible in consideration of such loose talk as, "See, what those people who are asking for their daughter are proposing seems like lies," or, "They gave her away so quickly!" as if anyone might get her with no need to ask.

Moreover, even very small people will make themselves inaccessible when their superiors come asking for their daughter.

Additionally, they will make themselves inaccessible because that's the way the world is. Since that is so, is it even necessary to give any other reasons for their becoming inaccessible?

So the heroine becomes distraught when she hears that the hero's proposal has been refused, and her friend will stand with honor to her mother. The foster mother will stand with honor to the real mother, who will stand with honor to the father and brothers, with words like suggestions. Here are some poems for her speaking like that:

Standing With Honor

We must consider
the arrival of these eminent men,
the nobility of those who sent them,
and our own lineage
that reaches to the heavens,

for if we think of wealth,
the very seas
filled with fish
    and wedded to the scepter
    of Māṟaṉ, who conquered the Cōḻa,
    whose fragrant garland
    is as though dipped
    in honey,

would never be price enough
for this tender natured girl![462]

We must agree
and accept this
offer, according
to social custom,
for if we do not—
the whole world
    of the Supreme One,
    him whose ancestor
    is the cool rayed moon,
      held in the matted locks
      of Him who wears fresh laburnum,[463]
    of the Emperor
    with the white canopy
    of cool pearls,

---

[462] *Pāṇṭi-k-Kōvai*, 211.

[463] Lord Siva.

of him whose army
triumphed at Naṟaiyāṟu,

even that whole world
would never be price enough
for this girl with her brilliant forehead![464]

It would be best
for you to accept the mountain
filled with beautiful gemstones,
and give away her chest, with
its budding breasts:
consider the sufferings
of the eminent ones,
and your own lineage
that reaches to
the heavens.
Otherwise, if you think only
of what wealth you might gain,
even Uṟaiyūr City
with its Ulli festival
and Vañci City
with its Paṅkuṉi celebrations
of the Cōḻa king
with fine chariots,
who annexed Kaḻumalam
and its canopy

would be far too
little![465]

When they hear her mother speaking in this vein, they realize that their lineage would most likely be disgraced if they did not give the girl away in marriage.

Implied is the excellence of standing with honor.

* * *

---

[464] *Pāṇṭi-k-Kōvai*, 212.

[465] Unidentified poem.

Verse 29.

> **If desire increases when guarding becomes excessive,**
> **if the time comes for a stranger to marry her,**
> **if her relatives refuse to accept then the offer of marriage,**
> **and if a time comes when they fear harm to him:**
> **in all four of these, shedding her bodily modesty,**
> **the standing with honor belongs also to her friend.**

What does this declare, you ask? In the last verse he explained "standing with honor;" now he describes the situations of standing with honor. That is what this verse declares.

What is its connection with the previous verse, you ask? There, standing with honor was the principal topic.

Its meaning:

If desire increases when guarding becomes excessive—if desire swells when her guarding becomes extreme.

if the time comes for a stranger to marry her—if it comes time for an outsider to wed her.

if her relatives refuse to accept then the offer of marriage—if they do not accept the marriage proposal, and refuse at that time.

if a time comes when they fear harm to him—when they are afraid of some harm that might come to him.

in all four of these, shedding her bodily modesty—in all four of those situations, that modesty which lives within her body leaves her.

the standing with honor belongs also to her friend—her friend also stands with honor.

The phrase, "If desire increases when guarding becomes excessive:"

Guarding is of two kinds: "mental" and "prison."

Of those, mental guarding means one's own conduct, in which one preserves what is to be preserved and forsakes what is to be forsaken. This we get from the saying,

> What is the use of prison locks? Guarding
> women with their own conviction is better.[466]

Next, "prison guard" means these things: the mother not sleeping, the dog not sleeping, the town not sleeping, watchmen hastening, the moon coming out, an owl hooting, and a cock crowing.

Of those, it is prison guard that he takes up here: it becomes an obstacle to Stolen Love when it increases, and then a great change comes over the heroine. Her friend will notice that change, and so will her mother. She will consult the

---

[466] *Tirukkuṟaḷ*, 57.

pundits, and they will tell her that it came about through God. They will attribute it to God because it is their function to speak about Him, and because this lineage is not such that anyone can point out and understand its nature. She then places the heroine before her and has her worship God, and with that the heroine loses her fidelity to the hero.

Her friend is distraught over the heroine's loss of fidelity and her mother's anguish: she recognized the heroine's loss, and she had watched her mother's anguish grow as the heroine changed upon hearing that her languor had a divine cause. The heroine's grief is inconsolable. Distraction such as her friend experiences means anguish with no other emotion at all; and such anguish grabs onto something in consolation. Since there is nothing else, she will ask the pundits herself, but before she does, she thinks to herself, "She will ask me before she goes to anyone else. And I know what to tell her when she does." At this point she will not seek to set up any more rendezvous for the lovers.

Carrying a mirror, her mother comes in while she is in this state and looks her daughter over from head to foot. "Dear," she says, "how did this change come over my daughter?"

"I do know a little something," her friend replies, and stands with honor as described above, with no contradictions. Then the foster mother stands with honor to the real mother, and all the rest.

Next, the phrase "if the time comes for a stranger to marry her:"

"Stranger" means an outsider. The heroine becomes distraught when she hears that he has arrived with a marriage proposal.

At that, her friend stands with honor to the foster mother, as described above.

Next, the phrase, "if her relatives refuse then to accept the offer of marriage:"

The hero's relatives approach them with the marriage offer, sending Brahmins and eminent men on ahead with gifts of precious jewels. As they approach, her relatives refuse them once; they will not agree immediately, like some others who have a girl they can't sell! They say, "The bride price is too small," or, "She is too young," or, "Why don't you come back when the day and the bird-omens are more auspicious?" and the heroine grieves. How does she grieve? The heroine grieves as she thinks to herself, "Our lord is not the sort of man who asks others to accomplish anything for him; rather, he does things for others. It is not through any graciousness on my part that these people have come to me to accomplish this deed, is it? Oh, poor me! I have brought him such disgrace!" or, "They have refused my lord: what will become of him now?"

Her friend will notice this change, and she will stand with honor as described above.

The phrase "if a time comes when they fear harm to him:"

She undergoes some changes while the hero comes to nighttime trysts, because she thinks to herself, "Along the path our lord travels there are bears, white-tusked elephants, snakes, thunder, tigers, mountain nymphs and celestial nymphs—and it is the nature of the gods to snatch people up! Will he come to some harm?"

Her friend notices that change, and she stands with honor as described above.

The phrase "in all four of those:" in all four of the cases mentioned above.

The phrase "shedding her bodily modesty" means that the modesty that resides within her body forsakes her; she would not stand before her mother and speak while her modesty remained.

The phrase "standing with honor belongs also to her friend:" Honor is propriety; it means that her friend also stands up and says that which is proper. Moreover, honor in women is fidelity: that is, it means standing foremost in fidelity.

Next, by using the word "also" in "...belongs also to her friend," he meant to imply that it is appropriate for the heroine as well to stand with honor. Here is how that works: Following either natural union or the union arranged by his friend, she decides to leave her family in order to attain him through marriage. But then, by definition, they will refuse, whereupon she becomes upset and undergoes changes, thinking to herself, "What will become of our lord now that he has been refused?"

Her friend will notice and ask, "Our lady, why are you suffering this change?"

Once that happens, the heroine will stand with honor and say, "This is what happened to me: One time while you and the other girls were getting leaf skirts and wreaths, you and I were separated for a while. I was standing by this magnificent mountain pool—there was a riot of lilies, glory lilies, water lilies, and lotuses—and I jumped in: I was so happy, and I wanted to play in it! But I slipped, and fell in over my head. 'Help, friend! Help!' I called out, but you didn't hear me. Just then a lord appeared to dispel my suffering, and he held out his hand. I was confused, and I thought it must be your hand, so I grabbed it. He took firm hold, hauled me up, and set me on the bank; then he left. I didn't tell you then because I thought it might upset you: you never fail me, you know, but that time you did. I'm out of sorts now, and changed, because I was just thinking, 'If that wasn't fate, what could it be?'"

And that is how the heroine stands with honor to her friend. Later on, her friend stands with honor to the foster mother, as described before.

But if that's how it works, does it not contradict her friend's chaperoning, you ask? No, it does not, because it is her friend to whom she stands with honor; and even if it did contradict her chaperoning, fate would protect her against dying of the thought, "I failed in my chaperoning!"

But it still amounts to telling a lie, since she conceals her real behavior and invents things, doesn't it, you ask? No, it doesn't amount to lying. Why not? There is no fault or sin here, because he has said,

> Even a lie may hold the place of truth, provided
> unblemished good results.[467]

The point of this verse is simply to lay out the names and order of the situations for standing with honor; we have presented its definition above, as well as exemplary poems.

* * *

Verse 30.

> **The speech out of much brooding over increased desire,**
> **the speech out of helplessness when prison-guard increases,**
> **the speech out of fear of what happens on the way,**
> **saying, 'Come at night or in the day,'**
> **telling the hero, 'Don't come!'**
> **the speech of placing her helplessness,**
> **other things as well collected in that line,**
> **all the speeches of her affliction**
> **have the meaning of a desire for marriage, they say.**

What does this declare, you ask? It collects and declares all the ways of demanding marriage.

What is its connection with the above, you ask? Here he explains further the particulars of leaving Stolen Love and turning to Married Love. Since this marriage shares in that, he placed it after Married Love.

Its meaning:

The speech out of much brooding over increased desire—"desire" means love; "increasing" means growing larger; "much" implies that it is intensified; "brooding" means pondering; and "speech" means speaking.

It indicates the poems she speaks out of deep pondering through intensified desire.

the speech out of helplessness when prison-guard increases—the uttering of a poem in the helplessness brought on by an increase of prison guard.

the speech out of fear of what happens on the way—poetry on her anguish in thinking of the dangers along the paths he travels.

saying, 'Come at night or in the day'—poetry asking, 'Wouldn't it be all right for you to come at night or during the day?'

---

[467] *Tirukkuṟaḷ*, 292.

telling the hero, 'Don't come!'—poetry declaring that the hero should come neither at night nor during the day.
the speech of placing her helplessness—poetry blaming her helplessness upon something else.
other things as well collected in that line—a collection of other themes defined as these are.
all the speeches of her affliction—all the poems she utters in her anguish.
have the meaning of a desire for marriage, they say—are poems uttered out of their desire for marriage, it means.

The Speech Out Of Much Brooding Over Increased Desire

Next, here is how the phrase "the speech out of much brooding over increased desire" works: While the hero conducts daytime or nighttime trysts, her desire is not satisfied with seeing him only once in a while. Why? Because she spends more time not seeing him than seeing him. Feeling such a desire, she speaks some poems in the hope that such things as these might alleviate her burden: a mastwood tree, a swan, the sea, the backwaters, and other such things. Here are some poems for that:

O, black ocean!
Suppose you approached
my lover and rebuked him,
suppose you said, "Is it right
for you, in your nobility,
to cause, like an enemy,
this anguish for her to suffer,
and to lament, when she went
to your trysts there in the sea grove
where flowers bloom,
on cool, pretty Cape Kumari
    of King Māṟaṉ
    with his garland
    and tall crown
    decked with fresh flowers?"

Where would the harm be
if you did that?[468]

O, she-heron,
you, with your
gleaming feathers!

---

[468] *Pāṇṭi-k-Kōvai*, 213.

You and your mate
go everyday
to the sea grove
with flowers
where bees drink nectar—
if you were to meet my lover,
and if you told him,
"We have come as emissaries
from your girl,"
and then rebuke him,

would they banish you
from the sea grove?[469]

Take it that these are addressed to the sea and the heron.

Will the hero overhear this, and will he come to her, you ask? This is how he will step forward, and later decide to marry her: he will realize, "My acting like this upsets her." If her friend overhears it, she will stand up to the hero and demand the marriage. Yet even if no one overhears her, she will still feel some consolation. Why? When you uncover a saucepan, the heat inside it lessens a bit; similarly, it will relax her tension some just to have let those words out. One of those three things is bound to happen.

Does she have a certain result in mind as she speaks—does she think, "If the hero overhears me, this will happen; if my friend overhears me, that will happen; and even if no one overhears me this other will happen?" you ask? She does not. The result is brought about by the excess of her desire as she speaks. It is like a baby crying: the baby doesn't cry out, "Give me milk! Bathe me!" It just cries because it is unhappy, and people who attend to its crying will cause the result to happen.

The Speech Out Of Helplessness When Prison-Guard Increases

The phrase, "the speech out of helplessness when prison-guard increases," indicates poems that she speaks when she is helpless because her prison-guard has intensified. Guarding is of two kinds: "mental" and "prison." Of those, mental guarding deals with what she says in anguish when she finds herself unable to hide the natural increase in her desire from others. Here are some poems for that:

It is decidedly mean
of that swan,
whose eyes never shut

---

[469] Unidentified poem.

while she hugs
her young mate:
she won't go and tell
of my sleepless nights
to my lord
of the rich ocean front
at midnight
in the thick
of the dark!
It feels like
  when enemy kings
  never shut their eyes
  out on the battlefields
  of Neṭumāraṉ, on whose
  sharp lance
  the gleam
  never shuts
  its eye![470]

Lily blossom, your mouth
is brimful of nectar,
yet you get to sleep, no
suffering, no
misery like my eyes
in the solitude
of my evenings,
which fan my pain!

Have you ever watched that cruel man
come to this sea grove in your
dreams?[471]

Prison guard, on the other hand, means these things: the mother not sleeping, the dog not sleeping, the town not sleeping, watchmen hastening, the moon coming out, an owl hooting, and a cock crowing. Among those, here is a poem for the mother not sleeping:

In dense dark
after the hot sun
in his unique,
single wheeled
fine chariot,
has set behind the mountain,
this girl, with her perfect jewelry,
cannot dim her thoughts
and fall asleep:

---

[470] *Pāṇṭi-k-Kōvai*, 214.

[471] *Cilappatikāram: Kāṉalvari*, 33.

it's too much like
    a battlefront
    of the Lion to His Enemies,
    with his righteous scepter,
    the King of Tamil,
    which people study!

Her mother, too, has forgotten
to fall asleep, on such a night.[472]

Here is a poem on the dog not sleeping:

She is like Vañci City
    of the Gift of the Gods,
    with his righteous scepter
    and thick, gold
    warrior's anklet,
yet even though the moon
has slid behind mountains,
and everyone else is asleep,
even her mother and
the town watchman
at midnight,
that dog is still
awake—

How can she join with the lord
of the cool, sweet mountains?[473]

Here is a poem for the city not sleeping:

O, you who are like
beautiful, cool Kūṭal City
    of the king who took up
    his sharp lance
    so enemy kings
    and their horses,
    elephants, and bejewelled
    grand chariots
    were cut down
    at Vallam!
Because of this festival,
like one up in heaven,
flowers, incense, and perfumes
exude their aromas,

---

[472] *Pāṇṭi-k-Kōvai*, 215.

[473] *Pāṇṭi-k-Kōvai*, 216.

and this great town
is still wide awake tonight.[474]

Here is a poem on the hastening of the watchmen:

You who are like Kūṭal City
    of the King of the South,
    the Lion to His Enemies,
    with his warrior's anklet
    resounding on his feet,
    who fixed the thunderbolt
    upon his banner
    for his foes to perish!
In this darkness,
the sharp eyes
of the young men
with sharp lances
who guard this rich city,
and the twin eyes
of their little drums

have not slept
a wink.[475]

Next, here is a poem on the moon coming out:

You with your tender nature,
like the Tamil lands
    of the king
    who swept the battlefield clean
    and conquered Cennilam
    so those who had come
    to fight with him
    sank in the red flames!
Where can the darkness
have gone, where can
it have found room
to hide itself tonight?

The moon sits up there in the sky
and smears its light about,
as though it were day.[476]

Next, here is a poem in which all of the prison guards figure:

---

474 *Pāṇṭi-k-Kōvai*, 217.

475 *Pāṇṭi-k-Kōvai*, 218.

476 *Pāṇṭi-k-Kōvai*, 219.

My dear friend!
There is no festival
today, and still
this noisy old town,
with all its drunks,
won't fall asleep!

Yet even when the rich bazaar
and the rest
of the streets
do die down,
mother won't sleep—
and she can speak
her harsh words
so harshly!

Yet when mother
does fall asleep—
she is like iron prison bonds!—
those watchmen
run all around
with their
sleepless eyes!

And if those warriors
with their sharp lances
should fall asleep,
our dog with its sharp teeth,
and tail that curves
to the right,
is exuberant!

But then if the dog
with its noisy mouth
finally calms down,
that big plate
in the sky sits
up there and shines,
showering moonlight
like the light of day!

And if the moon sets
behind its mountain,
and thick darkness
really sets in,
an owl preying
on house mice
with its strong beak
hoots, portending
ruin at midnight

when ghouls are out
and about!

Then if that he-owl
subsides quietly
back into his owl-hole,
a rooster raised
in our home
crows in his stupendous
voice!

Still, one day,
all these things
do die back—
and on that day
he doesn't come,
his heart
wavers.

So it's like rocky brambles
set about Uṟaiyūr City
    of Tittaṉ, who built
    a palisade of fortress walls,
    whose fine, fast horses
    gallop and run straight
    where they must, adorned
    with tinkling anklets!

Our stolen love
faces so much.[477]

The Speech Out Of Fear of What Happens On The Way

Next, the phrase, "the speech out of fear of what happens on the way:" "Way" means path; "what happens" is being distressed; "fear" is a trembling that appears involuntarily; "speech" means words.

Here is how it works: It is her worrying while the hero conducts nighttime trysts. She thinks to herself, "The trail our lord follows to come to me is very rough—it has streams, stones, thorns, and ups and downs!" Now, one school maintains that this is what the speech out of fear of what happens on the way amounts to, but they do not realize that it simply describes what there is along the way. Saying that it is a speech out of *fear* means that it is to be spoken out of a worry that his path leads through thieves, tigers, bears, white-tusked elephants,

---

[477] *Akanāṉūṟu*, 122.

thunder, and snakes. Of those, here is a poem that delineates just what there is along the way:

In those Kolli Mountains
of the Supreme One
with his horses
and grand chariots
whose wheels never falter,
the strong king
whose righteous scepter
bears the grace
of guarding the world,
through gorges in groves
where bees buzz
like music,
your long trails
are always dark
and painful
to travel—

Please, don't come,
for my sake.[478]

When he hears this, the hero will marry her.

Next, here are some poems for the speech out of fear:

In bamboo jungles
where bears roam,
on the long ranges
of the Potiyil Mountains
of the King of the South,
the king whose lance
drilled out wounds
in those who opposed him
on the western coast,
the Scholar,
the Emperor
on whose white canopy
cool pearls
glisten,

please, don't travel at midnight,
for the sake of your girl
whose voice surpasses music.[479]

---

[478] *Pāṇṭi-k-Kōvai*, 220.

[479] *Pāṇṭi-k-Kōvai*, 221.

Lord!
In those Potiyil Mountains
where clouds settle,
mountains of him
    who conquered Cēvūr,
    to make those who had
    opposed him
    die in tough battle,
there, where the he-bear
takes with relish
bits of food
cached in ant mounds
covered with glowworms
that look like scatterings
of gold,

even if you're overwhelmed with love,
don't come through the dark—
that would really be cruel![480]

Here are some more poems on those themes:

Lord of the mountains
with beautiful bamboo!
In the Potiyil Mountains
where clouds settle,
    mountains of King Māṟaṉ,
    who won the Battle of Naṟaiyāṟu
    and took the whole world,
along those narrow trails
where all the spirits
have settled, never to leave,

please! don't come at midnight,
in the dense darkness, with the lance in your hand as your only lamp.[481]

Lord of the mountains
that dip into sky!
In those Potiyil Mountains
where clouds settle,
those mountains
    of Māṟaṉ, who conquered
    the Cēraṉ king,
    and fought so his foes
    spilled from the edge
    of his sword at Naṟaiyāṟu,

---

[480] *Pāṇṭi-k-Kōvai*, 222.

[481] *Pāṇṭi-k-Kōvai*, 223.

there you go,
during the daylight,
there where young lions
who never miss their mark
roam at all hours,

your girl's shoulders are already sapphire—
she will grow thin yet.[482]

Lord of these cool,
beautiful mountains,

don't come through these Potiyil Mountains
whose peaks brush the sky,
  mountains of the Scholar,
  the Emperor—
don't come through those cool, sweet hills
along dangerous trails
where lions roam,
don't come at night,
for the sake
of the innocent girl
whose tender fingers
are like glory-lily buds—

it would be cruel
wouldn't it?[483]

Through depths of darkness
where even ghouls dare not go,
no more than they dared
visit the battlefield
  of our King Neṭumāṟaṉ,
  on whose red lance
  oil mingled
  with his enemies' fate—
Lord, do not come!
for the sake of this girl
who weeps, laments,
and suffers,
don't come!

---

[482] *Pāṇṭi-k-Kōvai*, 224.

[483] *Pāṇṭi-k-Kōvai*, 225.

I pray, I beseech,
I request you![484]

Lord of those brilliantly
rich hills
with dark clouds
at their peaks!
Ghouls fold their hands
beneath their heads
and doze off
in the depths of the dark
    as they did at the battlefront
    of our King Neṭumāṟaṉ,
    whose lancehead
    is anointed with oil!

For the sake of her whose hair is so soft—
stop coming here:
you, with your false grace![485]

Those belong to her friend; next comes one that belongs to the heroine:

Lord
with your pretty garland!
Through these Potiyil Mountains
where the sun and the moon set,
    mountains of the king
    who took up his lance
    to make ghouls leap
    and grab pieces of the men
    who refused to obey him and live,
    but opposed him and died
    in a corner of the battlefield—
through bewildering darkness,
when hunters chase elephants
tossing off gems
that cobras spat out
of their mountain fissures,

don't come.[486]

When they speak poems like these, the hero will marry her if he overhears; if her friend overhears hers, she will demand their marriage; and if no one hears

---

[484] *Pāṇṭi-k-Kōvai*, 226.

[485] *Pāṇṭi-k-Kōvai*, 227.

[486] *Pāṇṭi-k-Kōvai*, 228.

she will still feel some relief, since she spoke them herself. But this occurs only during a period of nighttime trysts.

Saying, "Come At Night Or In The Day"

Next, the phrase, "saying, 'Come at night or in the day:'" It is addressed to the hero, as he is conducting daytime or nighttime trysts. It simply means, "Come at night or in the day;" here is a poem for that:

> There in the pretty sea grove
> at Cape Kaṉṉi of the king
> whose feet are worshipped
> by his foes, the Supreme One,
> the Emperor who owns
> the world, wrapped up in the seas,
> your girl is unhappy—
> you come to your trysts
> only during the daytime!
> If you came at night as well,
> after the hot sun
> disappears over the hills,
>
> what disgrace would harm
> your sweet grace?[487]

He decides to marry her when he hears this, because he thinks, "It seems she addressed me in this manner because she cannot bear my coming and acting like this."

Next, one body of teachers maintains that "come at night and in the day" amounts to saying, "Come in the daytime," to one who comes at night, and, "Come at night," to one who comes during the day. They even adduce poems for these two themes. Of those, here is a poem for saying, "Come in the daytime," to one who comes at night:

Saying, "Come In The Daytime"

> Through depths of darkness
> filled with the crashing
> of the thunderbolt
> on the flag that was raised
> in days of old,
> the flag of Neṭumāṟaṉ,
> who made the whole world
> bow at his feet,
> who even struck the crown

[487] *Pāṇṭi-k-Kōvai*, 229.

of the king of the gods
with his armlet—
don't come!
From now on,
please come
in the daytime,
so you can feel
happy!

If you do, my girl with all her bangles
will like it.[488]

He decides on marriage when he hears this; he thinks to himself, "She has asked me to come in the daytime because she cannot bear my coming at night."

Next, here is a poem to address to one who comes in the daytime, to say, "Come at night:"

Saying, "Come At Night"

Lord of the misty mountains!
Slander will grow monstrous
if you keep on coming
in the daytime
to this girl
whose broad mound of love
is covered in cotton cloth,
she is like the good lands
of the King of the South,
who took up his lance
with its gleaming tip
dipped in poison
to make those
who fought him fearlessly
die in the wars,
and lose their lands!

What disgrace would you face
if you came when the darkness is deepest?[489]

He decides on marriage when she says this, as he thinks to himself, "She is telling me to come at night instead of the daytime, as I now do, simply because she cannot bear my conduct."

---

[488] *Pāṇṭi-k-Kōvai*, 230.

[489] *Pāṇṭi-k-Kōvai*, 231.

Telling The Hero, "Don't Come"

Next, the phrase, "telling the hero, 'Don't come:'" It means telling the hero, "Do not come—neither in the daytime nor at night." Here are some poems for that:

Saying, "Don't Come At Night Or In The Daytime"

Lord!
In these Potiyil Mountains
of Māṟaṉ,
King of Pūḻi
who commanded the goblins,
and churned the ocean
to hand out ambrosia
for celestials to eat,
for the sake of this girl
who holds her tender glance
and her love just for you,
don't come at night,
nor in the daylight.

You will just reap harm
and disgrace.[490]

When you come
in the daytime
with your dog
trotting along,
you who are like
Murukaṉ walking
through our small town
on the seaside,
where men and women mingle
and dance in the streets
to the raiders' drum,
sporting bunches of kino flowers
fragrant with honey
from the slopes of the hills
where resounding
whitewaters glisten,
we are scared
of the gossip!

---

490 *Pāṇṭi-k-Kōvai*, 232.

But when you came alone
through the depths of darkness
at midnight
when murderous tigers
roam all about,
tigers that missed
felling elephants
with great mouths
and long trunks
in the company
of their black cows
and their calves,
yet still forced the elephants
to hide in hatred,
we were even
more scared!

She kept so many trysts
on so many days with you,
there in the millet field
with its sheaves
of ripening grain!
But now she no longer sings
to chase parrots
away from the field—
what will happen
to her?

She has nothing but your grace,
poor thing.[491]

Take it that she refuses both types of trysts in order to make him think of marriage, since if she refused just one, he might turn to the other.

The Speech Of Placing Her Helplessness

The phrase, "the speech of placing her helplessness," means the declaration that her helplessness is due to some other cause; here are some poems for that:

You're just like me,
you old sea—
deep in your waves
you yearn all night long,
you can't sleep,
any more than I can!
Are you really like me—
does it hurt when you look

---

[491] *Akanāṉūṟu*, 118.

in that sea grove
with its mastwood blooms,
like gold doubloons,
by deep tide pools
at Cape Kaṉṉi
    of the king
    who grasps a bolt of thunder
    as angry as himself?

Did you lose your head too,
over a man?[492]

Roar on, ocean—
you're perturbed,
you cannot get to sleep,
you're like those men
    who would not join together
    by the triumphant feet
    of the Scholar,
    Emperor of the Wide World,
    him who vanquished Cennilam
    in hard fought war!
Do you have someone, too,
who gave you golden
beauty marks and
such a pretty complexion,

who loved you and left?
Tell me.[493]

Ocean, boom on
like the kettledrums,
and may you live long!
You never get to sleep,
even when everyone else
in this little town
by the leaping seafront
near Pantar does—
do you, too, have
a seaside lord
who left you,
like me,

---

[492] *Pāṇṭi-k-Kōvai*, 233.

[493] *Pāṇṭi-k-Kōvai*, 234.

in the miserable evening,
shattering my strength of mind?[494]

She is saying, "You don't get to sleep at all, do you? Just like me! Have you, too, lost you senses over a lover?" If the hero overhears this, he will marry her; if her friend overhears it, she will demand their marriage; yet if no one overhears it at all, she will just say it to herself, and feel comforted.

The phrase, "other things as well collected in that line, all the speeches of her affliction," means the utterance of all other poems along the lines of her affliction.

The phrase, "have the meaning of a desire for marriage, they say," means their desire for marriage as well as all poems spoken to declare that desire. The desire for marriage encompasses all of the heroine's poems, whereas all those poems that her friend utters to the hero are poems declaring that desire for marriage.

Since he said, "other things collected in that line," include all poems that the distraught heroine and her distracted friend utter to the hero as he conducts daytime or nighttime trysts, with the intention of effecting their marriage. There are many of these poems; some of them are as follows:

Spoken After Seeing The Situation

When you come, my lord
into our pretty, cool
little village
here on Mount Nēri
where clouds stand,
  Mount Nēri of our king,
  King Neṭumāṟaṉ
  whose lance
  is forever anointed,
people will not think of you
as the god of these mountains
and clasp their hands in worship—
they will realize the truth
in time,

and then how will your girl
with her tender nature
survive?[495]

---

494 Unidentified poem.

495 *Pāṇṭi-k-Kōvai*, 235.

She is saying, "If you keep coming to these nighttime trysts, nobody will take you for Lord Murukaṉ: they'll figure you out. And she has such great modesty that this would kill her!"

When the hero hears this, he thinks to himself, "Look how disgracefully I have behaved!" He will step forward that very day, and marry her later on.

Here is another poem illustrating "other things as well in that line:"

Speaking Words Of Invention

Know what happened yesterday,
dear friend?
I said
that a grand chariot
decked with gems
flashing like lightning
came by last night—
came to that pretty
flower grove
at Cape Kaṉṉi
    of Neṭumāṟaṉ
    whose golden
    warrior's anklet
    other emperors worship—
it came, and it went back
I said!

Mother's face went red,
and she stared at me, too.[496]

Her friend invents this and says it to the heroine when she knows the hero is within earshot, during a period when he is conducting nighttime trysts. But how does it work, you ask? She is saying, "My mother got angry yesterday—she looked me in the face and asked 'Why did that chariot come into the grove where you were playing, and then leave?' I didn't know what she was talking about."

Then he thinks to himself, "All right: it seems my conduct has become known to others." Later, he decides on marriage.

Here is another poem illustrating "other things as well in that line:"

This girl
whose words
surpass music
went one day
into the Potiyil Mountains,

[496] *Pāṇṭi-k-Kōvai*, 236.

mountains that dip
into the sky,
    mountains of Neṭumāṟaṉ
    the King of the Sword
    the king whose majesty
    surpasses the earth,
    the King of the South,
    who subdued his foes at Pāḻi—
there she played in the cataracts,

and watched a black bull elephant
as he stood by his loving mate
under a kino tree.[497]

This one is an invention by her friend to demand that the hero marry the heroine; it applies to the period of daytime trysts. When she sees a she-elephant standing under a kino tree with her bull like that, she remarks, "Will our lord not decide to worship us in that way as well?"

Here is another poem illustrating "other things as well in that line:"

Girl, in whose garland
fresh buds bloom
as they are woven in!
There in that
pretty seaside grove
at Cape Kaṉṉi
    in the land of the Goad to His Enemies
    who destroyed them at Kōṭṭāṟu
    and brought the southern nations
    under his sway,
    the king of the Grand Dynasty,
    who churned ambrosia
    and gave it to the gods—

will the birds speak as emissaries
to the lord of the seacoast,
without disgracing him?[498]

Comment upon this also as appropriate to that sense.

Thus there are just three types of poems discussed in this verse: those spoken only by the heroine, those spoken only by her friend, and those spoken by either of them. The "speech out of much brooding over increased desire" and the "speech of placing her helplessness" belong to the heroine alone. "Saying, 'Come at night or in the day,'" and "telling the hero, 'Don't come!'" belong

---

[497] *Pāṇṭi-k-Kōvai*, 237.

[498] *Pāṇṭi-k-Kōvai*, 238.

only to her friend. The "speech out of fear of what happens on the way," and the "speech out of helplessness when prison guard increases" belong to them both.

But then, why did he use the singular[499] instead of the plural, "all the speeches of their affliction," as it ought to be, you ask? He fixed upon the singular so as not to differentiate between the heroine and her friend; they are to be thought of as one person, not two.

* * *

Verse 31.

> **Unpleasantness along the path, fear of obstacles,**
> **and blaming himself do not exist for the hero.**

What does this declare, you ask? It presents an understanding of the definition of the hero in Stolen Love. What is its relationship to the above verse, you ask? In case someone thinks that the hero as well fears what might happen along the way, since the above verse says "fear of what happens along the way," he enunciated this verse in order to declare that it is not so.

Its meaning:

Unpleasantness along the path—"path" and "trail" are synonyms; it means his path has ups and downs, slippery spots, boulders, and thorns.

obstacle—means something that comes in his way, such as tigers, elephants, celestial nymphs, thieves, and bears.

fear—involuntary sensation of fear when one sees things that are to be feared; it means he has no fear.

blaming himself—blaming himself for his own misery thinking, "I took upon myself a conduct that does not become me."

does not exist for the hero—the hero does not have such things.

Then, you ask, is it a fact that they do not exist for him because he simply does not think of them, although they really do exist; or do they not exist for him because they simply don't exist at all? If they exist, but he doesn't think about them, then they will eventually come to pass: for example, all species here on earth avoid thinking about death, don't they? Yet it will come to pass. Just like that, all these things will come to pass even though he doesn't think about them, assuming they really do exist. But suppose they do not exist: now what is the use in declaring that a non-existent thing doesn't exist? Why? You don't have to mention that a sky-flower doesn't exist, and this is just like that.

The author is saying that these non-existent things "do not exist for the hero" for the benefit of people who take the position just enunciated; he did it to point

---

499 In the phrase, "all the speeches of *her* affliction."

out that this hero is not a man of the world, but a hero created by the poets: if he were a worldly hero, these things would not be non-existent.

Further, since he said only that they do not exist for the hero, it follows that they do exist for the heroine and her friend. They are afraid that he may encounter unpleasantness and obstacles along the way; further, they blame themselves, thinking, "Doesn't all this amount to the fact that we caused our lord to act disgracefully, and to adopt a conduct that is not proper to him?"

But a person who owns a diamond has no fear that it might rot; and just so, wouldn't these people also be free of such fears, since those things do not really exist for him, you ask? Not so. Since their femininity dictates their misunderstanding things, they will think those things exist for him, even though they do not.

Then again, it was stated above that he is beyond comparison, was it not? Could we not take it directly from that statement that he has neither fear nor self-blame, since all emotional afflictions arise through a lack of understanding?[500] That is the question. The answer is this: It points up that they do not exist, in case one were to think they did; that would imply that fate had debased his wisdom and conduct, and rendered him a man of limited understanding.

* * *

Verse 32.

> **Remaining in Stolen Love and deferring marriage**
> **are within two months, they say.**

What does this declare, you ask? It places a definite time limit on the conduct of remaining in Stolen Love.

Its meaning:

Remaining in Stolen Love—staying in Stolen Love.

and deferring marriage—extending the time until he attains her through marriage.

are within two months, they say—take it as occurring within a two-month period.

It follows from this verse as well that all this is not of the nature of the world, since the world places no such limit on the time of conducting Stolen Love.

This verse also indicates their ages at the point of their natural union. He has to have wanted the union to occur between a heroine who was eleven years and ten months old, and a hero who was fifteen years and ten months old. Thus, after she has conducted Stolen Love for two months, she becomes twelve, which is the childbearing age; the author eschewed the childbearing age as inappropriate

[500] That is: What is the point in bringing it up here?

for Stolen Love. And the hero will turn sixteen when he has conducted Stolen Love for two months; as that is the age at which he becomes confirmed in manhood, it also was eschewed as inappropriate for Stolen Love.

But why did he say "within two months" instead of just "two months," you ask? Because he will cease his conduct of Stolen Love when there are five or six days left to complete the two months, and begin asking for her in marriage—and being refused. When those days are over, his new age would arrive; and that would contradict the earlier statement that these people suffer no old age, sickness, or death. How, you ask? Because when those two months are gone, she would be twelve, and later thirteen; she would eventually reach a hundred and twenty, and have to die. Take it in the same way for him as well. Now the question remains, "When there is old age and sickness, is there necessarily death as well?" What is the answer to that, you ask? Nothing happens here except that she becomes twelve and he sixteen when those two months are over. Take it that it accords with the world to a certain extent, but no further. It continues throughout, does it not, partly in accordance and partly not in accordance with the world?

But then, there are poems such as this one, are there not, you ask:

> My lord of this town
> dazzling with flowers,
> take good care of her!
>
> May you never forsake her,
> even when her pretty,
> highset breasts begin to sag,
> or when her fine,
> long hair, cascading
> like sapphires down
> her golden body,
> is braided in with gray.[501]

Such poems mean to say that there is no old age, etc.; yet if there were, then so on and so forth.

Next, there is a group that says "within two months" means this: The waxing moon and the waning moon are "two." Of those, it is first light and then dark during the waxing of the moon, and first dark and then light during the waning of the moon.[502] "Within two months"[503] refers to the period of dark nights at the

---

[501] From *Naṟṟiṇai*, 10. The full poem was quoted on pages 185–186.

[502] That is, on each night during the waxing of the moon there is moonlight in the early evening followed by darkness after the moon sets; the process is reversed during the waning of the moon. There is practically no moonlight at all during the nights that occur near a new moon.

[503] **Tiṅkaḷ** is the word used to mean both "moon" and "month."

juncture of those two moons. That, however, is inappropriate. For what reason, you ask? Because it concerns nighttime trysts only. Moreover, it would require Stolen Love to occur only during the dark of the moon, and would place no time limit upon it.

Next, another group maintains that "within two months" refers to one part of fifteen days, as fifteen days divides a month into two parts. May you understand the inappropriate nature of this idea also.

* * *

Verse 33.

The hero has no interruption in Stolen Love.

What does this declare, you ask? It declares a characteristic of the hero during the period of Stolen Love.

Its meaning:

The hero has no interruption in Stolen Love—there are no interruptions due to the hero during Stolen Love.

By saying, "due to the hero," it is implied that there are some due to the heroine.

Further, by saying, "The hero has no interruption in Stolen Love," he implies that there will be no interruptions due to the heroine during the period of Married Love. Why? Because he will no longer encounter problems caused by a heroine who has to get herself to and from trysts at specific times, and on specific days. Also, they say that no heroine wants separation in Married Love; it is only the manly hero who does.

But there is no need to mention that. What is the reason, you ask? We get the idea that obstacles are caused by the heroine from his having said,

> There is a breach in Stolen Love if guarding increases
> when there is a delay in marriage,[504]

and,

> False signs also belong there
> as signs for knowing of his coming.[505]

And we get the idea that obstacles due to the hero do actually occur during the period of Married Love because these things are in his nature: learning, defense, and peace-mission. It is not necessary to comment upon them here.[506]

---

[504] *The Study of Stolen Love*, 16.

[505] *The Study of Stolen Love*, 17.

[506] They will be commented upon when he takes up verses 35–40, pages 245–274.

It could all have been brought in through the literary device of commenting upon extraneous words, but he wanted the student to understand it well, so he took it up and presented it here.

Or, says one sort of scholar, this verse means that the hero in Stolen Love doesn't stay with the heroine and leave her after a while; but that is inappropriate. If the hero were to stay on and on, stretching out his visit without coming and going, that in itself would create an obstacle, because it would become known to others.

What, then, is the correct interpretation? "Interruption in Stolen Love" means ceasing to be alone: we say "ceased" in the sense of "the disease ceased," or "the heat ceased."

Next, the hero acts without clarity during those two months; but if there are any times and places at which the heroine lacks clarity, she will come to understand later. But isn't it the hero who is supposed to be clear, and the possessor of great wisdom? And isn't she the one who is to lack clarity and to be less intelligent than he, you ask? It is not so. There is no way for him to avoid the quality of loneliness, and that is why it is pointed out in this way. But she avoids it, doesn't she? What she manages to avoid is her worry over his sadness and disgrace. Therefore, that is the reason both for her clarity and for his lack of it.

End
of
The Study of Stolen Love

PART II
The Study of Married Love

Verse 34.

> **In Married Love, departure is neither rebuked nor eschewed.**

What does this declare, you ask? It declares an understanding of the characteristics of Married Love, beginning here.

Its meaning:

In Married Love, departure—the departure that occurs during Married Love; renunciation, departure, separation, and moving away are all the same.

is neither rebuked nor eschewed—is not rebuked or eschewed by authors.

But why did he say, "In Married Love, departure is neither rebuked nor eschewed," instead of "in Married Love departure is not rebuked, and it is not eschewed," you ask? It is to say that neither do authors eschew it, nor do they limit it to a certain number of times.

Thus it amounts to saying that departure occurs only once during Stolen Love. But since the hero comes and goes many times, with all those daytime and nighttime trysts, departure must occur often in Stolen Love, you think? Those are not actually "departures," say the authors, since they are not undertaken with a particular goal in mind, and also because they are subject to a limit.

* * *

Verse 35.

> **Learning, defense, peace-mission,**
> **service to the emperor, amassing wealth, and courtesans:**
> **these six are the separations in that case.**

What does this declare, you ask? Above he said that there are many separations in Married Love; this verse declares their names, order, and number.

Its meaning:

Learning—leaving in the cause of education.

defense—leaving for the defense of the nation.

peace-mission—leaving to mediate between two kings, when they are warring between themselves.

service to the emperor—the emperor is the king; it means departing in his service.

amassing wealth—leaving for wealth.

courtesans—leaving for other women; the word 'courtesan' comes from an Aryan word meaning 'outside.'

these—a model for counting.
There is an empty word at the beginning of the third line.
six—their number.
in that case—at that stage.
separations—departures.
There is an empty word at the end of the verse.

Take it that the names of the departures are the names mentioned here, their order is the order in which they were given, and their number is six.

Next, the departure for learning was placed first because it is the best of all the departures, and because it belongs to the highest people. Departure for courtesans is placed last because lust is considered at the end.

So this verse contradicts the claim made above that these people are beyond comparison. Why, one asks? If he leaves for education after he has attained her, it implies that he was ignorant before. And since good conduct follows wisdom, and membership in a good family depends upon good conduct, he must have been deficient in all of those things.

Next, defense: He must be short in manliness if he departs to drive out others who enter his lands to harass and plunder.[507]

Next, peace-mission: He becomes an ambassador when he leaves to mediate, and ambassadors make their living by obeying the commands of others, so where is his incomparability?

Next, when one says that he leaves in the service of the emperor, it means that he runs errands. Now running errands is a very lowly occupation: it would mean that he doesn't have his own desires, but must follow the wishes of others, so where is his incomparability?

Next, if you say that he leaves to amass wealth, then he becomes someone who had no wealth before. Since people who have no wealth cannot command scorners, nor give to beggars and so on, he must also have all of those shortcomings, and where is the incomparability of a man like that?

Next, if you say he leaves for courtesans, he seems vulgar to those who see him; moreover, he must not love the heroine. Besides, he must have no strength of mind, since he sends his heart wherever he looks, and then trots along after his heart! And where is the incomparability of a man with no strength of mind?

All these points, then, show great contradictions, you claim? They do not. And why do they not, you ask?

His departure for learning is not to study. He had long ago learned from his teachers all the books on virtue, wealth, pleasure, and release. Now he travels to

---

507 The Bavanandam edition adds this further explanation: "... since it would mean that he suffers from base things done by others."

foreign lands to find people there who are strong in those books; if there are any, he goes to put their knowledge down and demonstrate the superiority of his own.

Next, his departure for defending the country: This does not mean that he will depart in order to remove suffering wherever there are sufferers; rather, he leaves his village to listen to the complaints of old people and women who cannot explain well what has happened to them, and of the lame people of the towns, the hunchbacks, the blind, the sick, and so on, in order to set things right. He leaves in order to bring the wicked to justice in the jungles, where one species terrorizes another; he leaves in order to free creatures that have been caught at the ocean front in nets of vines; he leaves to create wealth where there was none; to examine temples, town halls, rest houses, and so forth; and to help families that are going downhill. Moreover, he will leave simply to show his face to the living beings under his protection, since they will rejoice in seeing him, just as an infant is happy to see its mother, and in order to display his vigor before the spies of enemy kings whenever they come: because of this, even hostile kings will pay him tribute.

Next, the peace-mission: This does not mean that he departs to mediate as an ambassador would. Take the situation where two kings bear each other enmity and think, "We shall fight tomorrow! We shall fight today!" As he is sovereign over both of them, he thinks to himself, "It would be a great calamity for both families if all those people and animals died. Therefore, I am bound to prevent this war." Thus he entreats them both, and makes peace. That is one way. Moreover, just as the Pāṇṭiyaṉ King Mākīrtti made peace between the gods and the demons when they were at war by shouting, "Stop it! Drop it! Or I shall punish the victor!" he will declare here, "I will punish whichever of you two prevails over the other." Thus he will make peace. That is another way, since he really does have the strength to punish them both. But if he really has that much power, would it not be proper for him to sit back and send someone else? Why should he go himself, you ask? He must go: There is no greater example of perseverance than completing a task that takes you away from your lover. Therefore, he will depart for mediation.

Next, leaving in the service of the emperor is not done to run errands for him. He will leave in order to remove a danger that is threatening some emperor who is a friend of his, simply because he thinks it would be nice to do.

Next, departing for wealth does not mean he has none. All the various types of wealth that his parents had amassed may lie there for him to use, but he does not think it manly to enjoy his life in using that up; so he departs to amass wealth by his own enterprise, that he might live on that. Moreover, affairs of the gods and the ancestors will not bear fruit unless they are carried out with wealth that one has amassed by his own enterprise. Why? Gods and ancestors are not pleased with rites performed with inherited wealth. Thus, he departs in order to make them happy as well.

Next, courtesans are common women. But he is not one who goes and bows down before them, lacking love for the heroine; nor does he lack strength of mind. Why not? He leaves the heroine thinking, "I shall go and watch some singing, and some dancing." But then the emotions that he puts into the performance mask his feelings for the heroine. Why? Because those two emotions cannot coexist. He stays on with the courtesans, then, when he covers his feelings in this way. Why? If people who are naturally beautiful and attractive take it specifically upon themselves to attract a man with their songs and their dances, is it even necessary to say he will be attracted? You didn't know what you were talking about when you asked that question!

Take it that this is the meaning of those various departures. Next, we shall present poetry for each departure when we come to detailing the things that pertain to it.

* * *

Verse 36.

> **Of those,**
> **learning and defense belong to the highest people.**

What does this declare, you ask? It declares that of the above mentioned departures, in the order in which they are given, the first two pertain to such and such a type of people.

Its meaning:

Of those—among the six types of departure mentioned above.

learning and defense—the departures for learning and protecting the land.

belong to the highest people—the highest people are the Brahmins and the royalty; it means that they pertain to these two groups.

Take it by their respective order that Brahmins depart for learning, and kings depart for defense. To those who think that an improper interpretation, since he did not say "respectively," and maintain that learning and defense ought both to pertain to both Brahmins and kings, the answer is this: Even though he did not state it in that way, it is appropriate when one looks at the sort of meaning involved. Why? Because it is said that they pertain to the highest people, who are the Brahmins and the royalty. All right then, since he said they pertain to the highest people, shouldn't we assign them to Brahmins alone, you ask? It should not be taken that way: defense is not a Brahmin's job. Thus we get that they apply to both of them. Moreover, we also get that they pertain to both of them through the literary device of interpreting through the commentary.

When he leaves for learning, the hero will inform the heroine through her friend; here is a poem for that:

Making Known His Departure For Learning

You bewitching girl
from the good lands
of the King of the South,
the Scholar
who showered
a rain of arrows
from his mighty bow
upon Cennilam,
to destroy those
who did not join with him,
but instead made war!

Your man whose words cannot lie
is about to leave
to advance his immaculate
education—

that's what it looks like.[508]

A hero who is about to depart for defense also will inform the heroine through her friend; here is a poem for that:

Making Known His Departure For Defense

You with your thin waist,
you, like the cool and
pretty city of Kūṭal
of the king whose mere glance
at his fine, shining sword
caused emperors who made war
with him in their anger
to reach warriors' heaven!
Your lover loves
to go out and protect
this wide world, circled
by the sea with its
full, clear waves,
and keep from it
all evil.[509]

* * *

508 *Pāṇṭi-k-Kōvai*, 239.

509 *Pāṇṭi-k-Kōvai*, 240.

Verse 37.

The nature of imperial action belongs also to the Brahmins.

What does this declare, you ask? It declares that there is yet another departure for Brahmins, beyond that for increasing education previously mentioned.
Its meaning:
imperial—royal.
action—deed.
The nature—the quality.
belongs also to the Brahmins—is also a right of the Brahmins.

In saying this, he means that mediating peace, which is properly royal, pertains to Brahmins as well. But he would only have to say that the nature of imperial action belongs also to the Brahmins if he had already said that it belongs to kings, you say? Indeed he has said so. How? When he placed defense and peace-mission together and declared that those two both belong to kings, that is what he meant. How do they appertain to kings, you ask? If a king did not go and mediate between two others who differ and bear each other enmity, all of their dependents and their lands would suffer tremendously, wouldn't they? Such an act appertains to royalty because it is sin and a disgrace not to get rid of such a situation when one has the power to, but to sit back in acquiescence. The mediating function that pertains to them in that way, then, pertains to Brahmins as well. Why? Because they also have nobility. Here is a poem for that:

You with your perfect jewels,
you who are like the lands
full watered by the River Vaiyai
  of the king
  who deprived emperors
  flaunting great warrior's anklets
  of their honor—and
  the town of Veṇmāttu—
  in harsh battle!

Our man loves to mediate
between two mighty emperors
when they attack each other in war.[510]

* * *

Verse 38.

Other than kings, for others also
it becomes proper in one place, they say.

---

[510] *Pāṇṭi-k-Kōvai*, 241.

What does this declare, you ask? It declares that the departure for mediation belongs not only to kings, but also to merchants and farmers.
Its meaning:
Other than kings, for others also—the others, beyond the royalty, are the two remaining caste groups: merchants and farmers.
it becomes proper in one place, they say—it is appropriate, they say, when they are not available.

Merchants and farmers also get to depart for mediation between two who have had differences and enmity, providing there are no kings to do it. Other than the fact that they are merchants and farmers, they equal the royalty in wealth and perseverance. But then the previous verse must be superfluous, since saying "Other than kings, for others also" here would include Brahmins as well. But to those who say that, the answer is that it is not so. He said " other than kings" in order to include merchants and farmers, who are to be listed after kings. Otherwise, he would not have said,

> The nature of imperial action belongs also to the Brahmins.[511]

Take it that the poems adduced above are appropriate for these two as well.

* * *

Verse 39.

> **Departure for service to the emperor and amassing wealth,**
> **those two also belong to the lower people.**

What does this declare, you ask? It declares a departure that pertains to merchants and farmers.
Its meaning:
service to the emperor—service to the king.
Departure for ... amassing wealth—departure with a desire for wealth.
those—a model for counting.
There is an empty word at the beginning of the second line.
two—the number.
also—completion.
belong to the lower people—are rights of merchants and farmers.

You think it contradicts their incomparability to say they are low? It does not. Since this treatise both accords with and does not accord with the world, these people are called "low" by virtue of the worldly distinctions of caste types. In all other worldly respects, incomparability accords with these people as well.

---

[511] *The Study of Stolen Love*, 37.

Of those departures, a hero who leaves for service to the emperor informs the heroine through her friend; here are some poems for that:

Making Known His Departure For Service To The Emperor

You with perfect jewels,
you who are like the southern lands,
well watered, and ever growing in wealth,
    of him whose chariot's wheels
    reddened as they rolled
    across corpses of those
    who wouldn't think,
    and opposed him
    at Cennilam!
Our man is ready to leave
for a battlefront
filled with enemies
for the sake of a king
whose crown is adorned
with fragrant flowers,
whose drum is tied tight
with leather straps![512]

You with your innocent words,
rich, like the sweet Tamil
of Kūṭal City, that city
    of the king who fought
    the Battle of Naṟaiyāṟu,
    and made his foes perish,
    the King of the South,
    with his history
    of victories!
Your lover,
his longbow on his shoulder,
has set off to destroy enemies
in the battlefront
of our king,
whose shoulders
are like rock.[513]

Here is a poem for the heroine to address to her friend when the friend is worried about the anguished changes she has undergone after the hero has left in the service of the emperor; she tells her friend that she will be all right:

---

[512] *Pāṇṭi-k-Kōvai*, 242.

[513] *Pāṇṭi-k-Kōvai*, 243.

Placing It Upon The Clouds

Friend, with your fragrant wreath
and garland!
When dark clouds climb
into the sky,
having drunk from the deeps
of the southern seas
at Cape Kumari,
the cape
　of the Lion to His Enemies
　who waged war
　with his reddened lance—
will they go and appear
above the tents
where he, with his garlands
of cool flowers and leaves,
is staying?[514]

When her friend hears this, she thinks, "Her changes are not due to anguish at the absence of her hero: it seems she is upset because she fears those clouds beckoning above his tent. She fears he might return without completing the task he undertook. It is true that he had set the monsoon season for his return. I misunderstood her." She then condoles with the heroine:

You with your fragrant wreath
of sweet mango,
where bees buzz!
Those moist clouds
that took up the good waters
of Cape Kaṉṉi
　of him who loosed arrows
　from his magnificent bow
　to rout the navy
　of the Cēraṉ king
　at Kōṭṭāṟu—
would they go and appear
above the battlefield of swords,
filled with strong kings and grand chariots,
their horses galloping?[515]

Here are some poems for the hero to address to his charioteer on their return home; he has completed his task in service to the emperor, and the season he had set for his return is at hand:

---

[514] *Pāṇṭi-k-Kōvai*, 244.

[515] *Pāṇṭi-k-Kōvai*, 245.

Speaking With A Thought Of The Situation

On that dreary, dewy day
when the swan takes his darling young
under his right wing,
and hugs his mate with his left
in love,
and shivers,
what will become of that girl,
with all her brooding?
She is like the Vaiyai lands
    of the king who fought
    to make opposing kings
    head south from Iruñciṟai,

and her jewels
are perfect.[516]

When the heron
puts his pretty young to sleep
beneath his right wing,
and hugs his tender mate
with his left,
and keens,
in this Tamil land
    of him who crushed
    enemy kings
    until they perished
    at Āṟṟukkuṭi,

will she see the dew fall,
and will my loving girl feel reassured?[517]

Once the charioteer hears this, he agrees to drive faster.

Further, a hero who has completed his tour of duty in service to the emperor may also speak like this:

Thoughts On Having Completed His Task

The soft face of that girl
whose glance is like that
of a young doe,
whose waist is like a vine
with flowers where bees buzz,

---

[516] *Pāṇṭi-k-Kōvai*, 246.

[517] *Pāṇṭi-k-Kōvai*, 247.

a vine in the Kolli Mountains
    of our King Neṭumāṟaṉ,
    whose lance is sharp—
her face smote me that day
in the grand, fragrant grove!
And today her melancholy face
appears

above the high walls of these enemies
who will not submit, nor turn hospitable![518]

She is like Vañci City
    of our king,
    who ran off the armies
    of those who did not praise him
    but would oppose him at Naṭṭāṟu,
    who pursued them eight leagues[519]
    then sheathed his sword,
    flashing, and victorious!
And it was
her moonlike face
with her dark eyes
flitting like flowers in a pool
and her white ear studs shining,
that appeared today
above the battlefront
of our foes![520]

That girl's beautiful face
where lie the bow,
and the red carp
    of the King of the South
    who subdued his foes
    at Pāḻi, full as it is
    of waters where young carp
    leap among the flowers—
her face, it appeared today
with its ever shining
bright ear studs—
it appeared above their high fortress walls

---

518 *Pāṇṭi-k-Kōvai*, 248.

519 Eight **kātam**. Each **kātam** is approximately ten miles.

520 *Pāṇṭi-k-Kōvai*, 249.

just to make those rebellious emperors
drown in the flames![521]

The result of this is that the charioteer drives faster when he hears the hero say it.

Does he speak this way when he has not completed his tour of duty, as well as when he has, you ask? He does not. Why? He is to speak only after the completion of his mission, because it says,

They do not speak of the state of the heroine during the task;
it will be expressed when he has been victorious.[522]

Here are some more poems for him to speak to his charioteer while he is returning, after he has completed his tour of duty in the service of the emperor:

Speaking To The Charioteer

We went to the battlefront
of the foes of Neṭumāṟaṉ
    whose red lance rejoices
    now in its victory!
We have finished
our mission,
and now we come home.
The clouds are just
darkening a bit—
drive your strong chariot
up to the grand home
of the innocent girl
whose fine, curving waist
stands up like a young vine.
Let us arrive today.[523]

We went to his huge tents
that took the battle
through perseverance,
tents of the Pāṇṭiyaṉ
    with his proud horses,
    his army great as an ocean,
    and his indestructible
    white canopy
    that grants shade

---

[521] *Pāṇṭi-k-Kōvai*, 250.

[522] *Tolkāppiyam: Kaṟpiyal*, 45.

[523] *Pāṇṭi-k-Kōvai*, 251.

to all the earth,
and now we have finished
our mission—
Look, the season is here—
look there, in the woods
so pleasant to look at,
the woods that flourish
in these winter rains,
bees with pretty wings
swarm fragrant jasmine blooms
this evening!

Let us get to the shoulders
of that girl with her bright bracelets,
whose hair is as fragrant
as that grove in Vāṇaṉ's
Ciṟukuṭi village
where the sound
of a taṇṇumai drum,
covered with buckled leather,
drives birds from a pool
filled with flowers,
and where there are oh,
so many fields full of rice
ripe for the harvest—

Drive! Drive your well decked chariot fast!
Now![524]

Further, he says other things as well; here are some poems for that:

In the southern lands
of the Lion to His Enemies,
who fought the scorching
Battle of Pāḻi,
the descendant of the king
who gave a thousand elephants
in alms,
winter piṭavu is blooming now,
like a fragrant, woven
wreath in the cool woodlands.
I watch the dark clouds:

is that doll, that girl,
whose wide mound of love
is covered with silk

[524] *Akanāṉūṟu*, 204.

watching them too?
I wonder.[525]

That luxuriant woodland,
where stags with strong antlers
wander, yet never leave their does,
grazing on the putavam grass
that grows in such clumps
in those southern lands
    of the king
    whose sword witnessed
    the flight from war
    of all who opposed him
    at Vallam—

will those woods upset my girl,
with her soft, flowing hair?
I wonder.[526]

A flowering woodland
where a gamecock,
speckled handsomely
like milk sprinkled
on melting butter,
has his hen scratch
the white sand of a river bed
after a flood—
that woods swelled desire
in the eyes of our girl
with her fragrant garland,
she who is like
the southern lands
    of Māṟaṉ who conquered
    the Cōḻa and the Cēraṉ,
    and whose warrior's anklet
    fits tight.[527]

Look! Grief shows
in these flowering woods,
where a gamecock
with his handsome comb
scratches up food from the dust

---

[525] *Pāṇṭi-k-Kōvai*, 252.

[526] *Pāṇṭi-k-Kōvai*, 253.

[527] *Pāṇṭi-k-Kōvai*, 254.

to feed his hen, then
stands back to watch
her eat.
Drive that strong chariot,
that chariot like
the caparisoned elephants
    of those who lost at Āṟṟukkuṭi
    to the Wonder King,
    Tirumāl with His discus![528]

With her perfect, dark hair,
she is like Kūṭal City,
well watered,
    that city of Neṭumāṟaṉ
    with his well oiled lance!
But those heavy clouds
high in the sky
will bring no relief
to my girl,
so race this strong chariot
to the front of the line!
And may all those rapturous she-elephants
in heat, their eyes spitting fire—

may they follow the footprints of their bulls,
with strong trunks, through these woods![529]

Her nature is tender,
she is like the lands of waters
in the South,
the country
    of the Scholar
    who crushed his foes
    with the strength
    of his shining lance,
    so those disagreeable warriors
    died at Pāḻi in the South—
if your strong chariot
can fly no longer,
if thorns have pierced the hooves
of your surging horses,

528 *Pāṇṭi-k-Kōvai*, 255.

529 *Pāṇṭi-k-Kōvai*, 256.

will she mark this day down,
beside all those she has marked already?[530]

The charioteer drives faster because of his saying these things.

Clouds neared the banners
flying on the open terrace
of her rich, grand home,
decked with gems,
and then they
thundered—
Her eyes are tender,
like mango fruit,
she is like Muciṟi City
    of the Emperor
    whose fortress is triple walled,
    who destroyed other emperors
    with their fragrant wreaths
    at Āṟṟukkuṭi,
    and wears the wreath
    of war flowers
    upon his crown!

She suffered.[531]

This one also accords with those given above.

Next, here is a poem for the hero to speak as he gazes at the clouds; he intends his charioteer to overhear:

Conversing With The Clouds

Long may you live,
fertile cloud!
Just don't get
to her grand, guarded
home before I do!
You see,
she is like
the lands of waters
    of him who vanquished enemy kings:
    they bloated in blood
    from their own wounds
    there at Pāḻi,
    where winged bees
    buzz music in the groves!

---

[530] *Pāṇṭi-k-Kōvai*, 257.

[531] *Pāṇṭi-k-Kōvai*, 258.

She would see you, and cry,
and her beauty would fade.[532]

The charioteer drives faster because he hears this.

Here are some poems for her friend to utter to the heroine when she apprehends the return of a hero who had left in service to the emperor, his task complete:

Announcing The Arrival

You with your tender,
young breasts,
you are like Kūṭal City
in the South
    the city of King Neṭumāṟaṉ,
    whose lance
    the blacksmith keeps
    to perfection—
Horses with golden garlands
drawing the rich chariot
decked with gems
of our lover
who took tribute
from his foes
have arrived at our front door
with such a clamor—

go on:
you can shine![533]

You who are like Māntai City
    of Māṟaṉ
    who ravished the Cēras,
    and whose fragrant wreath
    drips with honey,
    that wreath woven
    of mountain ebony,
    pretty, tender palmyra,
    and neem blossoms![534]
Clouds are mingling,
roaring, and flashing lightning

---

[532] *Pāṇṭi-k-Kōvai*, 259.

[533] *Pāṇṭi-k-Kōvai*, 260.

[534] Mountain ebony, **ār**, is the flower characteristic of garlands worn by Cōḻa kings. Similarly, palmyra, **pōntai**, is the Cēraṉ's flower, and neem, **vēmpu**, is the Pāṇṭiyaṉ's.

now that the chariot of our lover enters
our grand mansion, to all that clamor![535]

Next, her friend speaks to a heroine suffering in the absence of the hero; she tells her that the season he had specified as marking the completion of his tour of duty has arrived as his emissary. Here is a poem for that:

Her Friend Announcing The Ambassadorial Season

These huge clouds
gathering darkness,
like the sapphire throat
of Him who stands atop the crown
    of Neṭumāṟaṉ the Scholar
    who conquered Pulippai
    in the South—
they have come as emissaries
to foretell the return
of him who once
tightly embraced
your budding breasts
and devoured your smile,

but left you![536]

Next, here is a poem for the hero to address to her friend, when he has finished his mission and sits sweetly with the heroine:

The Hero Speaking To Her Friend

That time we spent
in our tents sortying out
to battle the foes
    of him
    whose army conquered Kuḷantai,
    the noble King Neṭumāṟaṉ,
    whose canopy
    is of glistening pearls,
passed pleasantly enough,
but only because she
with her vine-like waist
came along:

---

535 *Pāṇṭi-k-Kōvai*, 261.

536 *Pāṇṭi-k-Kōvai*, 262.

With her long eyes that look like lily blooms
filling an aqueduct with tears—
she stood by my side![537]

Next, here is a poem for the hero to speak as he prepares his departure to amass wealth; he informs the heroine through her friend:

Making Known His Departure For Wealth

You with your tender nature,
who are like
the lands of waters
in the South,
  lands of the Scholar
  whose bow showered
  fierce arrows
  over Nelvēli
  to extinguish those foes
  who opposed him
  in their anger!
Our man knows
that no have-not
will ever feel comfort
in this life, nor the next:

so he's made up his mind to travel
through those rocky wastelands
for great wealth.[538]

Here is a poem for the heroine, who felt anguished as she heard that, to address to her friend:

The Anguish Of The Heroine

Across the wastelands
where bamboos burn hot
like the battlefronts
  of the enemies
  of this king
  whose righteous scepter
  rises far above
  the world's meanness,
  the king who distressed
  his foes in war at Vallam,

---

[537] *Pāṇṭi-k-Kōvai*, 263.

[538] *Pāṇṭi-k-Kōvai*, 264.

and demolished their honor,
the Supreme One,
the Emperor
with a grand canopy
rising far above blemish—

is our lord to make his fortune
out there?[539]

Here are some poems in which her friend lets the hero know the state of the heroine:

Her Friend Relating The State Of The Heroine

As soon as I said,
"Our lord will travel
through scrubwood hills,
hot like the battlefields
of the Scholar,
the Emperor
with the ever fragrant,
tall crown,"
row upon row
of conch bracelets fell
from the arms of that girl
with her brilliant brow,
pearls spilled from her eyes,
and the loose jewelled band
slipped from her waist,

fell on her soft feet,
and wailed![540]

Lord of great renown!
When I said,
"Dear girl,
with your waist prettier
than a lightning streak,
you who are like Māntai City
of Neṭumāṟaṉ,
the king with the famous sword,
the king of great renown—
our man is to travel
through hot deserts,"
her lotus eyes spilled pearls

539 *Pāṇṭi-k-Kōvai*, 265.

540 *Pāṇṭi-k-Kōvai*, 266.

on her golden, pert
young breasts!

That fortune you mean to make:
what good is it now?[541]

This also accords with those given above.

Next, her friend says to the hero, "How will she pass such long nights alone, while you are gone?" Here are some poems for that:

Blaming It On The Night

Once it disappears
behind those special,
tall mountains we call
the setting mountains,
and wanders the whole earth
    like the enemies
    of our king
    with his grand army
    that crushed them
    at Vallam,
the red sun
will not rise again
until it crosses
those beautiful,
tall mountains
in the East—

How is she to get through
those long nights ahead?[542]

Dusk must spread
    like the victorious battlegrounds
    of the king
    with the poisonous bow
    who conquered Pāḻi,
    the Goad to His Enemies,
    whose elephants wear
    headgear slung low
    on their huge faces,
yet it must leave again,
but only after
the darkness of midnight

[541] *Pāṇṭi-k-Kōvai*, 267.

[542] *Pāṇṭi-k-Kōvai*, 268.

has passed on,
only after that grand
eternity of the last watch
crawls slowly by,

before the burning sun
can reappear![543]

This also is the same.

When she consents to the hero's departure, her friend utters a poem; she says, "You have done well. The woods he will travel through are like this:"

Her Friend Describing The Nature Of The Woodlands

Girl with your hair
perfumed with musk,
he who wears his garland
dripping with honey
will see a black elephant
that never takes its trunk away
from its mate,
there in the woods
adorning the Kolli Mountains
    of the Gift of the Gods
    who holds his proud,
    gleaming lance,
    whose tip has ripened
    in conquest—
he will go
no farther:

You did right when you agreed
to his leaving.[544]

Next, her friend says to the heroine, "Our lord has finished making his fortune! He has returned!" Here is a poem for that:

Her Friend Announcing The Hero's Arrival

You with your
gleaming bracelets!
The clouds,
dark as always,
have started to pour out

---

[543] *Pāṇṭi-k-Kōvai*, 269.

[544] *Pāṇṭi-k-Kōvai*, 270.

their rains,
and he with his garland
where bees buzz
mountain melodies
has returned!
He has entered
our golden mansion
with riches
like cool, beautiful
Kūṭal City
    of the Lion to His Enemies
    with his righteous scepter
    that always grants grace
    to the people
    of this great earth![545]

Additionally, at this point she reassures the heroine by noting that the season has come for his return; but the heroine has grown thin and distraught by this time, and answers with a broken heart. Here are some poems for that:

Answering A Reassurance With A Broken Heart

You, with your unguented hair,
look:
This woman
with all her bracelets
traipsing from door to door,
hawking spring flowers
dear to the god
with the fish emblem
upon his banner,
    here in Kūṭal City
    in the South
    of Neṭumāṟaṉ
    with his righteous scepter and mountainous elephants,
    who conquered Caṅkamankai—

really, she's quite
obnoxious.[546]

Like skewering a lance
deep in the raw flesh
of a gaping wound
in the chest,

---

[545] *Pāṇṭi-k-Kōvai*, 271.

[546] *Pāṇṭi-k-Kōvai*, 272.

this river
with its lucid water
is crueler
than the cries
of the cuckoo
that never leave me alone
in my pain—
but, worse yet,
this gorgeous little farmgirl
from the fruit orchards
traipses around
with her palmleaf basket
swarming with bees,
and keeps calling,
"Wouldn't you like
some little champak flowers,
tied in with fresh kurukkatti buds,
their outer petals are pretty
like cotton cloth?"[547]

See for yourself, then, all other poems that pertain to this context, wherever they occur.

* * *

Verse 40.

Mistresses is appropriate for everyone.

What does this declare, you ask? Above he detailed all departures in their specifics; here he declares that the departure for courtesans is appropriate for anyone.

Its meaning:

Mistresses is appropriate for everyone—departure for courtesans is appropriate for men of all four castes.

Men are quite intelligent enough to recognize it when courtesans see them and love them, and it would be ungracious of them to leave without uniting with them: take it that this applies to men of all castes. But this interpretation is not proper. For what reason, you ask? All people, high or low, love a great man when they see him; and by this argument he would have to depart to unite with everyone! He would then bear all sorts of shortcomings, which would contradict his greatness. Moreover, it is also claimed here that they depart through grace, not love; therefore it would be inappropriate for him to depart and go to a woman who really loves him.

---

[547] *Naṟṟiṇai*, 97.

Next, one school argues that a "mistress" is a courtesan who really loves him. What is their reasoning, you ask? A man who enjoys milk every day will realize its superiority only if he eats sour gruel now and then; and just like that, a man who continuously enjoys the wonderful qualities of the heroine day after day will feel increased love for her if he visits mean natured whores from time to time—otherwise he could not know that her qualities are incomparable. Why? Because it is through the existence of something unpleasant that we know the pleasure of the sweet. But their comments also are improper. For what reason, you ask? If he needs them as a comparison in order to appreciate her greatness, then he must have doubted her qualities even when he was not with them; but that would contradict the statement that he and she are non-different. Why? Because no one doubts his own good qualities.

What, then, is the true commentary, you ask? Take it that the hero loves his mistress. But if that is so, might he not fall in love with anyone he sees, you ask? He does not. We shall explain how it works: The hero conducts his life principally in these three arenas: virtue, wealth, and pleasure; he divides his day into three parts to accommodate them. He spends the first ten nāḻikai[548] in the pursuit of virtue, the middle ten in the pursuit of wealth, and the last ten for pleasure. Now such a hero, who performs his activities with an eye upon the time, wants the same things the heroine does: he enters his audience hall, attends to expositions of virtue, and continues in the line of virtue. Still attentive to the time, he listens to matters of taxation and justice during the middle ten nāḻikai, as he lives in the realm of wealth. And when those times are past, he comes back to the heroine for the last ten nāḻikai. On his way, the courtesans see him coming and play their flutes and string their lutes, beat their taṇṇumai drums and play their muḻavu drums to advertise their dancing to him. Why? Because the author of *A Treatise On Dancing* also has said,

> ...
> stringing the lute after playing the flute,
> and beating the muḻavu drum after the taṇṇumai
> drum: that is the āmantirikai performance
> ...[549]

When the hero learns of their performance in this manner he thinks to himself, "We'll have a look at this for a while." They make him stay with them then, once he enters.

---

[548] Ancient Tamils divided the day into sixty **nāḻikai** of equal length; that corresponds to twenty-four minutes per **nāḻikai**.

[549] Unidentified verse.

Now it must work in only one of these two ways: the hero has them either after he has attained the heroine through marriage, or before. Of those two, if one were to say he has them after his marriage, he must be one of those people who think people other than the heroine can please him; but that would contradict the saying,

> Seeing and hearing, tasting, breathing, and touching:
> these exist only in her whose bracelets gleam.[550]

But if one were to say he had them before he attained the heroine in marriage, he would turn into a lusty reveler who had no time for study during his youth; that is, he would have had a poor upbringing.

Then what other interpretation is there, you ask? He had the courtesans even before he attained the heroine in marriage. But if you say that, won't the shortcoming noted above apply to him, you ask? It does not. His parents would have provided for him without his knowledge, and set things apart saying, "This is his girl, these are his elephants and horses, and all these things are his." In the meantime, they themselves would have sported with them. Thus they were his possessions before he ever attained the heroine, since they were raised by his parents in that way. How does he first become aware that they belong to him, you ask? The hero leaves the heroine, completes his pursuit of virtue and wealth, and returns. They play their flutes, lutes, and drums, as we noted before, and he says, "What's this?"

"It's all yours," they answer, "isn't it?"

"How is this mine?" he asks.

"It was given to you by your parents," they tell him, "as your right."

He realizes that he should not cross his parents' commands, and he goes to see them: and then they make him love them. That is how the departure for courtesans comes about.

All right then: the author needed all those other departures to confirm the hero's perseverance, but what did he need this one for, you ask? Here is what occurs when the hero departs for courtesans: jealous love quarrels, sulking, and loathing. After they occur, they are removed, and then the hero and heroine experience tremendous pleasure as they make up and reunite. Take it that these things bring out this pleasure, and that he needs this departure because he is an author who has a taste for such subtleties.

All right, but why doesn't the verse read "Mistresses are appropriate for everyone" instead of "is appropriate," with the singular form of the verb, you ask? Since this comes in his section on departures, he means that the *departure* for mistresses is appropriate for everyone.

---

[550] *Tirukkuṟaḷ*, 1101.

Here is a poem on his departure for courtesans:

Her Friend's Refusal At The Door

I said,
"You with impeccable jewels,
who are like the lands in the South
 of Neṭumāṟaṉ with a well-oiled lance,
 who granted heaven to his enemies at Vallam,
 with its great groves
 where clouds settle!
Our lover
is coming this way."

And right in front of me,
her red lips quivered,
and her black eyes reddened.[551]

A hero who had departed for courtesans asks her friend to let him through the door of the house, but she refuses. What does she say as she refuses him, you ask? She says, "She has come to this pass because she understood what I meant when I told her about you. Now it's up to you to figure out what is proper, and do it!"

Next, here is a poem to be uttered by a bard who has come to the door on the hero's behalf, and been refused by the heroine:

What The Bard Says In Anger

Go on, my lord,
lord of this town
decked with fields,
go on, stay with them
for years and years!
The calf you gave me to eat
will do fine,
you needn't hurl rocks
at me too—
this grand world,
 owned by him who crushed
 angry enemies
 and annexed Viḻiñam
is plenty big enough,
isn't it?

---

[551] *Pāṇṭi-k-Kōvai*, 273.

Pray, let this slave
take my honorable leave of you![552]

Further, here are some poems for her friend to speak. She watched as he was refused at the door after his return from the courtesans, only to be allowed to enter later with his son as his pass. She now hopes to banish the heroine's jealousy:

Her Friend Speaking To Remove Jealousy

You with a waist like
a lightning streak,
you who are like Cape Kaṉṉi
   of him who watched ghouls bathe
   in his enemies' blood
   at Iruñciṟai, and eat
   their half-gelled fat!
Since our lord has waltzed on in
with his son
who is wearing
his little cowrie-shell belt,
crying and climbing all over
his father's nape,
you'll have to worship
and obey him!

Don't think any more
about his flaws.[553]

You who wear
so many bracelets,
who are like
the lands of waters
in the South
   of the king with worldwide renown
   who simply thought
   about his oiled lance,
   and enemy warriors
   fled Neṭuṅkaḷam—
he's here with his son
perched upon his shoulders,
his son who bears the name
of his grandfather—
he's wearing his belt of gems

---

[552] *Pāṇṭi-k-Kōvai*, 274.

[553] *Pāṇṭi-k-Kōvai*, 275.

and golden coins, and he's
holding his little drum
with the leather straps—

Don't think any more
about his flaws.[554]

This is similar in meaning to the one just above.

The heroine's anger cools down when the hero comes through the door with his son as his pass. Her friend recognizes the indicators of this fact, and tells the hero that the heroine is now in such and such a state; here is a poem for that:

Her Friend Telling Of The Heroine's Cooling Down

She is like Cape Kaṉṉi
    of him who has elephants
    whose bells beat
    against their legs,
    who won at Viḻiñam
    and made kings decked
    with myriads of gems
    flee!
And since you came back
with your son
sporting that jeweled belt,
her eyes, like fighting carp,
lost their redness
and regained
the pretty coloring
of huge sapphires—

they blossomed![555]

When the hero has returned from a visit to the courtesans and regained admission to the house, the heroine will lose her jealousy; here is a poem for her to speak then:

Telling Him To Come On In After
He Has Dried Himself Off From His Bathing

Lord of those large baths
in the sapphire colored
River Vaiyai
    of him who made misery

---

554 *Pāṇṭi-k-Kōvai*, 276.

555 *Pāṇṭi-k-Kōvai*, 277.

for the wives of his enemies
at Pāḻi,
the Goad to His Enemies,
the lord of this land
with beautiful lotus pools!
I know you got wet
when you splashed my little sister
in those refreshing waters—
now go on, dry yourself off,
then come and touch
my little feet with your palms:

then do what you do
with such grace![556]

What does this mean, you ask? She is saying, "Dry off the moisture from your bath with your mistress yesterday; then come and do that precious thing you do for me!"

* * *

Verse 41.

It is not appropriate to delimit in years
the length of departure for those who stay in a different land.

What does this declare, you ask? It places a limit upon the length of time during which a hero remains away.

Its meaning:

It is not appropriate to delimit in years—a departure delimited in years is inappropriate.

the length of departure—a departure that extends over a long period of time.

for those who stay in a different land—for those who leave and remain off somewhere beyond countries and forests.

What meaning are we to get from this, you ask? When he departs, he specifies days, months, or seasons for his return: he says, "I will return on this day," or, "in this month," or, "in this season."

Here is a poem for her friend to address to the heroine when she has learned that a departing hero is to return on a specified day:

Her Friend Relating The Specification Of A Day

You with your large eyes,
like swords

[556] *Pāṇṭi-k-Kōvai*, 278.

of the Lion to His Enemies,
who wields the righteous scepter,
and whose killing elephant
burns men
with its fiery eyes!
Our man has marked a day
in a good month
for making that precious fortune
which enhances the number
of one's relations—

he is thinking of leaving.
What do you think?[557]

The heroine suffers changes when the departing hero sets a certain month for his return; and her friend worries that she can not be comforted. Here is a poem for her to speak to her friend, assuring her that she can:

Girl with such soft,
long, thick, dark hair!
He left to seek his fortune,
wearing that cool garland:
Will he see, tonight,
the budding crescent moon,
the ancestor of him
who just the other day
saw the backs
of those who arrived
in Cennilam
intent on victory,
and repulsed
their strong chariots,
then came back home?[558]

What did she say in that poem, you ask? She said, "It's not out of anguish that I have suffered these changes: I was upset when I thought about the month he had set, because I wondered if he might end up coming back without finishing the task he undertook to make his fortune."

Next, the hero may specify the rainy season when he departs. Then the heroine undergoes changes when the monsoon arrives, and her friend worries that she might not be able to comfort her. Here are some poems for her to address to her friend, assuring her that she can be consoled.

Girl, you whose hair
is surrounded

---

[557] *Pāṇṭi-k-Kōvai*, 279.

[558] *Pāṇṭi-k-Kōvai*, 280.

by the buzzing
of bees' wings!
Billowing clouds
that took up good water
from Cape Kumari
    of him who unsheathed
    his shining white sword
    by the edge of the sea
    at Viḻiñam, so that
    enemies who stared at him
    just died—

the clouds have darkened like the sapphire throat
of the God who made the River Ganges
descend into his flowing, matted locks![559]

These clouds
are like the hands
    of Neṭumāṟaṉ,
    the king who crushed
    his enemies at Naṭṭāṟu
    and turned the pools
    of their blood
    into lakes!
These clouds darkened
and brought the monsoon—
but then when they thought
of the cool woodlands
where young forked thorns
on wild berry bushes
look like cobra tongues,

they suffered.[560]

What does she mean by that, you ask? She said, "It isn't because I'm anguished that I have suffered these changes: I was upset because I wondered if he might come back without finishing his task of making his fortune, when he notes the arrival of this season he had set for his return."

Her friend will worry that the heroine will languish when she notes the arrival of the dewy season, when that is the one the hero had set for his return; here are some poems for the heroine to address to her friend:

You who are like
the lands of waters in the South
    of the Lion to His Enemies,

---

[559] *Pāṇṭi-k-Kōvai*, 281.

[560] *Pāṇṭi-k-Kōvai*, 282.

whose elephants burn
with anger, and make
striped bees circle
and buzz as rut
streams down their cheeks
to their mouths!
The lingering dew
that blankets red flames
from a fire, cools it down,
and turns it to powder,
it's here—
it will save
your pretty bracelets,
and keep them from
slipping off.[561]

Now, as thorns
on fruiting berry bushes
in the Koṅku forests
of the king
who conquered Āṟṟukkuṭi
with his solitary,
curved bow,
gather scattered dewdrops
upon their tips,

will they string them like shiny pearls
just to afflict lonely women?[562]

Her friend worries that she might not be able to comfort the heroine when spring arrives, if that is the season the hero had set for his return; here is a poem for her to speak in that vein:

Her Friend Speaking In Worry

The beauty of this girl
who is like Māntai City
of Māṟaṉ the King,
whose hands have usurped
the greatness of rainclouds,
passed away with the winter—
now how will spring pass,
when cool south breezes
mix with cool water lily blossoms

---

[561] *Pāṇṭi-k-Kōvai*, 283.

[562] *Pāṇṭi-k-Kōvai*, 284.

dripping with nectar, only
to kindle heartfires,

how will it pass
for this delicate-natured girl?[563]

The heroine suffers changes when the departing hero sets the summer season for his return, and her friend worries that she will not be able to comfort her. Here is a poem for the heroine to speak to her friend, assuring her that she can be consoled:

What The Heroine Says To Her Friend

Tender natured friend!
Sweet asoka blossoms
fall hot upon us,
bursting with red flames
from the fire that burnt
the God of Love,
with his practiced bow,
flames used by the God
who holds the moon
in his matted hair,
who rests on the head
    of the king
    whose shoulders
    are like those
    of a wrestler,
    and who prevailed
    at Viḻiñam—

those flowers have fanned out
as though to invade him![564]

How does this show she can be comforted, you ask? She is saying, "These asoka blossoms, which bloom when summer starts, are so hot to us; but won't they seem just as hot to him? I fear he may return without finishing his task of making his fortune: that is what makes me feel bad."

This verse is linked in frog-jumping fashion with the one that begins,

Departure for service to the emperor...[565]

* * *

[563] *Pāṇṭi-k-Kōvai*, 285.

[564] *Pāṇṭi-k-Kōvai*, 286.

[565] *The Study of Stolen Love*, 39.

Verse 42.

The departure for courtesans has no change in lands.

What does this declare, you ask? It declares that when he departs for courtesans he does not leave the country and stay away, unlike what we have taken from the above verse.

Its meaning:

The departure for courtesans—his leaving her to go to a prostitute.

has no change in lands—there is no change of location.

That is, he does not get to leave his home town to meet her. It means that during the departure for courtesans he does not travel through countries and forests. Thus, he implies that it all occurs within one city and one place.

Next, members of one school say that it must occur in his own home; but that is inappropriate because there are poems by eminent poets as follows:

> ...
> leaving his door,
> as great bells
> of exquisite workmanship
> toll
> ...[566]

and

> ...
> may he come
> and reach
> our quarters
> ...[567]

Next, by saying that he doesn't leave the country, he implies that it occurs within a single town; therefore it must be either his own home town, or some other one, farther off.

Next, by thus indicating a single town, he implies that the hero's place is large, and that the heroine's and the courtesan's are different and removed from it. The courtesan's place will have an artificial playhill, a playground, a pool, and all.

* * *

[566] From *Akanāṉūṟu*, 66.

[567] From *Akanāṉūṟu*, 276.

Verse 43.

> **The hero who has departed for courtesans**
> **leaving and remaining away from her**
> **for two times six days after the appearance of his wife's menstruation**
> **is not the way of virtue.**

What does this declare, you ask? It declares how the hero acts if the heroine menstruates while he is with courtesans.

Its meaning:

The hero who has departed for courtesans—a hero who has departed for outside women.

for two times six days after the appearance of his wife's menstruation—for twelve days beginning with the day of his wife's menstruation.

leaving and remaining away from her ... is not the way of virtue—leaving her and staying away is not the path of virtue.

Thus it implies that the path of virtue is not to leave her and stay away. This means that he is to stay and pay attention to her, and to unite with her. It says that staying with her like this is what he must do.

Here is how it works: The hero knows about it if his wife's menstruation appears while he is away with the courtesans. How does he know about it, you ask? Go-betweens let him know. And how do they do that, you ask? He has go-betweens who stay with the heroine, and she has go-betweens who stay with him; it is they who let him know. Moreover, the heroine's go-betweens come to the hero every morning bearing a mirror; but on that day, they bring red clothing as well: some say this is how he comes to know about it.

Next, there is a school that maintains he realizes it when a maidservant clothed in red brings him some red flowers in water in a small copper vessel on the day that menstruation appears, and pours them over his feet. This, they say, is how high born people make menstruation known in their homes. It is up to you to decide which commentary is better.

Here is a poem that the hero addresses to his heart when he learns of his wife's menstruation:

What The Hero Says To His Heart

Here comes her friend,
dressed in red
and wearing red jewels,
with red makeup
on her large breasts:
she tells me the state
of her whose wide mound of love
is covered with a cotton cloth,

she who is like the wide world
of him whose warring elephants
rejoice fearlessly,
him who destroyed kings
and their swords
in war at Vallam
with its large groves,
where clouds settle![568]

When the hero thus realizes about the menstruation, he returns with the go-between and stays at the heroine's place for three days, paying careful attention to what she says; he then continues to stay, uniting with her during the remaining nine days.

Why does he stay with her and pay attention to her for those three days, you ask? There is jealousy because he has been with courtesans, isn't there? Such anger will leave if he stays with her and pays attention to her for three days. Then once it is gone, union will occur, and the embryo thus formed will be splendid. All this was explained with that in mind; that is why it is called the way of virtue.

Otherwise, the jealousy developing within the heroine because he has just returned from courtesans will breed anger, and that anger will create great heat: because of that heat, the embryo cannot become splendid. That would be a slip in virtue, it implies; and that is why he remains and pays attention to what she says for those three days.

What would be wrong, you ask, if we were to say that he remains united with her during those three days as well, since we conclude that those days are comprised within the twelve that follow the appearance of her menstruation? Any embryo developing at the onset of menstruation will disintegrate in the womb; one that develops on the second day will die in the womb; and an embryo that develops on the third day will have a short life: if it lives at all, it will not prosper. Therefore, we are told not to have intercourse then.

Also, this commentary is appropriate because others have said,

They shall not copulate for three days beginning with menstruation.
If they do, rites formulated by the sages and the gods in the formulation of tradition
will perish, they say.[569]

* * *

---

[568] *Pāṇṭi-k-Kōvai*, 287.

[569] Unidentified verse.

Verse 44.

> **Yet if a hero who has departed during Married Love**
> **comes back from the courtesans**
> **and follows that theme, it will not be eschewed.**

What does this declare, you ask? It presents a behavior that is an exception to the above verse.

Its meaning:

a hero who has departed during Married Love—a hero who is in the courtesans' quarter and hears of the menstruation.

If he does not return to stay with the heroine and pay attention to her for those three days after the onset of menstruation, he is termed one who has departed during Married Love. "Married Love" here stands for menstruation: it is because menstruation occurs only during Married Love and not during Stolen Love that he calls it "Married Love."

Yet if (he) ... comes back from the courtesans—his return from the courtesans' quarter after those three days.

and follows that theme—and follows the path of virtue.

Following the path of virtue means that he uses go-betweens to cool down the heroine's anger; then he enters and unites with her.

it will not be eschewed—even though it is not so great, it will not be considered a flaw.

Here is a poem on cooling down the heroine's anger through the use of go-betweens:

Cooling Down The Heroine's Anger

She reddened
the moment I said,
"The lord of the town
with golden waters
has come, he's here
at your back door!"
Yet though she reddened,
her anger cooled
when I said,
"Dear! That's not
like you!"
Such a tender girl she is,
like the lands of waters
in the South
    of the king
    whose lance gleams
    like a lightning streak,

who extinguished
all other kings
at Vallam![570]

* * *

Verse 45.

Honor and baseness are in the hero.

What does this declare, you ask? It presents a definition of the hero.
Its meaning:
Honor and baseness—honor means calling him an honorable person; baseness means calling him dishonorable.
are in the hero—both of these exist in the hero.

Thus it means that the hero is to behave in such and such a way; that is, he is an honorable man when he remains with the heroine and dishonorable when he stays with courtesans.

Who speaks these poems, you ask? Take it that they are spoken by the go-betweens. Here is a poem for saying that he is honorable:

Saying He Is An Honorable Man

The wilting sorrow
of his young wife's
lovely bamboo arms,
she with long
arched eyebrows,
he understood,
and came home.
Like those who thought
they could attack
the Lion to His Enemies,
but gave over and left,

this very lover who stayed away
is really a great man
in this great world![571]

Next, here is one declaring that he is dishonorable:

Enemies from everywhere
died at Viḻiñam
when the king unsheathed

---

[570] *Pāṇṭi-k-Kōvai*, 288.

[571] *Pāṇṭi-k-Kōvai*, 289.

and grasped
his shining lance
in his right hand!
And she is like the Vaiyai River lands
of that king,
this conch bracelet
honeybee garland
of a girl—
she grieves
that he stays on
in those nice folks' home:

that dandy of this town
with cool, watered fields all around
is just a big misfit![572]

* * *

Verse 46.

There is no baseness in the heroine.

What does this declare, you ask? It declares the heroine's greatness.
Its meaning:
There is no baseness—one does not call her a dishonorable woman, only an honorable one.
in the heroine—in the heroine.

It implies that the heroine maintains the same character throughout.

Might she be considered honorable when the hero comes and lives with her, and dishonorable when he goes to live with courtesans, you ask? No. Here is a poem for that:

Proclaiming The Greatness Of The Heroine

Phalanxes of foes
fell at Nelvēli
when he loosed arrows
from his long bow.
And she who is like the Tamil lands
of that conqueror
concealed, even from us,
his lack of good quality,
that dandy of this
well watered town!

---

[572] *Pāṇṭi-k-Kōvai*, 290.

All the wide world honors
such a faithful woman.[573]

This is spoken by a bard who comes to the heroine while the hero is in the courtesans' quarter; he addresses his dancer when they note the state of the heroine.

* * *

Verse 47.

The heroine's self-praise before the hero,
even in times of quarrel, is not great.

What does this declare, you ask? It declares that a certain quality exists in the heroine.

Its meaning:

The heroine's self-praise before the hero—the heroine praising herself in front of the hero.

even in times of quarrel, is not great—that should be proper in times of quarrel, shouldn't it? It is not proper, even then.

The heroine will never get to praise herself; and thus we see her greatness.

Next, by saying that the heroine never gets to praise herself, he implies that the courtesan does get to praise herself. Here is a poem on the courtesan praising herself:

If I do not
make him turn to me,
like a thistle
turns to face the sun,
right in front of her
with her white teeth,
and her sunshine face,
then may my white
conch bracelets break
like the army
of gleaming swords
that broke
for those who fled
the fertile lands
taken by the Lion to His Enemies,
who clutches
that glistening lance![574]

---

[573] *Pāṇṭi-k-Kōvai*, 291.

[574] *Pāṇṭi-k-Kōvai*, 292.

Take and note down others like this as well.

* * *

Verse 48.

> **If she cites the country, the town, or the house**
> **while speaking of herself, it denotes sulking.**

What does this declare, you ask? Let the heroine not praise herself; yet this presents the root of her sulking when she speaks in this way.

Its meaning:

If she cites the country, the town, or the house—considering the country, the town, or the house.

while speaking of herself, it denotes sulking—if she speaks of herself, it denotes sulking.

The heroine is not to praise herself by naming the country in which she lives, nor her town, nor the family in which she was born. This means that if she does mention them, it denotes sulking. Here is how it works: She says, "Our country is inhabited by very mean people," and,

> That country's little towns
> are circled with tiny forts,
> it is married to valor,
> it eats its gruel
> for sustenance,
> it has its few hills,
> and there
> in that country
> our town is an impediment
> with lost wealth—
> where even a tiger skin
> turns to rags!
>
> In that town, the house where I was born
> is full of little, ignorant people,
> isn't it?[575]

and, "The conduct of such little people is not for you—and besides, it is so magnificent for our lord, is it not? People like him can stand such unions, can't they?" If she speaks this way, it is because she is sulking. Here is a poem for that:

---

575 Unidentified poem.

The Heroine Praising Herself

Lord of this town
with its waters and waves!
We do not live
within the boundaries
where the Pāṇṭiyaṉ's righteous scepter
holds sway, in those lands,
bounded by the seas,
    of the Scholar
    with his garland
    of fragrant flowers—
our home is a village
where mannerless
little people live.

How could we presume to deserve
your sweet grace, even a little?[576]

* * *

Verse 49.

If she speaks of him, it denotes union.

What does this declare, you ask? It declares that if she speaks in this way, it denotes union.
Its meaning:
If she speaks of him—when she cites the country, town, or house when speaking of him.
it denotes union—union is the meaning to be settled upon after rejecting a false inference.

What is rejected, you ask? Sulking is rejected. How do we get that, you ask? Because the theme of the sulks follows from the previous verse.

After the hero has returned from the courtesans, he enters, through the good offices of go-betweens; she accepts him, receives him, and worships him. Then she gets to her rationale for that unreasonable jealousy she had felt, and says to the hero, as a pretext, "Is it proper for one of such great conduct as yourself, born in your great country in such a very great city, and into a noble house, to grant sweet grace to us who are so little?" She says this in order to banish her sulks. Here is a poem for her to speak in this vein:

---

[576] *Pāṇṭi-k-Kōvai*, 293.

Saying, "This Is Not Proper For Someone As Great As Yourself"

Perhaps behaving as you do
is not natural
to you in your nobility,
since you belong
to such a great house
in this great, good city
of this great, good land,
like the earth
surrounded by the seas
    and protected by the king
    who took up his sharpened lance
    to char his foes at Vallam,
    the Gift of the Gods,
    whose garlands are swarmed
    by little striped bees,
    who owns chariots
    and horses![577]

There are also those who say that this verse is set like the falcon's dive, and has to do with marriage in Stolen Love; but that is not appropriate since that theme was treated in the verse that says,

...have the meaning of a desire for marriage[578]

in the line,

other things as well collected in that line.

Moreover, it would be inappropriate to bring in Stolen Love while commenting upon Married Love.

* * *

Verse 50.

If a quarrel not settled through conciliation occurs,
then they do not eschew sulking in the hero either.

What does this declare, you ask? It declares that one of the heroine's exclusive characteristics pertains, in one context, to the hero as well.
Its meaning:

---

577 *Pāṇṭi-k-Kōvai*, 294.

578 *The Study of Stolen Love*, 30. This is the last line of Verse 30.

If a quarrel not settled through conciliation occurs—if a quarrel that leaves no room for conciliation manifests itself in the heroine.

then they do not eschew sulking in the hero either—they do not eschew speeches of a sulking nature for the hero as well.

It is not the heroine's alone; such things, on occasion, belong to the hero also.

When quarrelsomeness appears in the heroine, it does so in one of three ways: she will think, "Has he done it?" or, "Is he doing it?" or, "Will he do it?"

Of those, the origin of her wondering if he has done it is this: She wonders, "Did he take the courtesan out in his chariot, adorn her with flowers, and dance with her, before he left her?" Her thinking, "Did he do it?" occurs with all the certainty of the past tense.

Next, she thinks, "Will he do it?" when she wonders, "Will he do it in the future?" Between those two, there is no room for conciliation in the case of something that happened in the past; but in this case it can cure itself. It will do so as she thinks, "How can I distress our lord when I am not sure?" It will also cure itself if others give her bits of advice.

Next, here is how something that might happen in the future can cure itself: She thinks to herself, "It isn't right for me to think that this might happen some time, when I am not sure." Why? People do not bundle their clothes on top of their heads just because they are nearing a river they will have to cross, do they?

Next, there is still the case of what actually happened with certainty in the past, isn't there? Since he did it, and everyone knows he did, there is simply no room for conciliation. If he were to say, "I didn't do it," that wouldn't hide it; and it would be cruel for him to deny it, like adding insult to injury. That is why there is no room for conciliation when this type of quarrel occurs.

When, then, will this appear, you ask? We shall explain: He takes her friend with him as a go-between when he returns from the courtesans' quarter, and she goes on in and gives the heroine many reasons for accepting the hero back. She says, "We stay in our houses, worship God, raise children, and entertain our guests, but we have nothing else but sensual pleasure: so we had better not indulge ourselves in sulking, quarreling, and loathing!

"Moreover, men are like bees and women like flowers. Why? When bees suck nectar they never say, 'We'll only suck the nectar from good flowers, not any others!' Nor do those flowers sulk and say, 'They suck all those flowers, not only us!' do they? In the same way, it is in the hero's nature to meet with all women. We know he is like that, so we ought not to fight with him: we should worship his back as he leaves and his front when he returns, and receive him whenever he comes. There is nothing superior in us if we fight back, and behave like this!"

In addition, her friend also says, "This is what will prove true: We must accept him and worship him, and we must think to ourselves, 'What can we do? We can't help worshipping him. What do we gain by distressing him?'"

Then the heroine says, "All right," and her anger departs.

She then tells the hero, "Enter," and he does.

But once he enters and they are within their bed chamber, her anger that was bottled up inside her comes out again: her eyes show red, and her brow changes. He becomes exceedingly distressed when she exhibits these signs: he laments, and speaks of the way things used to be. Here are some poems for him to address to his heart, saying, "In the old days, she would turn sad when I was sad, and when I was consoled, she would be, too. But today that very same girl has not consoled me. She probably does not know that I am hurt! Or maybe she is not my lover: it must be some spirit who looks like her! And you thought it really was her, o my heart, in your stupidity! But then, who is she?"

The Hero Addressing His Heart

Heart, don't simper
and shrivel up
like a house that says "No!"
and refuses a beggar!
This girl
with her conch bracelets
is like the Tamil lands
    of him who seized Viḻiñam,
    his sword wedded to killing,
    who made the Cēraṉ king,
    wearing his war garland,
    displaying his emblem
    of the single bow,
    wither—

But who is she
to us?[579]

I was mixed up—
I wondered
if she might be
a bewitching goddess
from the shining Potiyil Mountains
    of the Supreme One,
    the Emperor of Tamil,
    with its bewitching words,

---

[579] *Pāṇṭi-k-Kōvai*, 295.

who won Āṟṟukkuṭi—
this girl with her proper jewels:
she stood there,
her dark eyes dripping tears
like bewitching dewdrops,
lined up in a row,

and her waist was not troubled
by any clothing at all![580]

That is what the hero says to his heart. When she overhears it, the heroine thinks to herself, "He would always let me do little things for him, through that tremendous grace he showed, wouldn't he? It is not right for me to hold a grudge against him who has been so gracious to me!" and her anger leaves.

* * *

Verse 51.

When it is fixed in mind,
if a speech occurs that is appropriate to Stolen Love,
they will not eschew using names from the modes for the hero also.

What does this declare, you ask? It declares another characteristic of the hero during the time of Stolen Love.

Its meaning:

When it is fixed in mind—when it is fixed in mind.

if a speech occurs that is appropriate to Stolen Love—if the heroine has a speech that would be appropriate in the period of Stolen Love.

they will not eschew using names from the modes for the hero also—they will not eschew the changing of modes, nor the taking of names for the hero from them, either.

That is, it says that the hero's mind speaks to him at some point after he has attained her through marriage and is conducting Married Love; it says, "Let us depart for wealth."

His mind said, "Poor men cannot consolidate their friends, nor can they destroy their enemies; therefore, let us remove this lack! Let's depart for wealth!"

And the hero responds, thinking, "We shall go only if she can stand it; if not, we shall give it up." He agrees with his mind as he approaches the heroine; he enters their bed chamber and performs his very gracious deed.

But now the heroine feels upset; she thinks to herself, "Our lord has often done these gracious things before, but this time it was different. It all seems very

---

580 *Pāṇṭi-k-Kōvai*, 296.

sweet, but it also seems like the deceit of someone who is about to leave me. It seems those words he spoke, 'I will not leave you; if I did, I would languish,' have proven false. Falsehood is always just an aberration of good conduct."

The hero senses her distress and thinks to himself, "She must have understood my intent to leave: that's why she's upset. If I really left now, she'd die for sure!" Here is such a poem for him to address to his heart:

What He Says To His Heart

O, heart!
This girl with her select jewels,
cannot even endure
such excellent grace
as the righteous scepter
    of the king called Supreme,
    with his sword of
    bright light—
she suffers!
If we told her today
that I'm to be off
through hot wastelands
that reject every drop of water,
her brilliant brow
would just wither—

she'd never survive,
would she?[581]

Here are some poems on his tarrying after speaking to his heart like that:

The Hero Delaying His Departure

O, heart,
drops drip
from her dark eyes,
she stands in sorrow—
this girl with oiled hair
weeps!

How could we leave
for those wastelands,
hot like the enemies
    of Him Who is Cruel to The Angry Saturn,
    the God of Love in these latter days,
    who wields the righteous scepter,

[581] *Pāṇṭi-k-Kōvai*, 297.

and holds his cruel bow
in his hands,
who stood in triumph
at Naṟaiyāṟu?[582]

O heart!
That long
and tortuous road
is like the battlefront
of Māṟaṉ, King of Pūḻi,
who strung his warring
long bow so the Cēraṉ king
and his great, fighting navy
was demolished at Naṟaiyāṟu—
it's no good
traveling that way
to make a fortune—

not when her very black, cool eyes
dropped pearls to perturb us.[583]

He also says this to his heart as he tarries:

If it's medicine
I need, she's it—
if I want my fortune,
she's it!
with her big, young,
pretty breasts, alluring
with their golden beauty marks,
her broad shoulders,
and her tiny waist!

my girl, given by that man from the woods
where rocks jut out.[584]

Take it that a man from the wasteland mode switches to the river-plain mode when he delays his departure like this: that is how the hero uses names from the modes. Although it is primarily the heroine who does not want his departure, in this case the hero does not want it either.

Further, saying "when it is fixed in mind" means when the hero has decided, "I will take her along with me."

---

[582] *Pāṇṭi-k-Kōvai*, 298.

[583] *Pāṇṭi-k-Kōvai*, 299.

[584] *Kuṟuntokai*, 71.

Saying "a speech that is appropriate to Stolen Love" means a poem that belongs to the period during which they conduct Stolen Love; specifically, it refers to standing with honor.

"If ... (it) ... occurs" means if such a thing appears; it is spoken by the hero to her friend.

Saying "they will not eschew using names from the modes for the hero also" means that a hero of the wasteland mode may become a river-plain hero.

By the word "either" in "they do not eschew ... for the hero either," take it that they do not eschew it for the heroine either: in agreeing to go along, she also becomes a heroine of the wasteland mode, and take it that she becomes a heroine of the river-plain mode when he says he will delay his departure.

Take it that these points are also considered in the earlier verse about elopement, because of the saying,

> The departure for wealth, and the elopement,
> and speaking about those departures, occurs in the wastelands.[585]

* * *

Verse 52.

> **All departures of remaining in changed places,**
> **with those left out knowing and not knowing,**
> **have the nature of his leaving and staying far away, they say.**

What does this declare, you ask? It declares yet another characteristic of the departed hero during the time of Married Love.

Its meaning:

All departures of remaining in changed places—all departures except that for courtesans.

with those left out knowing and not knowing—the heroine and her friend either knowing or not.

have the nature of his leaving and staying far away, they say—it is his nature to remain far away, past countries and forests, say the poets.

Thus, because he has said,

> Learning, defense, peace-mission,
> service to the emperor, amassing wealth, ...[586]

he must sometimes inform the heroine and her friend when he leaves for these purposes, and sometimes he must leave without informing them; it means that both are defined.

---

[585] Unidentified verse.

[586] *The Study of Stolen Love*, 35.

But of those two, it is improper for him to leave without letting them know; it is proper only if he lets them know beforehand and says, "I shall come back when I have finished such and such a mission in such and such a place," and she consents.

If he leaves without telling her, she worries; she wonders, "Why did he leave me like this, without saying anything?"

The author has formulated a period comprising several days; he declares, "Heroes leave thus, complete their missions, and return; and the heroines are consoled until they have finished their missions and come back home: such is the nature of the world."

If, then, you respond by asking, "All right, but might it be the case that heroines cannot be consoled while their heroes are away making their fortunes?" he replies, "She would then be a hindrance to his perseverance: therefore the only thing for her to do is to be comforted until he finishes his mission and returns home, isn't it?" Why? All living beings know about death and decay, yet they are not always morose, thinking, "What if I die?" And so it is with her: she says, "I shall be consoled, so I am not a hindrance." That is how it is appropriate for her as well.

But she still feels suddenly grieved and distraught on the day he leaves, even though he told her beforehand that he was going. And he also, since he realizes his departure will be like death to her, is likely to leave without actually coming before her, carrying with him her earlier reaction instead.

Then again, he might say, "The other day you told me you could take it, didn't you? Now, since you never tell a lie, you have no reason to feel so bad!" In this case, he steps forward to comfort her, and entrusts her to her friend; and then he gets to leave. That is the best way for him to depart: letting them know as he goes.

Here is a poem for the heroine to speak when her hero has left without her knowledge:

I underestimated him:
I thought he would not go!
And he underestimated me—
he thought my eyes too weak
to follow him through those deserts!
These two things
weaken my heart,
like enemies
    of him who holds his bow
    that conquered Kuḷantai,
    Neṭumāṟaṉ the King
    whose lance

is wedded
to killing![587]

All right, then, you ask, why did he add the word "all" instead of simply saying, "departures of remaining in changed places, with those left out knowing and not knowing?" There was one departure noted during Stolen Love, was there not? It was the departure of a hero who did not marry, but left her and stayed away in other places; it was termed a departure for wealth, and in it he traveled great distances. "All" was added here to suggest that it is appropriate to consider that as well as one of the departures that may occur either with or without their foreknowledge.

Still, why was he not content simply to say, "the nature of his staying far away?" What did he say "leaving" for, you ask? He does not change modes halfway through, hopping from one land to another, and leaving the desert. Why? Only a stupid person would give up a task he has undertaken before his finishes it, isn't that so? Also, others have said,

> The frenzy dance and desisting from departure,
> when you examine them closely, do not exist, they say.[588]

Here is another poem on his leaving without their knowledge:

I underestimated him,
I never thought
he'd really go,
and he underestimated me,
he thought I'd never agree!
But now from this huge
two-sided struggle
for dominance,
my sore heart spins,

as though caught
by a cobra![589]

* * *

Verse 53.

All of the go-betweens, when the hero has departed,
seek to comfort in many ways.

---

587 *Pāṇṭi-k-Kōvai*, 300.

588 Unidentified verse.

589 *Kuṟuntokai*, 43.

What does this declare, you ask? It declares how the go-betweens comfort the heroine, who is distraught while the hero is gone.

Its meaning:

All of the go-betweens—all go-betweens except the hero and house guests, including her friend, Brahmins, and male and female bards.

when the hero has departed—during a time when the hero has traveled past countries and forests.

seek to comfort in many ways—think of many ways to comfort the heroine.

That is, when the heroine is distracted by the arrival of the season the hero had set for his return, her friend says, "He will not delay, once the monsoon comes: he has come, he is coming, he will come!" or, "If you slander this season and say it's not when he said he'd come back, and if you think some other season is, you're wrong. Why? Because he cannot tell a lie. We just don't understand." Her friend diverts her by showing off the season, by interpreting omens, by playing the lute, and by all other stratagems. Then, too, she comforts her by saying, "He doesn't love you! He's cruel!" and so on.

Of those, here are some poems in which she invents things when the season arrives; she tells the heroine that the season has not really come at all:

Saying It Is Not The Season

Like the crashing
of thunderstorms
rutting elephants roar,
smashing down walls
  of enemies of the Emperor
  whose white canopy
  is of bright pearls,
  who wields his righteous scepter
  that Saturn may be rubbed out,
  the God of Love
  in this age of decline
  who drives grand chariots—
and piṭavu bloomed,

But why grow thin when you see these things,
my bewitching girl?[590]

My precious!
Our lover
has traveled mountain trails
hard as the battlefronts

[590] *Pāṇṭi-k-Kōvai*, 301.

of the enemies of the Emperor
whose canopy is unique
and scepter righteous,
who rules this wide world,
the Scholar,
whose sharp lance
is covered with flesh!
He never lies,
don't worry!

This stupid laburnum mistook that freak cloud
for the start of the monsoon,
that's why it bloomed.[591]

You with your tender,
burgeoning breasts!
In the Kolli Mountains,
that dip in the sky,
of Him With the History of Victories,
whose garland drips honey,
who fought the Battle of Pūlantai
the other day,
there in those hills
a thunderhead angered
a strong elephant,
who struck it
with his trunk,
and the rains poured down—

so this jasmine smiles:
and you are going to grieve over that?[592]

Ask, girl—
ask me if this
really is the monsoon,
when he told you he'd be back,
as he left to cross
that hot wasteland
with its long, endless trails,
dry, with never a drop of water,
where the heat of the sun
spreads over you like a blanket,
and makes you shiver in fright!
I tell you, girl, these lilies,
laburnum, and piṭavu blossoms

---

[591] *Pāṇṭi-k-Kōvai*, 302.

[592] *Pāṇṭi-k-Kōvai*, 303.

are crazy—
in their own little minds
they thought it was
the monsoon, but it's
just a heavy shower
that some foolish,
pregnant clouds could not bear
any longer, and shed,
after they had scooped
the water up from the seas—
they forgot it's not
the monsoon yet,
you see?

It's just because they're so stupid
that these flowers are blooming
in such profusion![593]

Thus she reassures a heroine who is distraught at seeing the arrival of the season he had set for his return. She says, "This is not that season! Why, he would never lie to us! It must be just a freak: in their foolishness these lilies, laburnum, and piṭavu have mistaken this freak for the monsoon; they're just confused, and that's why they're blooming now."

Reassurance Through Saying That He Will Come

Girl, with your large,
darkened eyes,
don't grieve!
Black clouds took up water
at Cape Kaṉṉi
    of the king
    whose hand holds his bow,
    who raised a cloud of red dust,
    like smoke, to make
    his foes fall in battle
    at Neṭuṅkaḷam—
then they poured it out
upon the battlefront
of swords:

He, with his oiled lance,
he will see that rain.[594]

---

[593] *Naṟṟiṇai*, 99.

[594] *Pāṇṭi-k-Kōvai*, 304.

That is how her friend reassures the distracted heroine during his period of departure; she said, "The season he set has arrived; he, too, will not fail us: he will come."

You, your waist
like a little drum,
you who are like
rich Kūṭal City
  of Māṟaṉ,
  he who defeated the Cēraṉ,
  whose lance is sharpened,
  who demolished the confederacy
  of kings at Kōṭṭāṟu,
  with its grand walls
  and banners!
Don't grieve—
huge clouds have come
and thundered,
and he who wears those flashing
warrior's anklets
upon his feet,

he who had left you—
he will come back, now![595]

This also is the same.

You with your deer-like eyes,
don't grieve—
huge clouds are thundering
  like the thunderbolt
  upon the flag
  of the king of those
  who live by rich, sweet Tamil,
  Māṟaṉ, the Sapphire Colored One,
  who conquered Pāḻi in the South
  with his grand chariots
  and surging horses!
They will present him to us,

him whose fragrant wreath
is made of sweet mango leaves,
but who left us.[596]

This also is the same.

---

[595] *Pāṇṭi-k-Kōvai*, 305.

[596] *Pāṇṭi-k-Kōvai*, 306.

Don't grieve,
girl, don't feel
like a battlefront
    of Neṭumāṟaṉ
    whose great, cool canopy
    is decked with little pearls,
    the King of the South
    whose munificent hand
    is like a cool, dark cloud!
Clouds are thundering here,
white jasmine crawls up
the wild lime, its buds
bloom sharp, like teeth:

our lover
will come.[597]

This also is the same.

Girl, with your fitting jewels
you are like the Tamil lands
    of him whose righteous scepter
    rules all the world
    surrounded by that noisy sea,
    Māṟaṉ, who took up his lance
    to make the families
    of all who opposed him
    at Naṟaiyāṟu
    suffer!
All fields face
the cool rains now,
their color is changing to gold—

their beauty is ripe,
and you will see the beauty of his return.[598]

This also is the same.

You are like the world,
bounded only by the seas,
    of the king who took up
    his gleaming, bloodsoaked lance
    in his right hand, who crushed
    that king with jangling
    warrior's anklets,
    and made him climb
    into the fire

---

[597] *Pāṇṭi-k-Kōvai*, 307.

[598] *Pāṇṭi-k-Kōvai*, 308.

at Āṟṟukkuṭi!
Beautiful clouds have thundered,
and the chariot of him who left you
to give you firmness of mind,
is coming back:

those striped bracelets will fit your wrists
once again.[599]

This also is the same.

Note that he added the extra phrase "in many ways" to his statement, "All of the go-betweens, when the hero has departed, seek to comfort..." Therefore, include here what the foster mother reports to her real mother on the status of the hero, and that of the heroine, after she has paid a visit to their marital home, during Married Love. Here are some poems for that:

The Foster Mother Speaking To the Real Mother

Woman with large black eyes,
you who are like
beautiful, cool Kūṭal City
of the Lion to His Enemies,
whose huge army is unique,
who wields the scepter
of unfailing righteousness!
The girl with her long,
pretty hair, never
worships the gods!
And the lord
with his very broad shoulders
always comes home, he never
stays long, even
when he fights
his own foes!

That's how their love is.[600]

In the cool Kolli Mountains
of the Goad to His Enemies,
the king of this world
with his righteous scepter,
she, her hair dark
as a raincloud,
is as constant

599 *Pāṇṭi-k-Kōvai*, 309.

600 *Pāṇṭi-k-Kōvai*, 310.

as the pole star,
and those magnificent horses
harnessed to the grand,
golden chariot of the lord
whose lance never rests in war—
they don't know what it means
to stay long in the battlefield,

even when he goes to carry out
his king's commands.[601]

She who is like Vañci City
of him who was born a Gift of the Gods,
whose chariots are victorious,
who plundered great wealth
from his foes
with his sharp lance,
she has never depended
on gods—
and the lord,
with his great qualities,
he never has known
what it is to stay
in the battlefield full
of enemies at Vallam,

even when the king himself,
wearing great warrior's anklets,
commands.[602]

Include others as well.

She lives in a tiny village
where jasmine scents
the fertile woods
as raindrops fall cool
upon the spotted neck
of a wild gamecock
crowing brilliantly,
our daughter does!
And her lord's chariot
has never known
what it means
to stay away
in another town—

[601] *Pāṇṭi-k-Kōvai*, 311.

[602] *Pāṇṭi-k-Kōvai*, 312.

even when he leaves
on imperial affairs.[603]

Include here all other speeches from the period of Married Love as well, if they arise against this background.

* * *

Verse 54.

All go-betweens who seek to reassure,
if a speech occurs when her love has departed,
cite the prison, say the poets.

What does this declare, you ask? In the previous verse he presented the ways in which they comfort her. Now there are those who would say that this verse declares that the hero informs some go-betweens when he decides to depart, and that they inform the heroine when he leaves; also, if they are her go-betweens, they will tell her while he is still within earshot, hidden in a secret place.

Next, there are also those who say it declares that they comfort the heroine by speaking to her of the prison, while she feels distraught in the absence of the hero.

Its meaning:

All go-betweens who seek to reassure—all go-betweens who are fit to use the methods of comforting the heroine.

if a speech occurs when her love has departed—when the heroine is distraught during the hero's absence, it means; the implication is that they are unable to console her when they are supposed to.

cite the prison, say the poets—those who are well versed in learning say one should cite the prison in order to cool her down.

"Citing the prison" means comforting her by calling upon the prison of fidelity. How does it work? They think they can console the heroine in this way, when she would not be consoled by any of the methods noted above. They say, "The house to which our lady was born is noble, is it not? Its descent from ancient times betrays no degenerate conduct, and it continues to rise, forever, in grandeur. Would it be proper, then, for you to bring it ruin? Modesty and fidelity are a woman's jewels, are they not? Your family guards that prison of fidelity, and will not permit it to be destroyed! And you will earn yourself a disgraceful reputation, since you seem bent on destroying it!"

And they say, "Our lord has exhibited his manliness by leaving you; now you have to protect your fidelity until he finishes his mission and comes back."

---

[603] *Kuṟuntokai*, 242.

And they say, "Wise men say women are no mean creatures: they are great. And if they conduct themselves properly with regard to their families and safeguard their fidelity—there is nothing greater than that."

Comforting her in these ways is called "citing the prison;" here is a poem for that:

Citing The Prison

You with
your conch bracelets!
Behaving like this
is not suited
to our family,
great in wisdom,
nor to your modesty and devotion,
nor to your beauty,
which is like Kūṭal City
with its wide waters,
  of him who wields
  the righteous scepter
  that shines upon this earth,
  the Supreme One
  with brilliant chariots,
  the king whose shoulders
  gleam, like round boulders![604]

Cooling her down in this way is termed "citing the prison."

* * *

Verse 55.

There is also the occurrence of not citing the prison
when there are signs of his reuniting.

What does this declare, you ask? It presents a way of cooling the heroine down by telling her that the hero is coming, when she is distraught during his absence. Its meaning:

There is also the occurrence of not citing the prison—above, her friend cooled the heroine down by saying, "You have ruined the prison of fidelity!" did she not? But there are also poems of a different sort.

when there are signs of his reuniting—if there are indications that the hero is returning, his mission finished or his fortune made.

---

604 *Pāṇṭi-k-Kōvai*, 313.

This is how it works: Above, they cooled her down by treating her separation from him in that manner. Her friend has been comforting her during their separation, hasn't she? But in the meanwhile, the hero has also completed the task he had undertaken, has he not? And once it was finished, and the season he had specified was at hand, he returned home, did he not? Conches and drums sound when he arrives, and her friend realizes his return; she then speaks like this: "Our lady, you thought you would die, didn't you! Now, look: there is nothing a person can't have, is there? Since you let us comfort you, you get to worship your lord again this very day!"

This sort of poem is an example of "the occurrence of not citing the prison." Here are some poems blessing the conch when the conches and drums sound:

Blessing The Conch

You appeared
in the huge,
sky-colored sea
with its white capped waves
at luxuriant Cape Kumari
    of Māṟaṉ,
    he who defeated the Cōḻa,
    whose wreath is huge, colorful,
    and dripping with honey!
And the blue god
who measured the earth
holds you in his hand!
O conch,
white like sweet milk,
and like the color
of that god's elder brother—

who could be greater
than you?[605]

Take this one also:

Great conch
with fine curves,
you equal a god:
the god on whose chest
beauty sits
holds you,

---

[605] *Pāṇṭi-k-Kōvai*, 314.

and your color
is like that
of his brother's body.[606]

* * *

Verse 56.

The mode and conduct, the speaker and audience,
the person, time, elision, mood,
result, and analysis: these ten
are the ways of commenting on all five interior modes.

What does this declare, you ask? Above, he has presented both Stolen Love and Married Love. Next, this declares how to comment upon songs that have been composed about either of them, through these ten categories.

Its meaning:

The mode is a word that encompasses many meanings; they call lands, families, and conduct "modes." Thus, he has called the locations in which modal conduct occur "modes" as well. They are five: the mountain-country mode, the wasteland mode, the woodland mode, the river-plain mode, and the seaside mode.

Implied is their distinctiveness in first, matrix, and propriety aspects, when one knows them well. We taught these distinctions above, when we commented upon the phrase,

in five modes of affection...[607]

These are what are called "modes;" it means noting, as you hear an interior poem, that it deals with such and such a one of those five modes.

Next, **conduct** means Stolen Love or Married Love; it amounts to knowing that this poem deals with Stolen Love, while that one deals with Married Love.

Next, **the speaker**: Knowing who is fit to speak, and which of them utters this poem. Find the people who are fit to speak from Cempūṭcēyār's *Study of the Speakers* or Tolkāppiyaṉār's *Section on Meaning*:

Brahmin, his friend, her friend, foster mother,
eminently excellent hero and heroine:
these six types of people who mingle together
are fit to speak in Stolen Love, they say.[608]

Bard, male and female dancers, courtesans,
the learned filled with good, passers-by:

---

[606] Unidentified poem.

[607] *The Study of Stolen Love*, 1.

[608] *Tolkāppiyam: Ceyyuḷiyal*, 181.

> these six, along with the Brahmin, worthy of protection, and others mentioned above,
> are fit for speeches in the Married Love of ancient tradition.[609]

Take it that Tolkāppiyaṉār has composed this.

Know that each poem is a speech uttered by some certain one of those mentioned above.

Next, **audience**: knowing that such and such a person heard what such and such a one spoke. For example, it means commenting with the knowledge that the heroine hears what her friend says, or that her friend hears what she says, or that the hero hears what her friend says, or that her friend hears what the hero says.

The person: knowing the person of the audience, when one of those people speaks and one of them listens. They are: first person, second person, and third person. Of those, "I" is the first person, "you" is second person, and "he" is third person. It is the knowledge that a poems deals with such and such a one of these.

Time is of three types: past tense, present tense, and future tense. Of those, "he ate" is past tense; "he eats" is present tense; and "he will eat" is future tense. It is the knowledge that a poem deals with such and such a one of these.

Elision is the residue, and it is divided into two: word elision and sense elision. We shall explain later how these work.

Mood is of eight kinds: smiling, weeping, disgust, astonishment, joy, fear, pride, and anger. It means knowing that such and such a mood is in force.

Result is knowing that because this poem is spoken, such and such will occur.

Analysis: analyzing the structures of meaning in a poem. This is divided into five types: lock-tongue, shimmering, unstringing of beads, transposing words, and standing to one side. This analysis is the knowledge that a poem exhibits such and such a semantic structure. Of those, here is an example of lock-tongue structure:

> He will return—
> You with your
> shining jewelry!
> Like kings with war-eager armies
> who would not worship
> the beautiful gold warrior's anklet
> of the King of the South
> who raised his shining eyebrow
> to make those kings
> with their beautifully decked
> grand chariots,
> who fought him
> with their swords
> at Vāṭṭāṟu

609 *Tolkāppiyam: Ceyyuḷiyal*, 182.

fall—
he who went
to the hot
wastelands![610]

Next, shimmering construction is as follows:

You
with words
like music,
in the cool
Kolli Mountains
of the king
who fought his foes
so they left their horses
behind them on the battlefield
as they died!
Vines bend,
buzzing with bees
like your
swaying waist:
when our lover sees them,
will he cross
the woodlands?
He won't![611]

Next, the construction of the unstringing of beads is as follows:

I know
that he who left
is coming back.
Girl, don't
grow thin
like the enemies of him
who conquered Cennilam
in war!
Even this earth,
measured by him
who lifted the mountain of yore,
has cooled down!
Because of great clouds,
these pretty laburnum trees
blossom golden, as

---

610 *Pāṇṭi-k-Kōvai*, 315. In the Tamil, the initial "He" is absent.

611 *Pāṇṭi-k-Kōvai*, 316.

they themselves
glisten![612]

The construction of transposed words is as follows:

The lands to which our lord
with his shining lance
has gone—closer than
the Tūvai country by the seacoast
of King Neṭumāṟaṉ who has a white canopy
strung with cool, white pearls:
Will they[613] approach...
You equal the icon
at Cape Kumari
where waves clash!
All those clouds
that the god
the color of fresh bilberry blooms
stomached in ancient times,
then let back out?[614]

The construction of standing to one side is as follows:

Glory-lilies bloomed,
leaf buds sprouted,
laburnum spread pure gold,
and made sapphire bees
sing songs,
until,
like an enemy
of him who conquered
the cool, beautiful lands
of the Cōḻas,
the Lion to His Enemies,
whose chariots sport tall,
fluttering pennants,
who conquered Pāḻi,
it[615] sinks—

what shall I do,
you with such a pretty brow?[616]

---

[612] *Pāṇṭi-k-Kōvai*, 317.

[613] Refers to the clouds four lines below.

[614] *Pāṇṭi-k-Kōvai*, 318.

[615] Refers to "my heart."

[616] *Pāṇṭi-k-Kōvai*, 319.

Lock-tongue construction means that you link the first and last expressions together in order to interpret the poem; shimmering construction means you link the first, middle, and last expressions; construction by the unstringing of beads means that all expressions and lines are independently meaningful; construction with transposed words means that one must transpose some words in order to understand the poem; and the construction of standing to one side means that the meaning suggested in a poem has to be located somewhere within it.

these ten—ten is the count; there are empty words at the beginning and end of this phrase.

are the ways of commenting on all five interior modes—when one who is well versed in interior poetry recites, you should comment with full knowledge of the five interior modes.

> Lord of the cool mountains
> where hunters in the scorching summertime
> raise their clamor
> when hordes of clouds dump rain
> it is not worthy:
> Your girl
> with her bright, shining brow,
> who is like cool, beautiful
> Kūṭal City
>   of the Lion to His Enemies
>   whose righteous scepter
>   grants grace on earth,
> your girl grieves!
>
> Such behavior of yours![617]

For the above poem,

Mode—mountain-country

Conduct—Stolen Love

Speaker—her friend's speech

Audience—hero

Person—second person

Time—future tense, but as it is spoken to a man who is acting out his part right then and there, take it as present tense also

Elision—the word "you" is implied

Mood—fear, because she is in such a state that she would die if others came to know of her conduct

Result—demanding marriage

---

[617] *Pāṇṭi-k-Kōvai*, 320.

Semantic Analysis—since the ordering of the poem is, "Lord of the cool mountains...it is not worthy...(she) grieves! Such behavior," it is in the shimmering type of semantic construction

> My hands,
> —but don't quarrel,
> my precious!
> don't think vile thoughts
> like the sword-filled battlefront
>   of the Gift of the Gods,
>   who has horses,
>   and chariots,
>   and a famous,
>   quick bow!
> my hands smell
> —remember when I plucked
> and put them in your musky hair
> with love, there in the hot
> wastelands?—
>
> they smell of pretty
> kuravu buds![618]

For the above poem,

Mode—river plain

Conduct—Married Love

Speaker—the hero's words; this is what a hero says when he realizes the heroine has changed, thinking he has bedecked a courtesan

Audience—the heroine

Person—second person

Time—present tense, concerned with the past

Elision—"with me" is implied

Mood—trembling[619]

Result—the heroine gives up her quarrel when she hears this

Semantic Analysis—shimmering, because its meaning comes in three places: "my hands...my hands smell...they smell of pretty kuravu buds"

* * *

Verse 57.

> **Of those,**
> **the lack of elision and analysis also occurs.**

---

[618] *Pāṇṭi-k-Kōvai*, 321.

[619] Note that "trembling" is not included in the previous list of moods.

What does this declare, you ask? It declares that, of the ten items mentioned in the above verse, elision and analysis may also be lacking.

Its meaning:

Of those—among the ten mentioned above.

the lack of elision and analysis also occurs—a poem can stand well enough without either elision or semantic analysis, or both.

Of those, here is a poem with no elision:

You with your deer-like eyes,
don't grieve—
huge clouds are thundering
  like the thunderbolt
  upon the flag
  of the king of those
  who live by rich, sweet Tamil,
  Māṟaṉ, the Sapphire Colored One,
  who conquered Pāḻi in the South
  with his grand chariots
  and surging horses!
They will present him to us,

him whose fragrant wreath
is made of sweet mango leaves,
but who left us![620]

Next, a poem with no particular semantic analysis is as follows:

My lord,
with your noble qualities!
You are in no position
to bathe with girls
however bright
of forehead
in the Vaiyai River
  of him who removed suffering,
  protected the earth,
  and watched his foes flee
  from Vallam!
Nor are you
in any position
to stay there with them
in their beautiful groves!

---

[620] *Pāṇṭi-k-Kōvai*, 322. This poem is identical to that numbered 306, appearing in the commentary on Verse 53, page 300.

Tell me: just what position
are you in?[621]

* * *

Verse 58.

Word and implication are the two elisions.

What does this declare, you ask? It declares that elision, mentioned above, is divided into two types.

Its meaning:

Word and implication are the two elisions—word-elision and sense-elision are the two types of elision.

It means that there is yet another model for elision, beyond that of word-elision.

Elision means leaving something out.

Here is a poem with word-elision:

As soon as his chariot
leaves the seagrove
where bees drink gaily
from soft flower cups
on Toṇṭi beach
  of the king who placed a red lily
  upon the pool of blood
  from those who died
  at one end of the battlefield
  as that pool flowed on
  into trenches,

the roaring ocean steps in to destroy us—
and our hearts![622]

Next, here is a poem with sense-elision:

Though they know the suffering
of this girl whose eyes
are like the sharp lances
  of the Sun on the Battleground,
  the king who raised
  the thundering thunderbolt
  of the clouds,
still that flock of herons
keeps feeding

---

[621] *Pāṇṭi-k-Kōvai*, 323.

[622] *Pāṇṭi-k-Kōvai*, 324.

in the rich,
dark backwaters—

they are even crueler than that cruel man
who united with us in this sea grove,
and left![623]

* * *

Verse 59.

To all the understandings of meaning mentioned earlier,
examine where there comes a residue:
even if something other than what was said appears,
understand it and take it by means of what was said.

What does this declare, you ask? It instructs us to take this verse as a supplementary note, to bring in all poems that are not completely explained through the detailed expositions or the interpretations of extraneous words in this treatise, and to form our comments accordingly.

Its meaning:

To all the understandings of meaning mentioned earlier—for the meanings of all verses that have been commented upon thus far.

examine where there comes a residue—investigate the places where something is missing.

even if something other than what was said appears—even if another model different from those described should appear.

understand it and take it by means of what was said—it is to be understood and commented upon through the ten categories mentioned.

This entails recognizing what is a residue in Stolen Love and Married Love.

In the first verse, he did not explain love, beyond simply noting "the five modes of affection." Take this as the appropriate section in which to bring forth all its variations. He did not develop the distinctive features of the five modes that arise in love; bring them up in this section, and comment in accord with

God, food, animal, tree, bird, drum, and
activity, added to the division of the lute[624]

on the five lands, noting the place, time, god, food, animal, tree, bird, drum, activity, music, man's name, and woman's name; for each land the people, flower, type of water, season, and so on; the behavior features that pertain to the five modes and their causes; the variations pertaining to the five modes, and all these things.

---

[623] *Pāṇṭi-k-Kōvai*, 325.

[624] *Tolkāppiyam: Akattiṇaiyiyal*, 20.

Next, bring comments on the variations of the eight nuptials into this section in like manner.

Next, bring comments upon the Kantaruva marriage convention into this section in like manner.

Next, bring into this section comments upon how the two of them meet in natural union when the heroine's playmates go running off to different spots; the nature of their meeting place, noting that it occurs upon a mountain, in a grove filled with flowering branches and vines, like a painted cloth spread along a waterfront, while wasps, beetles, and bees sound like lutes and flutes, as ocean waves or forest rivers beat time like muḻavu and tuṭi drums, with shade as rich as the night, and sand as white as the moon, where people on the inside can easily see those outside, but it is hard to see in; in a grove beloved by celestials and such as have renounced desire; and how he comforts the heroine at the conclusion of their natural union, and leaves.

Next, bring into this section your comments upon the meeting through his friend, when he sees the hero's changes: what the hero says when his friend inquires; what his friend says in rebuke when he hears that; the protestations he makes to his friend; the worries his friend has about the hero when he sees his anguish at being thus accosted; how his worried friend says, "Where, and of what nature, is this form you saw?" how the hero says, "The form I saw is in such and such a place, and is of such and such a nature;" how his friend heads toward that place when he hears that; what he says when he enters the grove and sees the heroine; and his friend's return and showing him the place.

Bring into this section your comments upon the verse,

> Other than of that nature...[625]

Bring into this section and comment upon: the hero accomplishing what he wants through beseeching her friend; how the reconciliation of knowledge comes about; how her friend refuses his gifts as he beseeches her; how she realizes the truth about their union by grasping the signs they both exhibit when she encounters them; how her friend speaks to her heart after she realizes it; how her friend consents later to the hero's entreaty; how she tells the heroine about the hero's entreaty after she has consented; how she stands with honor in consideration of the ruination of fidelity, when she is shut up in the house; how her friend puts the hero off when he beseeches her, by telling him of the heroine's preciousness and greatness; the variations of her friend's standing with honor; the variations on the nighttime tryst; the variations of what her friend and the hero say during the period of daytime trysts; the variations of saying "Come to a nighttime tryst;" the variations of saying that the place assigned for

[625] *The Study of Stolen Love*, 4.

nighttime trysts is such and such a place; how both gesturing and gossiping belong to Stolen Love during the period of nighttime trysts; their speeches after it has become exposed; union and elopement; the variations of what her friend and the hero say in elopement; tarrying in the middle of the wastelands; how her friend entrusts the heroine to him and leaves, when standing with honor does not go right; how the hero accepts his charge and proceeds; the formula for what those who meet them in the middle of the wastelands say; how the foster mother follows them; how those whom she meets in the middle of the wasteland speak, when she follows them; how those who have seen them describe the state of the heroine in the middle of the wastelands, and make the foster mother return; how the hero becomes happy; how the hero puts off marriage as he goes to make his fortune and so on, and the things the heroine tells her friend, who consoles her; how the father and brothers refuse when the hero proposes marriage; how the real mother stands then with honor; the departures of the hero from the heroine during Married Love; the things with which her friend comforts the anguished heroine while he is gone; showing the season; how the hero returns when he has finished his mission; what her friend says when she realizes that he has returned; what the hero says to his charioteer and to the clouds, when he has completed his mission; what the hero says when he is with the heroine, for her friend to overhear; further, the variations on loathing, sulking, and quarreling during the departure for courtesans; how the heroine refuses the door to a hero who has gone to the courtesans; what the bard puts forward in demanding entrance for the hero; what the guests put forward; how the hero gains entrance through go-betweens; and everything else.

* * *

Verse 60.

> **What are thought of as Stolen Love and Married Love are the heightening of love**
> **that occurs in the hearts of people who live here.**

What does this declare, you ask? It is a supplementary note on Stolen Love and Married Love, which have been categorized above.

Its meaning:

What are thought of as Stolen Love and Married Love—the conducts labeled by poets as Stolen Love and Married Love.

people who live here—anyone who is born or moves about in this world.

are the heightening of love that occurs in the hearts—are the heightening of love that arises in the hearts of such people as the high-born hero and heroine.

It was to indicate that neither gods nor creatures in the netherworld[626] have this conduct in their realms that he said, "people who live here." Therefore, it follows that he means it happens from time to time to those people also, when they move about in this world. It was to mark it as a conduct established by poets as "the non-existent, the sweet, and the good," which does not occur by nature in this world, that he said "what are thought of."

Next, using a play on words, you may re-analyze "in the hearts of people who live here" with split words, in which case it would read "in one heart here." That would actually be appropriate, since he said,

> he and she[627]

and we take them as two bodies with one soul, as he is she and she is he.

Since he said "the heightening of love," we get that these conducts do not take place without love, that it is for high-born people, and that among them it is particularly for the royalty. But then wouldn't it read, "in the hearts of high-born people," you ask? Because of the saying,

> Be they servers or commanders,
> they are not eschewed, on the outside, say the poets.[628]

it is thought to have been extended occasionally to people of other castes as well.

The Study of Married Love
Is Complete

The Text And Comments Upon
The Study of Stolen Love
called
God's Interior Meaning
Is Complete

---

626 **Nākar**, or "snake-people," are the creatures of the netherworld to whom Nakkīraṉār refers here.

627 *The Study of Stolen Love*, 2.

628 *Tolkāppiyam: Akattiṇaiyiyal*, 23.

Bibliography and Works for Further Reference

Editions of *The Study of Stolen Love*:

Both of these Tamil editions include excellent introductions, and notations of variant readings:

Kaḷaviyal eṉṟa Iṟaiyaṉār Akapporuḷ. Madras: South India Saiva Siddhanta Works Publishing Society, 1976.

Kōvintarāja Mutaliyār, Kā. Ra. and Mē. Vī. Vēṇukōpāla-p-Piḷḷai, eds. *Kaḷaviyal eṉṉum Iṟaiyaṉār Akapporuḷ Mūlamum Nakkīraṉār Uṟaiyum*. Madras: Bavanandam Kazhagam, 1939.

Tamil texts for primary reference; these are editions of the works cited by Nakkīraṉār in his commentary of *The Study of Stolen Love*:

Aiṅkuṟunūṟu:

Cāminātaiyar, U. Vē., ed. and comm. *Aiṅkuṟunūṟu*. Madras: Sri Tiyākarāca Vilācam, 1957. Contains notes by Cāminātaiyar, who pioneered the work of publishing ancient Tamil texts in the modern era. As listed below, he produced editions of many ancient Tamil texts; all of his editions are still considered among the most authoritative available.

Kēcikaṉ, Puliyūr, ed. and comm. *Aiṅkuṟunūṟu: Marutamum Neytalum.* Madras: Pāri Nilayam, 1982.

———, ed. and comm. *Aiṅkuṟunūṟu: Mullai* Madras: Pāri Nilayam, 1983. These editions, like editions of other Tamil texts put out by Puliyūr Kēcikaṉ, are popularized versions, with notes by the editor.

Patippu Āciriya-k-kuḻu, eds. *Aiṅkuṟunūṟu*. Madras: New Century Book House, 1981. This is one of this publisher's complete set of Caṅkam texts, printed without commentary.

Akanāṉūṟu:

Cōmacuntaraṉār, Po. Vē., ed. and comm. *Akanāṉūṟu: Kaḷiṟṟiyāṉai Nirai*. Madras: South India Saiva Siddhanta Works Publishing Society, 1981. Like other SISSWPS editions, this is a standard reference edition.

———, ed. and comm. *Akanāṉūṟu: Maṇimiṭai pavaḷam*. Madras: South India Saiva Siddhanta Works Publishing Society, 1976.

Patippu Āciriya-k-kuḻu, eds. *Akanāṉūṟu*. Madras: New Century Book House, 1981.

Vēṅkaṭacāmi Nāṭṭār, Na. Mu., and Rā. Vēṅkaṭācalam Piḷḷai, eds. and comm. *Akanāṉūṟu: Nittila-k-kōvai*. Madras: South India Saiva Siddhanta Works Publishing Society, 1969.

Cilappatikāram:

Cāminātaiyar, U. Ve., ed. and comm. *Cilappatikāram, Aṭiyārkkunallār uraiyuṭaṉ*. Madras: Sri Tiyākarāca Vilācam, 1968 (first printed in 1892). Contains Aṭiyārkkunallār's classical commentary as well as notes by the editor.

Cōmacuntaraṉār, Po. Vē., ed. and comm. *Cilappatikāram: Maturai-k-kāṇṭam*. Madras: South India Saiva Siddhanta Works Publishing Society, 1984.

Kēcikaṉ, Puliyūr, ed. and comm. *Cilappatikāram*. Madras: Pāri Nilayam, 1958.

Kalittokai:

Iḷavaḻakaṉār, ed. and comm. *Kalittokai, Nacciṉārkkiṉiyar uraiyuṭaṉ*. Madras: South India Saiva Siddhanta Works Publishing Society, 1976. Contains Nacciṉārkkiṉiyar's classical commentary as well as notes by the editor.

Kēcikaṉ, Puliyūr, ed. and comm. *Kalittokai teḷivurai*. Madras: Pāri Nilayam, 1984.

Patippu Āciriya-k-kuḻu, eds. *Kalittokai*. Madras: New Century Book House, 1981.

Kuṟuntokai:

Cāminātaiyar, U. Ve., ed. and comm. *Kuṟuntokai.* Madras: Sri Tiyākarāca Vilācam, 1962.

Cōmacuntaraṉār, Po. Vē., ed. and comm. *Kuṟuntokai.* Madras: South India Saiva Siddhanta Works Publishing Society, 1978.

Patippu Āciriya-k-kuḻu, eds. *Kuṟuntokai.* Madras: New Century Book House, 1981.

Naṉṉūl:

Cāminātaiyar, U. Ve., ed. and comm. *Naṉṉūl.* Madras: Sri Tiyākarāca Vilācam, 1946.

Kaḻaka-p-pulavar-k-kuḻu, eds. *Naṉṉūl Kāṇṭikaiyurai*. Madras: South India Saiva Siddhanta Works Publishing Society, 1984. Contains a brief expository commentary.

Naṟṟiṇai:

Kēcikaṉ, Puliyūr, ed. and comm. *Naṟṟiṇai*. Madras, Pāri Nilayam, 1980.

Nārāyaṇacāmi Aiyar, A. and Po. Vē. Cōmacuntaraṉār, eds. and comm. *Naṟṟiṇai Nāṉūṟu*. Madras: South India Saiva Siddhanta Works Publishing Society, 1962. Includes notes on the individual poets represented in this classical Caṅkam anthology.

Patippu Āciriya-k-kuḻu, eds. *Naṟṟiṇai*. Madras: New Century Book House, 1981.

Turaicāmi-p-Piḷḷai, Auvvai Cu., ed. and comm. *Naṟṟiṇai mūlamum viḷakkavuraiyum*. Madras: Aruṇā Publications, 1966 (vol. 1) and 1968 (vol. 2). Contains the editor's detailed commentary.

Pāṇṭi-k-Kōvai:

Turaicāmi, Vē., ed. and comm. *Pāṇṭi-k-Kōvai*. Madras: Sṭār Piracuram, 1985. Contains the entire text, with introduction and comments. A few stanzas differ from the version found in Nakkīraṉār's commentary on *The Study of Stolen Love*.

Tolkāppiyam:

Kaḻaka-p-pulavar-k-kuḻu, eds. *Tolkāppiyam: Poruḷatikāram, Iḷampūraṇār uraiyuṭaṉ*. Madras: South India Saiva Siddhanta Works Publishing Society, 1982. Contains the text of pertinent sections of Tolkāppiyam, with Iḷampūraṇār's classical commentary.

Kēcikaṉ, Puliyūr, ed. and comm. *Tolkāppiyam (Muḻuvatum)*. Madras: Pāri Nilayam, 1970.

Patippu Āciriya-k-kuḻu, eds. *Tolkāppiyam*. Madras: New Century Book House, 1981.

Veḷḷaivāraṇaṉ, Ka., ed. and comm. *Tolkāppiyam: Kaḷaviyal*. Madurai: Madurai Kamaraj University, 1983.

———, ed. *Tolkāppiyam: Kaṟpiyal.* Madurai: Madurai Kamaraj University, 1983.

———, ed. *Tolkāppiyam: Poruḷiyal.* Madurai: Madurai Kamaraj University, 1983. these volumes contain pertinent sections of the ancient text with detailed comments by the editor.

English translations of Tamil texts cited by Nakkīraṉār, and other general reference works:

Balakrishna Mudaliyar, R., tr. *The Golden Anthology of Ancient Tamil Literature (3 volumes)*. Madras: South India Saiva Siddhanta Works Publishing Society, 1959–60. A translation of the 1903 Tamil collection of classical poetry entitled *Caṅka Ilakkiya Iṉkavi-t-Tiraṭṭu* by Iḷavaḻakaṉār, these volumes present Caṅkam poems in prose translation with detailed comments.

Bower, H., tr. *The Naṉṉūl (Part 1: Preface)*. Madras: South India Saiva Siddhanta Works Publishing Society, 1972. Annotated prose translations of these Tamil verses (**nūṟpās**) on grammar, with an Appendix discussing grammatical and rhetorical terms.

Cutler, Norman, and Paula Richman, eds. *A Gift of Tamil: Translations from Tamil Literature in Honor of K. Paramasivam*. New Delhi: Manohar, 1992. Includes a number of translated poems similar to ones cited in Nakkīraṉār's commentary.

Danielou, Alain, tr. *Shilappatikaram (The Ankle Bracelet)*. New York: New Directions, 1965. A popularized prose and poetry translation of *Cilappatikāram*.

Dikshitar, V. R. Ramachandra, tr. *Cilappatikaram*. Madras: South India Saiva Siddhanta Works Publishing Society, 1978. A careful prose translation with copious notes.

Drew, W. H., and John Lazarus, tr. *Thirukkural*. Madras: South India Saiva Siddhanta Works Publishing Society, 1982. One of a great many complete translations of *Tirukkuṟaḷ*.

Encyclopaedia of Tamil Literature (in Ten Volumes), Volume One. Madras: Institute of Asian Studies, 1990. Thorough discussions of many aspects of Tamil literature.

Gandhi, M. K. *An autobiography, or the story of my experiments with the truth*. Ahmedabad: Navajivan, 1927. Gandhi's classic, cited here principally with regard to its relevance to the Introduction, page xvii.

Hart, George L. *The poems of ancient Tamil, their milieu and their Sanskrit counterparts*. Berkeley: University of California Press, 1975. One of the best introductions to the context of ancient Tamil poetry.

———. *Poets of the Tamil Anthologies*. Princeton: Princeton University Press, 1979. Poetic translations of selected verses. The Introduction discusses the major forms of literary analysis for early Tamil poems, and also presents metrical and linguistic analyses.

Ilakkuvanar, S. *Tholkappiyam in English with critical studies*. Madras: M. Neelamanar, 1994. An English translation of Tolkāppiyam with discussions of issues raised.

Marr, John Ralston. *The Eight Anthologies*. Madras: Institute of Asian Studies, 1985. An in-depth analysis of the themes (**tuṟais**) and poetics of a major portion of Caṅkam literature. Large bibliography.

Meenakshisundaram, T. P. *A history of Tamil literature*. Annamalainagar: Annamalai University, 1965. One of the definitive references.

Nadarajah, D. *Love in Sanskrit and Tamil literature: a study of characters and nature, 200 B.C.–A.D. 500*. Delhi: Motilal Banarsidass, 1994. A recent study of the context of ancient Tamil love poetry.

Parthasarathy, R., tr. *The Cilappatikāram of Iḷaṅkō Aṭikaḷ*. New York: Columbia University Press, 1993. The definitive English translation. Its Introduction and Postscript provide a sweeping overview of literature and society in ancient Tamil Nadu. Large bibliography.

Popley, H. A., tr. *The Sacred Kural*. Calcutta: Y.M.C.A. Publishing House, 1958. Selected couplets from *Tirukkuṟaḷ*.

Rajam, V. S. *A reference grammar of classical Tamil poetry: 150 B.C.–pre-fifth/sixth century A.D.* Philadelphia: American Philosophical Society, 1992. The authoritative work on the grammar and wording of ancient Tamil poems.

Ramanujan, A. K., tr. *The Interior Landscape: Love Poems from a Classical Tamil Anthology*. Bloomington: Indiana University Press, 1967. Poetic translations of selected verses. The Afterword provides one of the clearest descriptions of the Five Modes of Love.

———, tr. *Poems of Love and War*. New York: Columbia University Press, 1985. Poetic translations of selected verses from ancient Tamil anthologies. The Afterword analyzes a number of poems in detail, with particular emphasis on the categories **akam** and **puṟam**.

Sastri, Nilakanta. *A history of South India.* London: Oxford University Press, 1955. One of the definitive references on the political history of the region.

Shanmugam Pillai, M. and David E. Ludden, tr. *Kuruntokai.* Madurai: Koodal Publishers, 1976. A complete translation of this classical Caṅkam anthology of **akam** poetry; each poem has its own commentary by the translators.

Singaravelu Mudaliar, A. *Abhithana Chintamani: the encyclopedia of Tamil literature.* New Delhi: Asian Educational Services, 1986. In Tamil. Encyclopedia-style entries on many of the characters, themes, authors, and traditions in Tamil literary history.

Subrahmanian, N. *History of Tamil Nadu (to A.D. 1565).* Madurai: Ennes Publications, 1986. A political history aimed at university student audiences.

Subrahmanyam Sastri, P. S., tr. *Tolkappiyam: The earliest extant Tamil Grammar. Porulatikaram—Tamil poetics.* Madras: The Kuppuswami Sastri Research Institute, 1994. A recent translation of the sections of Tolkāppiyam that pertain to poetics.

Takahashi, T. *Tamil love poetry and poetics.* Leiden: E. J. Brill, 1995. A recent and influential study of the subject.

Vanmikanathan, G., tr. *The Tirukkural (Complete).* Tiruchirapalli: The Tirukkural Prachar Sangh, 1969. Prose translations of the couplets, with short introductions to each of the work's three major divisions: Righteousness, The Body Politic, and Bliss.

Visswanathan, E. Sa., tr. Varadarajan, Mu. *A history of Tamil literature.* New Delhi: Sahitya Akademi, 1988. One of the standard references.

Zvelebil, Kamil. *Classical Tamil prosody, an introduction.* Madras: New Era Publications, 1989. One of a number of influential studies by this eminent scholar.

———. *Literary conventions in akam poetry.* Madras: Institute of Asian Studies, 1986.

———. *Tamil literature.* Wiesbaden: Harrassowitz, 1974. One of the standard reference works.

———. *Tamil literature.* Leiden: E. J. Brill, 1975. One of the standard reference works.

———, tr. *The smile of Murugan on Tamil Literature of South India.* Leiden: E. J. Brill, 1973. A fine collection of translated poetry, with analysis.